CONTENTS

"Dr. H. Leon Greene's knowledge and experience as a cardiologist has enabled him to produce a volume that once and for all exposes what he so aptly refers to as 'the cult of the near-death experience.' *If I Should Wake Before I Die* is clearly a valuable contribution to the field of near-death experience (NDE) research."

—RICHARD ABANES
Founder, Religious Information Center
Author, *Journey into the Light*

"In this ground-breaking book, a premier medical researcher and professor of medicine confronts what has been touted for twenty years as one of the greatest 'scientific' breakthroughs of the century—that of penetrating and solving the mystery of death. It has been a bestselling topic that has captivated the minds of an entire generation, turning it towards the East, if not within, for higher truth. Now Dr. Greene, a graduate of Johns Hopkins Medical School, takes us to an entirely unexplored field of medical research that throws new light on the popular understanding of so-called 'near death experiences'—from the tunnel of light to the being of light. He sounds a wake-up call to the medical community first, and the rest of us second. If you are among the millions who have read *Life After Life*, *Embraced by the Light*, or *Saved by the Light*, do yourself a favor and read this book! It stands apart from the spate of books to come out on death."

—TAL BROOKE
President, Spiritual Counterfeits Project
Author, *When the World Will Be As One*

"Using careful documentation and convincing medical commentary, Dr. Greene has written a remarkable book that will help us sort out fact from fiction, death from near-death. Dr. Greene skillfully combines medical science and biblical understanding to help us sort out the often confusing information and personal accounts surrounding near-death experiences. It is a landmark contribution to a sometimes murky subject matter."

—RONALD ENROTH
Professor of Sociology, Westmont College
Author, *Churches That Abuse*

"On solid logical, scientific, and theological grounds Dr. Greene has built, step by step, an irrefutable case against the near-death experience. This book is sure to rattle, if not topple, the flimsy ramparts now manned by the proponents of the NDE, sending the pseudo-scientists and New-Age pooh-bahs scurrying for cover. Every Christian—and non-Christian—should read *If I Should Wake Before I Die*."

—BRAD SCOTT
Adjunct Associate Professor of Communications, Golden Gate University
Author, *Embraced by the Darkness*

If I Should Wake Before I Die

The Medical and Biblical Truth About Near-Death Experiences

H. Leon Greene, M.D.

CROSSWAY BOOKS • WHEATON, ILLINOIS
A DIVISION OF GOOD NEWS PUBLISHERS

If I Should Wake Before I Die

Published by Crossway Books
a division of Good News Publishers
1300 Crescent Street
Wheaton, Illinois 60187

Editing: Leonard G. Goss and Ted Griffin

Cover design: Cindy Kiple

First printing, 1997

Printed in the United States of America

Library of Congress Cataloging-in-Publication Data

Greene, H. Leon, 1944-
If I should wake before I die : the medical and biblical truth about near-death experiences / H. Leon Greene.
p. cm.
Includes bibliographical references and index.
ISBN 0-89107-891-6
1. Near-death experiences—Religious aspects—Christianity.
I. Title.
BT833.G74 1997
236'.1—dc20 96-41250

05 04 03 02 01 00 99 98 97
15 14 13 12 11 10 9 8 7 6 5 4 3 2 1

Dedications are always seen, seldom read, and never understood.

Nevertheless, I dedicate this book to my precious family behind the scene who encouraged, humored, and coaxed me to complete this work. They believed that a message needed to be told, and they all surrendered part of me to the task.

To my wife Judy, who loves God first; *to David*, who is the Christian writer in the family; *to Julie*, who knows the music of God's heart; *to Elizabeth*, who discerns God's voice when others are deaf; and *to Matthew*, who quietly goes about God's work.

It is finished! What next?

PREFACE

Light of the World or Worldly Light?

Which newspaper headline is the most outlandish?

ELVIS SIGHTED BUYING GUITAR STRINGS
AT K-MART IN DES MOINES

LOCAL CONSTRUCTION WORKER ELECTROCUTED, DIES,
SEES JESUS IN HEAVEN, AND RETURNS TO TELL STORY

UFO SNATCHES ENTIRE THIRD GRADE CLASS FROM
EISENHOWER ELEMENTARY SCHOOL

All are equally implausible, but unfortunately the Christian community often chooses to believe the second. Man seeks answers. He desires to understand. He avoids the unknown. He learns about and prepares for a situation before it occurs. So it should not be a mystery that man has fashioned ideas about what occurs at the time of death. This "need to know" has been a major force behind most religions.

Those religions that promise happiness and peace for all have an immediate audience in the ranks of the seekers. Other religions that teach the concept of good and evil, of reward and punishment, are more difficult for people to accept. Who would choose a system of belief in which there is condemnation for the wicked over a theology that assures love, happiness, warmth, and light for all—even the rogue and the bandit? Therein lies the danger of the cult of the near-death experience (NDE).

For millennia man has feared death, in part because it belongs to the realm of the unseen and the inexplicable. What happens if we encounter a medical crisis and come close to death but are awakened by a medical team before we die? Are we treated to a celestial journey? Should we expect an NDE like the ones that have received wide publicity in the past few years?

Is the NDE a vehicle God uses to impart messages to us? Can we believe the stories allegedly brought back from the dead? The NDE teaches that there are no consequences to man's actions, that you might even get to cheat death and come back. Should we uncritically accept this theology that has generated both confusion in the Christian community and skepticism in the minds of the medical profession? Early comprehensive works on the NDE can be dated to the end of the 1970s, but the recent surge of interest in NDEs came with the 1990s. Authors such as Betty Eadie, Melvin Morse, and Raymond Moody have found themselves on the *New York Times* Bestseller List.

As a Christian cardiologist, I view these descriptions of the NDE to be at variance both with my own clinical observations of patients and with my Christian beliefs. It was thus that I began a study of the NDE. The purpose of this book is to evaluate the NDE in light of current medical knowledge and timeless Christian principles.

My approach to evaluating the NDE requires explanation. It is based upon Christian principles firmly entrenched in faith. These beliefs have molded and will continue to affect my interpretation of the medical "facts" at hand. I believe that the Bible is true and that its principles are unchangeable. Nevertheless, I acknowledge that interpretations of many biblical passages can be as diverse as the men and women reading them. However, the Bible has remained both infallible and immutable throughout the centuries, and it is only the human reading itself that is altered with time. Contrasting with biblical truth is the body of scholarship that we call medical "fact." Medicine is not only an imperfect science but an art, and our appreciation of the workings of the human body will change as the synthesis of medical information changes. Much of what is considered to be true today will most certainly be viewed as either false or incomplete by tomorrow. As new information is gained, the sum of opinion will progress toward absolute medical truth, but the process is often two steps forward, one step back.

We must reconcile accounts of the NDE with the Bible because so much has been written about the relationship of the NDE to a view of an afterlife. Do NDEs exist? Are they simply the figment of a vivid imagination, or perhaps a fabrication of men and women seeking attention, publicity, or income? Is the NDE really a glimpse of the hereafter? Does the NDE tell us anything about eternity? Can NDEs be explained by current medical knowledge? Is there any danger to the popular interpretations of NDEs? Why not simply believe what has been written about NDEs and accept that they have religious significance? Or are such stories of the NDE both medically unlikely and theologically incorrect?

If a single explanation encompasses both all that is known about the NDE and the biblical account of human life and soul, then we should readily accept such a solution. However, if a conflict exists between man's interpretation of the NDE and the Bible, then we must be willing to modify our interpretation of the NDE. Reassessment of our religious beliefs may also be necessary. But we must never compromise faith to accommodate a man-made concept. The Bible is the ultimate authority. Medical hypotheses must also be subject to scriptural truth.

Here are the principles I use in my analysis of the NDE:

1. All descriptions of bodily experience should be analyzed for their medical accuracy. Discrepancies between reported physical events and our knowledge of medicine must be resolved.

2. Miracles happen, and they are not limited to the past. They still occur.

3. God intervenes in our lives in ways we often don't understand.

4. An afterlife exists. We don't need "evidence" from the NDE to confirm this foundational principle of Scripture. This book is not written to "prove" or "disprove" the eternal existence of the soul. Faith is necessary, and faith by definition cannot be proven; nor can the object of faith be proven. In eternal matters, mankind must abandon the need to know as he clings to his faith.

5. Both angels and demons exist, though their manifestations may be hard to discern, and we must be cautious when we refer to them to explain earthly events.

6. Medical science is most incomplete when it comes to hypotheses regarding perceptions, the mind, memory, and conscious experience.

7. Though death is certain, universal, and final, many processes can lead to death, and many stages exist between a fully conscious, healthy person and one who dies. Some of these processes are reversible; some are not.

My interest in the NDE began when I finished my training as an internist, cardiologist, and subspecialist in treating patients with cardiac rhythm disturbances (arrhythmias). Arrhythmias are abnormalities of the heart's regularity that can lead to what physicians call "sudden cardiac death." In this condition the heart stops beating and pumping blood to the rest of the body. Without rapid medical intervention, the patient will die in a few minutes. With the advent of resuscitation techniques in the early 1970s, many of these patients were revived. Some of us objected to the term "sudden cardiac death" because these patients did not in fact die. They were resuscitated to resume a completely normal existence. Nevertheless, the term "sudden cardiac death" prevailed, and patients who survived a cardiac arrest are still called "sudden cardiac death victims."

Early in my experience with these patients—who had indeed suffered a documented cardiac arrest—I was impressed that none of them described anything that resembled an NDE. Hundreds of these survivors were unanimous in their opinion that they simply "passed out" and awoke with no memory of any NDE. Some who had read popular accounts of the NDE were disappointed that they had missed out on such a wonderful event.

This book is divided into three major sections: (1) a description of the NDE as reported by many popular investigators; (2) a summary of medical knowledge pertaining to the NDE; and (3) a review of biblical examples of death, resuscitation, resurrection, and the principles of the spirit, soul, eternity, and afterlife as they relate to the NDE. You will see that parts of the discussion to follow are technical and use necessary medical terminology. I urge you not to be intimidated by this language, as I have used only that which is essential to the argument and have also worked hard to explain any material that is technical in nature. I am not merely writing for other physicians or medical researchers but for all persons who are concerned about issues of the NDE. Each chapter begins with a story of a patient in my practice who illustrates a point about the NDE. The names have been changed, of course, as well as any other identifying characteristics. But the stories themselves are true.

Please join me as we explore the deceptive theology of the NDE from a Christian medical perspective.

SECTION ONE

■

The Near-Death Experience Defined

1

WHAT IS A NEAR-DEATH EXPERIENCE?

Dying to Live or Living to Die?

James Osborne was a man of faith. He had a strong conviction that heaven was a real place in a blissful eternity that was to be his someday. His confidence came from his belief in Jesus Christ, and he lived his faith day after day. When he suffered his first symptoms of chest pain, though, he did not anticipate that he might be starting a journey to his final reward.

The constriction in his chest on that Friday in January was actually rather mild. He had been walking down Fourth Avenue in the cool of Seattle's rainy winter. No shoveling snow. Not even walking uphill. But the pressure in his chest was unmistakable, and it caused him to stop walking for about three or four minutes. The pressure eased, and he continued toward his destination at the Federal Building.

That's the last he can remember, even though his coworkers said that he arrived at work at his usual time and worked for about an hour before he collapsed. John Fletcher, another office worker in the same complex, saw him suddenly slump onto his desk without any apparent warning. John had just completed a course in cardiopulmonary resuscitation (CPR) at the Ballard fire station, and he began working on James within thirty to forty-five seconds of James's loss of consciousness. Sue Thomas, another employee, happened by the scene and called the Medics, who arrived in four minutes, slightly slower than the three that it commonly takes in Seattle. (The Medics are emergency medical personnel working in Medic I, Seattle's city ambulance service.) The traffic had been heavy, and the rainy streets had slowed them a bit.

The Medics took over as soon as they arrived. Restoring James's heartbeat took nearly fifteen minutes. Soon thereafter, his blood pressure stabilized, and they transported James to Harborview Medical Center, where the Medics had done their training and where about one-third of all cardiac arrest victims in Seattle are treated.

The next two days were touch-and-go. James had obviously suffered a large heart attack, and it surprised James's family when the doctors told them that the heart attack probably had occurred a day or two before his collapse. The collapse was simply a late manifestation of the damage already done to the heart. James had told his family nothing about any chest pains, but he was not a "complainer." On the day of his collapse, his rhythm had become erratic and ultimately degenerated to cardiac arrest, or ventricular fibrillation, as the doctors called it.

James remained in a coma for nearly forty-eight hours, and the doctors felt that he might have suffered some brain damage from the prolonged period of time without blood circulation to the brain.

Over the next two weeks, James progressively recovered, and his heart rhythm and pumping capacity improved. But the lack of blood flow to his brain for nineteen minutes had obliterated from his memory the entire sequence of events. He could remember the walk down Fourth Avenue. He could vaguely remember the chest constriction that had interrupted his walking. But he had lost his memory for the entire two hours before the cardiac arrest and the subsequent three days. No recollection. Not even a hint of that horrible time in the Coronary Care Unit with all of its tubes and machines.

James was distressed. He had just been reading about cardiac arrest victims who had wonderful experiences during their unconsciousness. Trips to heaven. Blissful colors. A loving "being of light." The sense of forgiveness. A new purpose to life. Why had he been robbed of that experience? If he had to go through the heart attack and the subsequent cardiac arrest, at least God could have given him some memory that would reassure him he had been on the right track in his religious quest in life. But no. James felt cheated. James believed that "Man Returns from the Dead—Saw Heaven!" was not just a headline from the *National Enquirer.* He wanted an inspiring story to tell, and he had nothing but a huge blank in his memory.

Was he unusual? Should a near-death experience have been expected? He wanted to know.

Stories of NDEs are as old as mankind himself. But is the near-death experience real? Is the NDE a rehearsal for the real thing—death that is not interrupted? How can we assess the validity of an experience that is so intensely personal and that does not lend itself to investigation or experimentation? Is it sent from God as a revelation to mankind? Does it contain unique truths? Or is it the Loch Ness monster of religion—that elusive vision that everyone wants to believe but that no one is able to prove? Is the NDE sent from God, from Satan, or does it simply find its origin in man's imagination?

Historically, all cultures have feared death. Mankind ultimately wants love, peace, freedom from pain, release from the clutches of the unknown, and assurance of an afterlife. Most of us refuse to accept the notion that our lives might end at death. We all desire to live throughout eternity. Therefore, most cultures have reported previewing the afterlife through visions and dreams. Art in all societies has depicted the spirit or soul of man hovering above the body at the time of death. Tales of travel through time and space at or after death have been chronicled in all cultures.

What, then, is the NDE? Is it real? Can our faith hinge upon the insights revealed in the NDE? Can we trust the popular descriptions? These questions are all relevant to the Christian life today. In order to understand the issues raised by the concept of the NDE, we must evaluate the reports of this phenomenon.

Let's take each of the popular books in the sequence in which they were published and see if we can decipher their message.

2

THE GURUS OF THE NDE

Dying to Self or Dying to Sell?

Sam Lundquist had just been through the worst two weeks of his life. First came the cardiac arrest, then the five days in the Intensive Care Unit after his resuscitation, now the convalescence in the Telemetry Unit of the hospital where he was undergoing the many tests to determine why he had experienced the cardiac arrest in the first place. Would this ordeal never end?

The endless questioning by the medical staff was almost insulting. Where were you when you collapsed? What did your chest feel like just before you lost consciousness? What do you remember about awakening? How does your chest feel now? But the worst was that social worker, Sue Cook. She kept asking all of those questions about his memory for the events that had occurred when he was unconscious. Was she a fool? "I was unconscious. I don't remember anything!" Sam repeatedly told her.

But she would not take no for an answer. She kept drilling him. "What did you see?" "Did you pass through a tunnel?" "Was there a bright light at the end of the tunnel?" "Did you see your 'higher power'?" "Did your life pass before you?" Her questions were not only persistent, they were leading. She seemed to have an agenda to prove. And what did all of this have to do with social work, anyway? She was supposed to be helping Sam with his financial affairs and with his unemployment compensation.

Little did Sam know that Sue was writing a book about people who had experienced cardiac arrest. She certainly was located in the right place, though. Harborview Medical Center was the premier hospital in the world for such problems. The Medics in Seattle were based there, and they brought many of their cardiac arrest victims to Harborview for initial treatment

Sue visited Sam's room at least twice a day. Always the same questions. Sam was tired. He had absolutely no memory of the arrest. In fact, he had no memory of the two hours before his collapse or the three days thereafter. How foolish that Sue would think anyone could remember anything from a time when he was unconscious and oblivious to the events happening around him! After all, the doctors had told him that his heart had stopped and that his brain had been damaged because of the lack of blood flow. It had taken a few minutes for the Medics to arrive and restart his heart. Certainly Sam had no memory of any trips to heaven, as Sue was suggesting.

Finally, Sam could take no more. He was a polite man, but he couldn't tolerate this badgering any longer. He could endure no more of Sue's browbeating about this "near-death experience" she was trying to get him to describe. So Sam decided to give her what she wanted. He simply lied and agreed that all of her suggestions were true. Yes, he had seen a tunnel. Yes, he went to heaven. Yes, he saw his long-deceased mother there. Yes, there was a brilliant light that encompassed him and made him feel loved. They were lies, all lies, but at least that got Sue off his back. After she had heard all that she wanted, she stopped coming by his room. Peace at last!

So my experience with one of the proponents of the NDE

began. My patient told me this account as he was leaving the hospital, and he asked that I intervene so future patients would not have to suffer the indignities of Sue's questioning. Was this technique the basis for all of the NDE literature? Did all "researchers" behave this way? Were the accounts in the popular press similarly fabricated? Did all cardiac arrest patients have such complete and total amnesia for the events surrounding their crisis? I needed to know.

ELISABETH KUBLER-ROSS

Elisabeth Kubler-Ross began the popular analysis of death with her book *On Death and Dying* in 1969 (1). (Throughout this book a number in parentheses, as just previous to this sentence, indicates the bibliographic reference for the chapter being read.) Starting the discussion of a taboo subject, she published the book before she had much to say about the NDE. She outlined the stages of dying: denial, anger, bargaining, depression, and acceptance. Later it became obvious that the stages as described were too rigid. Many patients did not progress through all stages, nor did they necessarily pass through them in the order she suggested was the norm. Initial certainty was replaced with a lot of qualifiers and disclaimers.

Later Kubler-Ross was challenged (some would even say discredited) for some of her work, as she began to associate with mediums who dabbled in what many Christians would call the occult, including conjuring up dead spirits, crystal gazing, belief in reincarnation, out-of-body experiences, astral projection, seances, and sexual exploits. She even had her own spirit guide, named Salem (2-4). While she began the discussion of death and dying and taught compassion and concern for the terminally ill, it is difficult now to see the likeness of Christ in the totality of her work.

RAYMOND MOODY

The NDE became the subject of popular writing only about twenty years ago. In 1975, Raymond Moody published his book *Life After Life* (5), and it immediately became a sensational best seller. It went through many printings from 1975 through 1977, capturing the imaginations of its readers and fulfilling their desire for the fantastic. One of the later editions proclaimed on the cover: "Actual case histories that reveal there is life after death," and, "true experiences . . . so overwhelmingly positive that they may change mankind's view of life, death and spiritual survival forever." Quite a claim! But what was this book teaching? What was this experience?

Raymond Moody, raised a Presbyterian and later a Methodist, had no first-hand experience with the NDE. He denied any familiarity with the occult and acknowledged no proficiency in theological matters, having both a Ph.D. in philosophy and a medical degree (6). He claimed no intention to prove the existence of life after death, though his own identification of his religious affiliations may have been an attempt to attribute religious credence to some of his beliefs. The world attached a spiritual significance to the NDE in spite of his expressed intentions.

Moody described three settings for the NDE in this original volume (7):

1. Experiences of people who, by report, came close to death from some illness, accident, or injury and who were resuscitated from a state in which they were "thought, adjudged, or pronounced clinically dead by their doctors."

2. Experiences of people who had a "close call" with death, but who were not judged "clinically dead" by a physician.

3. Experiences of people who were dying and who related their experiences to bystanders as they actually died.

He described the sequence of the "dying" process as a number of separate stages, although admitting that very few people have all stages, that there is no defining feature of the NDE, that the order may be varied, and that many people report none of the stages (8):

1. "Ineffability"
Difficulty in reporting the event because of its uniqueness and the inadequacy of language to relay the essential features of the experience.

2. "Hearing the News"
Hearing the medical personnel say that the person has died, that "It's over."

3. "Feelings of Peace and Quiet"
Patients say that they are then overcome with an unimaginable calm or peace.

4. "The Noise"
Next is a sensation of a noise, variably described as a roaring, rushing, buzzing, or ringing that can be uncomfortable or unpleasant. However, some report the sound to be like bells or music that is actually comforting or pleasant.

5. "The Dark Tunnel"
The person's vision then begins to dim, often with loss of peripheral vision, simulating a trip down a long tunnel. During this time they may have the feeling of falling, tumbling, or moving toward the end of the tunnel at an ever-increasing speed.

6. "Out of the Body"
A detachment from the body; floating or even actually hovering around or over the body. Some reports describe the person giving a detached running account of events that were occurring during a resuscitation process. Moody describes these released entities as "spirits" or "souls" that have a new and altered perception of the surroundings.

7. "Meeting Others"
At this stage of the NDE, a person may encounter persons from the past, often long-since dead, though described as "spiritual beings."

8. "The Being of Light"
Moody then relates what he calls "the most incredible common element" in the NDE—the encounter with a bright light, almost always in the form of a person. It may begin as a "light at the end of the tunnel," but as the sequence changes and the person seems to travel toward the end of the tunnel, the light becomes brighter and more encompassing, and it often finally assumes the form of a person, sometimes in the form of an angel, a deceased relative, or an unidentified holy person. The all-encompassing nature of the light and the sense of warmth and love emanating from the light are fundamental. The identification of the person, though, "seems to be largely a function of the religious background, training or beliefs of the person involved."

While difficult to describe, the next element of this phase is the communication that takes place between the "dying" person and the "being of light." It is often said to be a direct transfer of feelings or thoughts, or a communication without words. The "dying" person then is asked if it is time to end his life, if he did on earth what he was supposed to do, or if his life was "complete." These questions are always asked in a loving manner, without judgment or condemnation.

9. "The Review"
Patients then conduct, in some fashion, a life review. During this time the "dying" person sees his past life displayed rapidly in great detail. Here Moody uses a description from a person who was only scared by an accident, was never in a medical crisis, but who nevertheless had an NDE with a life review.

10. "The Border or Limit"
Next the person encounters some obstacle to the continuation of the journey. The "dying" person must return to bodily life. Sometimes the person is given the choice to return to earth or to "continue dying," but in other NDEs the choice is made for the person by the "being of light."

11. "Coming Back"
The patient then returns to the body, frequently with unhappiness that he had to leave the "being of light" and the pleasant peace just experienced.

12. "Telling Others"
While Moody asserts that most people believe their experiences to be real, many are afraid to tell others for fear of ridicule or disbelief.

13. "Effects on Lives"
Moody claims that these NDEs have a profound effect on the remainder of the patients' lives, reorienting their goals. Patients become more philosophical and loving at the same time. They revere life more than they did prior to the NDE.

14. "New Views of Death"
Patients no longer view death as frightening, and they see their ultimate death in a more peaceful manner.

15. "Corroboration"
Some patients think their stories are supported by accounts of others who were nearby at the time of the NDE.

Moody's account is confusing to the reader. He didn't document the physical condition in most of his case examples, and many of those that were documented were definitely not near death.

Moody continued his account by alluding to some parallels between his subjects and descriptions in the Bible, citing Paul's encounter with the light on the road to Damascus. He noted that

Paul did not experience any near-fatal physical travail at that time. Moody further cited reports from Plato (9), from *The Tibetan Book of the Dead* (10), and from the scientist Emanuel Swedenborg (11-12). By citing these sources together, Moody attributed the credibility of the Bible to these occult or mystical sources. He blurred the distinctions among the various works, and by so doing he painted the NDE as a universal phenomenon with deep but undifferentiated historical and spiritual roots.

While some of his arguments are appealing, Moody's synthesis of the NDE leaves us with the impression that there is no sin inherent in mankind's existence, that there is no judgment, that a just and righteous God does not exist, that there is no system of rewards and punishments for our acts on earth, and—most importantly—that Jesus has no place in any redemptive strategy.

Nevertheless, it is always difficult to dispute personal experience. We are all truly experts on our own lives. In this respect, the world has appropriated the technique used by Christians as they witness to the power of God in their lives. Non-Christians now demand an audience to tell of their own experiences, and since experiences are not subject to rigorous examination, we often take them at face value. Discernment must guide us. We must not be misled simply by the intensity of the storyteller. Is the story of the NDE consistent with other evidence we have of the afterlife from the Bible? Is it even internally consistent?

Moody published a sequel to *Life After Life*, called *Reflections on Life After Life* (13), in 1977, even as his original book was maintaining its momentum. This subsequent book added little to his previous work except to elaborate on some of the theological issues. Many people were perplexed by the lack of divine judgment, reward, or punishment inherent in the NDE. Moody seemed to assert that the judgment in the NDE came from within the person himself, not from the "being of light" (14). Furthermore, Moody said, "In the mass of material I have collected no one has ever described to me a state like the archetypical hell" (15). He explained this singular lack of hellish experience in the following way: "However, I might remark that I have never interviewed anyone who had been a real rounder [an extremely dissolute person] prior to his close call. The people I have encountered have been normal, nice people. Such transgressions as they were guilty of had been minor—the sorts of things we have all done. So one would not expect that they would have been consigned to a fiery pit" (15).

Moody went on to cite the vision of St. Stephen as a possible NDE, as well as examples of similar events recorded from an English monk in A.D. 731, two examples from Irish tradition, a Polynesian account, an English vision, a Mexican story, accounts from Hemingway and Tolstoy, Mormon tradition, and one story from Plato.

Moody's second book concluded with a revised classification system for conditions and circumstances that might precipitate the NDE (16):

1. The person has a "close call," where there is no physical injury, even though there may have been a near-catastrophe.
2. The person is seriously ill or injured, but never experiences "clinical death" (cessation of vital function; loss of blood pressure, pulse, and respiration) and recovers.
3. The person is seriously ill, and he meets criteria for "clinical death." The medical personnel begin resuscitation, and the patient lives. No one ever actually "pronounced" the person dead.
4. The person is seriously ill (as in #3 with criteria for "clinical death"), and resuscitation is begun, but is stopped because it appears to fail. The person is "pro-

nounced" dead, or at least everyone thinks he is dead, but for some reason resuscitation is resumed, and the person lives.

5. The person is seriously ill, and "clinical death" is declared. Resuscitation is never begun because medical personnel think it will be useless. The person is "pronounced" dead. But later resuscitation attempts revive him.

6. The person is seriously ill. "Clinical death" supervenes. Resuscitation attempts may or may not occur. Medical personnel cease resuscitation efforts if they were begun because the cause appears hopeless, but the person recovers "spontaneously."

Moody, however, never used these criteria in a meaningful way, and there are both much overlap and subjectivity to this scheme.

To summarize these early works, Moody says that the NDE is a phenomenon that occurs as a person is close to death (or at times only seriously frightened from a near- accident), and a rather stereotyped sequence of events occurs. This sequence can range from *none* of the characteristics (in which case the person would have to say that he has *not* had an NDE) to any number of the components. While there are striking similarities to different persons' NDEs, no two are alike.

Moody's next book was an attempt to elaborate on some of the features of the NDE and to refine some of the concepts. In *The Light Beyond* (17), published in 1988, he cited a Gallup poll (18) that indicates that 8,000,000 people in the United States alone have had an NDE (19)! That's 8,000,000 round trips to heaven—lots of frequent flier miles. Is it likely that God would allow that many cookie-cutter glimpses into the heavenly realm? The poll further classified the components of the NDE, as reported by the respondents to this poll. Moody noted that no single element of the NDE was present in even one-third of those who reported having such experiences. Could all of these reports be authentic?

Moody alleged that in rare circumstances a person could have a component of a vision of the future, or what he called a "flash-forward," with a profound effect on the subsequent life of the traveler (20):

- No fear of dying
- Sensing the importance of love
- A sense of connection with all things
- An appreciation of learning
- A new feeling of control
- A sense of urgency
- Better developed spiritual side
- Difficulty reentering the "real" world

Moody admitted that the NDE has strong ties to Mormon doctrine, which espouses the validity of returning from death. He said:

> The Mormon doctrine supports the NDE as a peek into the spirit world. They believe that the spirit world is a dimension that can't be perceived by the living, but one that is inhabited by those who have left their physical body. (21)

Mormon tradition is replete with descriptions of the NDE, as chronicled by Lundahl (22). Many of the traits of the NDE are described by Mormon leaders themselves. One leader says, "The brightness and glory of the next apartment is inexpressible" (23), similar to the description of being engulfed by the soothing light. Another Mormon leader says that "there as here, all things will be natural, and you will understand them as you now understand natural things" (24), which is in keeping with many NDEers who claim to experience a kind of universal understanding. Mormon leaders say that "some spirits who have experienced death are called back to inhabit their physical bodies again. These persons pass through the natural or temporal death twice" (25).

We should examine further the background of the NDE researchers. Who is Raymond Moody? Often described as a medical philosopher, early in his career he dabbled in practices that would be considered occultic by many Christians. In 1991, with Paul Perry, he published *Coming Back—A Psychiatrist Explores Past-Life Journeys* (26). It is a treatise on reincarnation. Moody believes in "past-life regressions"—the ability to remember a previous existence, and he himself reports details of his nine previous lives. His major justification for his belief in "regressions" is that during the regression "something happens" (27). It is an experience-based phenomenon. He acknowledges that reincarnation is antithetical to the Christian faith (28), but also demands "reproducible evidence" of an afterlife to believe in it fully. While not willing to state unequivocally that he himself believes in reincarnation, the tone of this book supports his acceptance of it, simply disguised by calling it a "regression."

Most of his book, like many others in the NDE or spiritist realm, simply recounts personal testimonies collected during his psychiatric sessions with patients. He claims, for example, that a problem such as post-nasal drip could be related to the desire to cry in a "past life." When a patient "regressed" into that past life, the post-nasal drip "*almost* became a problem of the past" (29) (emphasis mine). Not a cure, but almost a cure. That is not good enough for me. And not much of "something happening." That is not a reason to abandon the Christian faith for idolatry either!

Furthermore, in 1994 Dr. Moody published *Reunions: Visionary Encounters with Departed Loved Ones* (30), a book dealing with communication with the dead, a practice he thinks is the logical extension of the NDE. If the dead exist "on the other side of the veil," then it should be possible to communicate with them outside the setting of the NDE. In his book he encouraged people to attempt to establish contact with the dead, while condemning the "religious fundamentalists" who oppose this practice on biblical grounds:

> Fundamentalists of whatever stripe, be it Christian, Jew, psychiatrist, or psychologist, are people who become transfixed by a cognitive structure, meaning that they obsess on an inflexible system of beliefs. They protest new ideas or inventions that somehow impinge on their rigid inner structures. Religious fundamentalists will voice their old refrain: "This is the work of Satan." Psychological fundamentalists have similar refrains as well: "I have never seen this, so it can't be true." (31)

He acknowledged that the Bible warns against these practices:

> *"Do not practice divination or sorcery."*
>
> *—Leviticus 19:26*

> *"Do not turn to mediums or seek out spiritists, for you will be defiled by them."*
>
> *—Leviticus 19:31*

> *"I will set my face against the person who turns to mediums and spiritists to prostitute himself by following them, and I will cut him off from his people."*
>
> *—Leviticus 20:6*

> *"A man or woman who is a medium or spiritist among you must be put to death. You are to stone them; their blood will be on their own heads."*
>
> *—Leviticus 20:27*

> *Let no one be found among you who sacrifices his son or daughter in the fire, who practices divination or sorcery, interprets omens, engages in witchcraft, or casts spells, or*

> *who is a medium or spiritist or who consults the dead. Anyone who does these things is detestable to the LORD.*
>
> —*Deuteronomy 18:10-12*

God gives us unequivocal warning against such occultic practices, but Moody claims that these examples are taken out of context and that these principles are outdated, in part because they come from the Old Testament. In Revelation, though, we also see New Testament admonitions against such practices:

> *"But the cowardly, the unbelieving, the vile, the murderers, the sexually immoral,* those who practice magic arts, *the idolaters and all liars—their place will be in the fiery lake of burning sulfur. This is the second death."*
>
> —*Revelation 21:8, emphasis mine*

> *"Blessed are those who wash their robes, that they may have the right to the tree of life and may go through the gates into the city. Outside are the dogs,* those who practice magic arts, *the sexually immoral, the murderers, the idolaters and everyone who loves and practices falsehood."*
>
> —*Revelation 22:14-15, emphasis mine*

Acts 16 gives us the story of a girl who had a spirit of divination. Paul recognized that this practice was forbidden, and he cast out the spirit within her, even at the cost of being beaten for this exorcism. Clearly the occult is dangerous and is condemned in the Bible.

Moody currently practices communication with the dead by divination techniques including mirror and crystal gazing at his headquarters, which he calls the "Theater of the Mind," in Anniston, Alabama (32). Here he conjures up the visions of the dead at his "psychomanteion" or "necromanteum," the names given to such a facility by the ancient Greeks. Moody reported such activity in a medical journal in late 1993, claiming that thirty-five of fifty-nine subjects who visited his psychomanteion were able to receive visions from the dead. While evaluation of Moody's conclusions about the NDE could be made in isolation, it is difficult to ignore his involvement in these other occultic practices. We must sometimes temper our judgment of a concept by the company it keeps.

But does anyone really believe in reincarnation or speaking with the dead? Why bother with this discussion? Aren't these practices simply the fascination of a fringe element of the general population, as well as the fringe of psychiatry? No; frighteningly they are almost mainstream religious belief. Colson (33), citing a 1994 Barna report, tells us that while 97 percent of Americans believe in God, only 67 percent think this God is the Creator. The same two-thirds deny the existence of absolute truth. The belief that God can be reached by achieving a plane of higher consciousness is embraced by most people in the United States. Fifty percent believe in the powers of extrasensory perception, and 25 percent have bought into the concept of reincarnation. Worse, half believe that your religious beliefs are unimportant as long as you have *some* beliefs. They embrace the concept that all religions are valid as long as you are "sincere." So we really *do* have a problem here.

IAN STEVENSON

Dr. Ian Stevenson is a psychiatrist with strong viewpoints about death and the death process. He has written extensively on the topic of parapsychology—that discipline dealing with phenomena that are difficult to explain within the bounds of normal human sensory and mental processes (34-42). This interest encompasses telepathy, extrasensory perception, and zenoglossia (communication with the dead). He believes strongly in reincarnation, and he wrote a summary of the principles of reincarnation in the *Journal of Nervous and Mental Disease* in 1977 (35). This article was followed by commentary from others in the field who were already generally supportive of Dr. Stevenson's thoughts (43-45). However, the editor acknowledged: "Extrasensory perception, reincarnation, and the paranormal in particular, carry an aura of abandonment of ordinary standards of logic and reality testing. For some they suggest rejection of the total body of knowledge accumulated by systematic observation and experiment" (46).

Stevenson published a summary of his concepts of the afterlife in 1977 (35), and he and Bruce Greyson evaluated the NDE in a special article in the *Journal of the American Medical Association* in 1979 (34).

The debate intensified when an article was published in the *Journal of the American Medical Association* that classified such reports as "fantasy" and challenged the concepts that Moody had popularized (47). Dr. Richard S. Blacher noted that the NDE occurred only during events that caused a gradual loss of consciousness and that the events of the NDE were remarkably similar to accounts of visions and sensory experiences observed with early anesthesia. He recognized that the NDE was an attempt by man to control and tame the frightening process of dying and to give it meaning in a way that would not contradict religious beliefs. He acknowledged that the NDE could even *generate* religious beliefs.

He was met with a response to his commentary by a letter from Dr. Michael B. Sabom, a cardiologist who had also investigated the NDE. Sabom disputed the notion that the NDE occurred only during gradual onset of cardiac arrest (48), though he agreed that the NDE should not be used as definitive evidence of an afterlife. He argued for a more controlled investigation of the NDE and warned that even "scientific" reports should be viewed critically. Blacher responded with sarcasm, warning us not to believe "the ideas of spirits wandering around the emergency room" and apologizing for saying that the NDE "never" occurred in patients undergoing open-heart surgery by saying that "never" only represented "several thousand patients" in whom he failed to find any evidence of the NDE (49)!

RALPH WILKERSON

An early Christian account of the NDE came from Ralph Wilkerson in *Beyond and Back*, published in 1977 (50). Wilkerson reported many NDEs of Christians who were profoundly affected by their experiences. These accounts were not as detailed as some of the other works being circulated at that time, but they became widely known because of the prominence of Wilkerson's ministry at Melodyland Christian Center, a church and school of theology based in Anaheim, California.

The first report in his book detailed a person who supposedly spent thirty minutes in heaven in 1971. The patient, Marvin Ford, suffered a heart attack and was being treated (with unspecified medications) when he had his NDE. He went to a beautiful city where he met Jesus. After some discussion in which he was given the opportunity to choose his next destination, Jesus told him to go back to earth with a commission to do Jesus' bidding. Though the patient tells us that the doctor told him he was "clinically dead," we are not told what that means, and we are not given any details of his medical condition during his NDE.

The next NDE reported is the experience of Dr. Irvine Harrison, a theologian who also supposedly had his NDE in the face of a heart attack. He describes a situation in which an unspecified "substance" was oozing out of every pore of his body, a condition that he likened to the life flowing out of him. He describes none of the medical details, and we cannot discern what actually happened to him at this time. Later he had another attack and died, though the details of this encounter are even more obscure. A bystander (without any reported evidence) interpreted the look on Harrison's face to mean that he had seen God and had decided that he did not want to come back to his life on earth. Thus, his death achieved finality.

The third NDE described by Wilkerson came from Dr. Michael Esses, another theologian who also had a heart attack. Medical details here are also lacking. Furthermore, Wilkerson says, "I cannot say whether Dr. Esses was clinically dead" (51).

Many other accounts of celestial journeys punctuate Wilkerson's book, but all are similarly vague with regard to the medical details, and none completely fulfill many of the stereotyped sequences attributed to the NDE by other authors. Some contain details that are discrepant with other accounts, such as the color of Jesus' hair, described as "brownish auburn (52)," contrasting with the description in the book of Revelation of "white" (Revelation 1:14). Another telling recounts the trip to heaven as being a ride in a "heavenly vehicle (53)," which is difficult to reconcile with the many accounts of others flying to heaven, being accompanied by angels, moving rapidly through a tunnel, or being led to heaven by the nail-scarred hand of Jesus.

BRUCE GREYSON

Greyson and Stevenson published their survey of the NDE in 1980 (40), in which they tried to evaluate the components and the aftermath of the NDE. They studied seventy-eight highly selected persons who claimed to have had an NDE. The study was terribly biased in the manner of recruitment for the interviews. They came from (1) letters written to a "national magazine" from people who had already read about the NDE and who claimed to have had a similar experience, (2) responses to requests from people interested in paranormal phenomena, and (3) responses of people who knew of the authors' interest in the NDE. The "control" population, to which the NDE patients were compared, was a group of psychiatric inpatients and a report of a survey of the general population obtained by mail responses to a questionnaire. This method of patient selection and comparison would today preclude publication in any reputable, peer-reviewed journal and indeed would be likely to provoke derision from the medical community.

Nevertheless, Greyson and Stevenson concluded that the NDE population was more likely to have had multiple close calls with death and to have experienced psychic or paranormal events (such as visions, memories of a "previous life," seeing auras or halos around other people, or communicating with the dead) than the control patients. Furthermore, Stevenson thought that the NDE had a more profound effect than other "psychic experiences" on the subsequent attitudes of the patients (54-58).

ERNST A. RODIN

As the interest in the NDE skyrocketed, a conversation was published in the *Journal of Nervous and Mental Disease* in 1980 that began with a report from a physician, Dr. Ernst A. Rodin, who claimed to have had an NDE (59-62). However, his report lacked many of the features of the NDE, and the event itself was questionable—he described his "personal death experience," which could have simply been sensations induced by anesthesia. There was no accounting of any physiologic parameters that would confirm that he was near death. His sense of "tremendous bliss" occurred after "the needle for the anesthetic [was] placed into my arm." He incorrectly rejected the notion that the event was anesthesia-induced by stating that he has had subsequent anesthesia without any similar reaction. He thought that his experience was a "toxic psychosis" and that the dying experience is created by the expectations of the person dying, without further influence. He says:

> It can be assumed that what is important for the individual in his dying moments is the mental content of this psychosis. . . . If the content of the final psychosis is pleasant, the individual who knows that he is dying is likely to accept it as his version of heaven. If it is terrifying and/or painful, one does not require medieval devils to realize that one has entered hell. There is no way of knowing whether our individual brain in its last moments will send us to celestial spheres or into the biblical bottomless pit. . . . The dying individual, however, acts as his own judge, jury, accuser, prosecutor, defense attorney, and witness. He or she alone renders the final verdict of guilty or not guilty. (63)

In other words, our mind-set controls our eternal destination, if there even is an eternity.

GLENN ROBERTS AND JOHN OWEN

Roberts and Owen reviewed the NDE in an article in 1988 in the *British Journal of Psychiatry* (64). They recognized that the NDE could occur in patients in whom imminent demise was not expected but who were simply experiencing emotional or frightening states. There appeared to be no predisposing demographic characteristics, but the interpretation of the NDE, the persons seen in the NDE, and the religious significance attached to the NDE varied according to the religious background of the patient (65-66). While a patient may not have a strong association with a religious organization, the cultural trappings of the society may indeed dictate the imagery contained in the NDE. They reported, "Cross-cultural studies . . . record the Navajo seeing a great chief in a beautiful field, a Hindu seeing a death messenger coming to take him away, and the Catholic meeting with the Virgin Mary in a great cathedral: the imagery corresponds to the concept of the after-life in the mind and cultural setting of the individual" (67).

The NDE seems to reinforce the notion that your choice of religious beliefs is of no consequence: whatever you believe is just fine. Your own religion will appear in a personal version of the NDE should you ever have one. This is a dangerous concept to the Christian, who has the imperative to "go . . . into all the world, and preach the good news" (Mark 16:15) because Jesus is the only way!

MICHAEL SABOM

Dr. Michael Sabom is a Christian cardiologist who was initially a skeptic of the NDE (48, 61, 68-70). He authored one of the early NDE books (68) and was the first vice president of the International Association for Near-Death Studies.

Sabom wrote his first two articles on the NDE in 1977 (69-70). Both apparently reported the same fifty patients, eleven of whom had experiences, described as either or both "transcendence" or "autoscopy." By "transcendence," Sabom meant an experience "of 'traveling' into another region or dimension." "Autoscopy" meant "viewing their body from a detached position of height several feet above the ground." These eleven patients generally experienced a cardiac arrest, though the medical details are not outlined in the papers.

Some of his reported NDE encounters quote conversations between man and God that seem a bit implausible. One patient cited in both articles (the two early reports are virtually identical in content, wording, and quotations) said that as she was being sent back to this life, "the good Lord popped up and he said, 'Go back, go back. Your kids and a lot of people are going to need you. We don't need you now.'" A strange way for a God who knows all (including the future) to act! Surely He would have known that the woman was needed on earth before her medical crisis brought her close to death. Was it necessary for her to go see God personally for Him to realize how necessary it was for her to remain on earth?

In his book, Sabom expressed his initial skepticism of the NDE by saying, "My indoctrinated scientific mind just couldn't relate seriously to these 'far-out' descriptions of afterlife spirits and such . . . . The kindest thing I could find to say at the moment was 'I don't believe it'" (71). He concluded the book with, "Does the NDE represent a glimpse of and afterlife, of life after death? As a physician and scientist, I cannot, of course, say for sure that the NDE is indicative of what is to come at the moment of *final* bodily death. These experiences were encountered during waning moments of life. Those reporting these experiences were *not brought back from the dead*, but were rescued from a point *very close to death*" (72, emphasis Sabom's).

Sabom recently restated and clarified his position regarding the scientific explanation of the NDE and how it should be integrated into our religious beliefs: "I am a Christian and believe in heaven and hell. Based on current knowledge, however, we have much to learn about the NDE, both distressing and pleasant, before we can say confidently just what this experience means and how it fits into our spiritual beliefs" (73).

MELVIN MORSE

Dr. Melvin Morse is a pediatrician who reported some of the first NDEs in children (74-79). His reports are primarily testimonials of patients who have had NDEs. Furthermore, his work generally is lacking medical detail regarding the illnesses supposedly precipitating the NDE.

Melvin Morse's first book, *Closer to the Light* (80), was published in 1990. It explored aspects of the NDE in children. He suggested that evaluation of children could yield useful, untainted information about the NDE because their memories are more reliable, they are less likely to fabricate a story (hardly a convincing argument to most parents), they are less encumbered by religious beliefs, and they are less likely to be biased or influenced by suggestion. He ignored the profound influence of early training, peer influences, and, most importantly, television. These influences are hardly neutral.

The foreword to the book was written by Dr. Raymond Moody, who emphasized that Morse "proves" that a person need be near death to have an NDE. He also claimed that Morse's researchers "have been able to isolate the area of the brain where near-death experiences occur" (81), though Morse presented no new data to support this theory. Morse quoted some of Penfield's studies, but he performed no original experiments on this subject.

This book consists primarily of short vignettes and anecdotes that Morse uses to illustrate his beliefs about the NDE. He cited his only three studies published in peer-reviewed and medical literature about the NDE (74-76). The first is his case report of "Katie," the case that first piqued his interest in the NDE. In fact, neither in his book nor in the original article in the *American Journal of Diseases of Children* in 1983 is there enough information about her medical illness—a "near-drowning"—to conclude whether the patient's heart actually stopped (though medical personnel on the scene performed chest compression and artificial respiration for her because it appeared that she had stopped breathing and presumably had no palpable pulse). There is no mention of whether an electric shock was administered to her chest to restart her heart. Other medical details surrounding her experience are quite sketchy.

Katie saw Jesus, God the Father, and an angel named Elizabeth during her NDE. Morse claimed that she had no concept of religion that would have biased her story but later points out that Katie was a "middle-of-the-road Mormon" (82), and the original article states, "The patient was from a deeply religious Mormon background" (83).

Morse claimed that it was necessary for the patient to be actually near death to have an NDE. He then proceeded to tell of the "predeath vision" experience, which does not depend upon physical manifestations of the dying process, and he reported or cited many cases of the NDE in which the patient was never close to death (84):

> A girl reports an NDE after falling to the floor and striking her head.
>
> A boy is rescued from a car being swept downriver in a flood, though no report of any physical injury is included.
>
> A boy walks on a fog-shrouded hill and sees a bright light that Morse thinks is the same spiritual force that is present in the NDE.
>
> A person has an NDE when swimming, though never drowning nor coming close to drowning, at least by Morse's report.
>
> A person has an NDE as a reaction to dental anesthesia, probably not a near-death complication of the procedure.
>
> Another boy is ill and later says that doctors had "given up," though no evidence is provided of any physical manifestation of a near-death experience.
>
> A girl has an NDE as part of a grief reaction to a friend's death. She has no physical illness.
>
> A woman has an NDE "from too much anesthesia" during an operation. She is not near death.
>
> A man siphoning gasoline swallows and inhales some gas, then has his NDE. He is not near death, and Morse provides no discussion about whether this experience could be related to the effect of the gasoline on the brain.
>
> A young boy has a fever after removal of a superficial fungus on his skin "and was barely holding on to life." Then he has his NDE. How could this experience ever be classified as near-death?
>
> A man passes out from blood loss and has an NDE. He was not near death by the account.

In many other cases, it is simply impossible to discern the physical condition of the patient at the time of the vision. In some circumstances, a person may have an NDE as a function of a "shared spiritual experience"—that is, a person not threatened by any physical disease or harm has an NDE when a *friend* or *relative* is in physical danger of death (80).

Dr. Morse includes "shared" NDEs in his classification scheme. His "telepathically shared" experiences certainly contradict earlier statements that the physical condition of death or near-death is required as one condition for the NDE. For proof, he quotes such authoritative sources as the United Press International news service and the television program *Unsolved Mysteries*, which in my view are not the best sources of medical information! Morse even claims that some people have the tunnel experience through dreams. All of its wondrous revelations are provided without having to endure any of the inconveniences of dying or having a serious illness. Finally, Morse even claims that NDEs can occur neonatally or prenatally!

A main emphasis in Morse's book is the powerful force in the bright light, by far the overwhelming aspect of the experience. He admitted that it can be influenced by the person's prior concept of religion and the afterlife. He attempted to homogenize religions—to arrive at a universalist approach—by citing examples of the light in various religions and cultures (85):

> Native American spiritual leader Black Elk had a near-fatal illness at age nine that put him in touch with the Light.
>
> In *Autobiography of a Yogi*, the Indian guru Paramahansa Yogananda describes his near-death experience at age eight, which then enhanced his lifelong devotion to religion.
>
> The religious implications of the Light were described more than two hundred years ago by Jonathan Edwards, the Calvinist theologian. . . .

The light described by Edwards, in fact, was not the light of the NDE, though Morse claims that it could have been because Edwards "nearly died of pleurisy as a child, an illness that may well have led to a near-death experience" (86). Edwards was talking simply about a "divine light, immediately imparted to the soul by God" (87). Furthermore, pleurisy is not a near-fatal illness, and there is no evidence presented to support the claim that Edwards might have been near death during this illness.

Note that Morse capitalized the word "Light" as though the light was indeed the supreme god, but he does not identify it as any member of the Trinity. The juxtaposition of the different examples of a light in the experiences of the lives of divergent religious figures seems to me to tie all religions together with a common thread, to universalize all religious experience, to say that the light can be *any* god.

Of course, the concept of God as light is well established in the Bible. Moses saw God as the Shekinah Glory—a pillar of fire by night and a cloud by day. When Moses visited with God on Mount Sinai, he returned to the children of Israel with a glowing countenance that reflected God's glory. In this respect, the NDE has a similar quality. But new religions or cults commonly borrow aspects from established religions to confuse the unwary.

In addition to reporting the NDE, Morse gives credence to other "visionary" processes. He says that "envisioning health" is useful. He states that "imagining" something can make it happen (87). Such concepts sound remarkably like New Age thought.

Morse's next book, *Transformed by the Light* (88), came in 1992. Its purpose was to demonstrate the long-term effects of the NDE on lives of those who experienced it. While he enumerated the interview testing instruments he used, he did not give any evidence of the reliability or reproducibility of these questionnaires when used in this setting. Most importantly, the entire set of data was not peer-reviewed, nor published in any reputable journal. Nevertheless, he claimed that his studies show that his NDE subjects have (1) "a decreased death anxiety," (2) "an increase in psychic abilities," (3) "a higher zest for living," and (4) "a higher intelligence." Who would not want to have an NDE if the researcher reported those benefits! He relied mostly on anecdotal stories that emphasized the fantastic. In my estimation, none of his data was conclusive.

Morse then tells us that survivors of an illness punctuated by an NDE acquire electromagnetic forces that influence physical objects, like stopping watches. While this "phenomenon" should be easy to document in a scientific fashion, Morse simply gave us a number that we are expected to believe: one-fourth of NDE patients have to give up wearing watches because the NDE-induced electromagnetic forces render the watches inoperable! He claimed other undocumented superpowers for these forces as well: healing of broken bones, cancer cures, limb regeneration, even the electromotive forces acting as "a second nervous system" for the NDE recipient. He then proceeded to give a simplistic "review" of the importance of electromagnetism in the body, concluding (without evidence) that the NDE confers these qualities to believing survivors, curing all manner of diverse illnesses. The title of the chapter concerning these phenomena, however, is appropriate: "The Circuit Boards of Mysticism."

The data presented by Morse are, in my professional opinion, only pseudo-scientific. While he purports to give us information about his "Transformations Study," the data are useless. Tests involving open-ended questions should have been obtained in a double-blinded fashion; that is, the researchers cannot know at the time of the interviews which persons were the controls and which persons had claimed to have had an NDE. Morse's book gives no such assurances. How were the "control" persons chosen? Were they matched for other clinical, medical, psychiatric, emotional, and spiritual characteristics? Were the NDE patients consecutive, or did he only test those whom he felt would exhibit the qualities he desired? One cannot assume lack of bias in such studies. These valid questions should be answered before we consider accepting his conclusions.

Morse recently published a comprehensive review article on the NDE, though it presented no new peer-reviewed data (78). Nevertheless, it is a good recent summary of the thoughts of the NDE proponents. Morse contended that the elements of the NDE can all be reproduced by stimulation of the temporal lobe of the brain and by hallucinogenic drugs and can be explained by physical characteristics of the neural connections. He generally avoided the lure to make definitive spiritual interpretations of the NDE, though he lumped the NDE appropriately with "ghosts, mediums, spirit communication with the dead, and death-bed and near death visions" (89). He also stated that the NDE has appeared "in the context of tremendous public interest in a wide variety of spiritual and paranormal issues, including spirit channeling, paranormal abilities, spiritual healing, encounters with UFOs, and even kidnappings by UFOs. Interestingly, the first wave of UFO sightings occurred in the late nineteenth century at the same time of the first modern accounts of deathbed visions" (89).

Indeed, Davis reported that UFO sightings themselves caused people to have more positive attitudes and an increased interest in spiritual matters (90). Morse claimed that from 10 to 90 percent of all medical crises are accompanied by the NDE—quite a range and quite at variance with estimates by Dobson et al. of 5 percent (91) and of less than 1 percent by Negovsky (92-93). Furthermore, he claimed that 11 to 14 percent of the American population has had an out-of-body experience, even the so-called normal segment of the population that does not experiment with illicit drugs.

Morse in his review article addressed the biases that prevail in the field of NDE research (94). He stated that Moody "readily acknowledges asking loaded questions," and he admits that Moody's book raised "issues of cultural contamination and examiner bias." As an example of the type of bias to which Morse alluded: Moody's book was "based on subjects who often approached Dr. Moody after lectures, no systematic interview format was involved, and no review of medical records or psychiatric or medical history was done." Morse cited Ring as another NDE researcher whose techniques are questionable. In Ring's book, the "interview format is filled with leading questions. The nature of the questions was heavily weighted toward answers that would please the interviewer by disclosing mystical events and personality transformations. The book is filled with impressive statistics based on a biased subject sample and poor data collection techniques."

Furthermore, the major supportive organization—and the major publisher of the "scientific" papers—was the International Association of Near-Death Studies (IANDS), which "itself developed a spiritual and political agenda, commonly referred to as 'New Age.' . . . The organization's therapeutic role made independent objective research difficult. The organization has dominated most near death research since 1977, and most of the studies are published in its journal, which is not refereed or indexed in the medical or scientific literature."

This means that nearly all of the near-death literature is not subject to close scrutiny for authenticity, objectivity, or accuracy before publication. Most medical experts view it as worthless, existing at best on the fringe of legitimate scholarship. Of course, the NDE proponents wear this label as a badge of honor and claim that the "medical establishment" is simply closed to new ideas. Finally, Morse admits that some view the NDE "at the level of campfire stories" (95), a summary with which Morse disagrees but with which I concur.

BETTY MALZ

An early report of the NDE was published by Betty Malz in *Angels Watching Over Me* and *My Glimpse of Eternity* (96-97). She described complications from a ruptured appendix (which included "gangrene" of her intestines and a " gangrenous infection in the . . . bloodstream"), slipping from a coma into death, and having a doctor pronounce her dead. She then had her NDE and was ushered into heaven, only to be returned to the earth twenty-eight minutes later. She enjoyed great popularity from these accounts. The most revealing statement of the book was her husband's comment, "You make dying sound like good news."

However, the accuracy of her account was later questioned. Lorna Dueck's and Ken Sidey's investigation suggested that the story was a fabrication, as outlined in both *Christian Week* and *Christianity Today* (98). All three physicians involved in her care disputed her story, and hospital officials provided admission and discharge dates that proved Malz's account inaccurate, if not completely false. Dr. Henry Bopp, one of her attending physicians and the surgeon who performed her appendectomy, said, "This is almost a complete fabrication. She did not die. She may have dreamt she did, but she did not die in the hospital." The anesthetist for her operation, J. Bopp (Dr. Henry Bopp's brother), also said, "I challenge [the publishers] to produce the medical records and let independent doctors look at the records. I'll flat guarantee you this didn't happen." Her primary physician, Dr. H. Clark Boyd, denied that Malz was ever close to death, coma, or even septic shock, as she alleges. He is quoted as saying, "I had a very good relationship with her. That was until I wouldn't believe her story, and she kept getting madder and madder. Then she didn't come in anymore."

At best, the details of her medical illness are unverifiable, and at worst, if the physicians are to be believed, she created the entire story herself. Malz's editors claimed that the physicians were covering up their actions by denying the story of her death, and the publisher of her book was unwilling to ask her for independent verification of her story before or after the publication of her books.

Leonard LeSourd, the book's editor for the publisher, Chosen Books, said, "The [medical] records weren't that important to me." The publisher seemed to be satisfied that she had a productive ministry, whether or not it was based on a true story.

BETTY EADIE

The most popular recent book on the subject of the NDE is Betty Eadie's *Embraced by the Light* (99). It remained on the *New York Times* Bestseller List for many months. Translated into twenty-one languages, it has sold over two million copies of the hardcover edition alone! It is purported to be an account of the experience that Eadie, an ex-hypnotherapist, had after a hysterectomy when she experienced serious bleeding and nearly died. However, she waited nearly twenty years after the events to write the book, she has refused to allow review of her medical records regarding the event, and the medical details of the experience are obscure (100). Nevertheless, she reports going on a fantastic voyage in which she leaves her body, travels around a bit, then goes down a tunnel to an encounter with a "being of light." She identifies this being as Jesus, though many of the aspects of her story have a Mormon orientation with a touch of New Age belief. Richard Abanes reports that "Dick Baer, founder of Ex-Mormons and Christian Alliance in Orangevale, California, says, 'This book is a carefully crafted book of deception . . . crafted to denigrate Christianity and promote doctrines that are mainline Mormon doctrines" (100). The book promotes the notions that there is no hell or judgment and that all religions are equally valid.

Eadie claims that all elements or particles of the universe are created by a spiritual power, and they have both intelligence and the power to experience joy. A rather strange set of attributes for the building blocks of the universe. She also claims that man starts his journey at death in a warm dark region and is allowed to progress in his spiritual quest by the process of progressive development. This concept is drawn from Mormon doctrine as well.

Betty Eadie, in a television interview (*20/20*, May 13, 1994), while not claiming to have talked with God the Father, discussed her visionary encounter with Jesus (she interpreted the person as Jesus, though "He did not identify Himself") as though she were talking with a very casual acquaintance, not the all-powerful Person of the Trinity that He is. Furthermore, she reported that Jesus said, "You died, but it's not your time," as though something about her "death" was beyond God's power. She claimed, "We are all divine. We are all perfect"—clearly an unbiblical interpretation of the state of man. She asserted that everyone is allowed to go to heaven and said that it matters not what we believe or do on earth; heaven awaits us when we die—unless, of course, we must return to the earth to finish our lives because God made a mistake in allowing us to die in the first place. She describes death as a "blissful experience," while depicting Jesus as simply a humorous tour guide in heaven.

As an article of literature, *Embraced by the Light* clearly met the needs of a large segment of the American population (101). As a testimony of religious truth, however, it falls short. The description of her journey is one of the most detailed yet published, but there are too many gaps in the story to allow us to analyze the medical aspects of the case. The reader is referred to Richard Abanes's extensive analysis of Eadie's work, entitled *Embraced by the Light and the Bible*, for a more in-depth discussion of the theological aspects of Eadie's book (4). He comprehensively analyzes the Mormonism and New Age belief present in Betty Eadie's *Embraced by the Light*. He reveals her Mormon roots, exposing the financial backing for the publication of this work, and he surprises most readers by revealing that two versions of the book were published—one for Mormon consumption and one for the larger and more profitable nationwide distribution (4, 99, 102)! He explains many false Mormon doctrines in Eadie's book, including:

1. We are literally God's physical offspring.
2. God is *just* a man.
3. Polytheism is acceptable.
4. We can become gods ourselves.
5. Everyone will be saved.
6. All religions are valid.
7. There is no judgment.
8. Everyone achieves peace at death.
9. Sins don't matter.
10. We can choose whether to return to our bodies after death.

DANNION BRINKLEY

Nearly each day, a new NDE book appears on the bookstore shelves. Recently Dannion Brinkley published *Saved by the Light* (103). It is an account of a man who experienced two NDEs, one after being struck by lightning, another after surgery for replacement of a defective and infected aortic valve. Brinkley—like Eadie—espouses Mormon philosophy and leanings, while referring to his NDE as a "deeply spiritual experience."

In his first encounter, Brinkley was talking on the phone during a lightning storm, and he apparently was electrocuted and lost consciousness. Transported to a city of crystal and light, he encountered a "being of light" and later thirteen "beings of light." The original "being of light" was a silver form surrounded by "energy fields." It had neither male nor female form, and it (Brinkley refers to it as "he") offered no harsh judgment but gave only "friendly counsel." Brinkley was then presented a detailed life review, for which he felt remorseful. He was also supposedly given the power of mental telepathy.

During his NDE, he saw a city of grand cathedrals, like those of France or the Mormon Tabernacle in Salt Lake City, as he described them. The thirteen "beings of light" filled him with knowledge, including the knowledge of important events of the future revealed in individual boxes. (Of primary importance is the fact that his prophesies [such as the breakup of the Soviet Union] were not revealed until *after* the events had occurred.)

He was told a number of things that were to guide his life after his "return": for example, humans are "great, powerful, and mighty spiritual Beings" (104). Brinkley was also told that he was "to create spiritual capitalism there [on the earth]." He was shown seven rooms that were to be the prototype for stress reduction clinics to be built on the earth, and each one was similar to an ancient oracle. When asked how he was to build them, he was told, "Don't worry. It will come to you" (105).

He saw the medical practice of the future, in which it will be revealed that every cell of the body vibrates at a certain frequency. When these frequencies become incorrect, disease supervenes. Medical tools of the future will have the capacity to change the vibratory frequency of the cells by special lights, bringing the frequencies back to normal, he was told.

During his NDE he became aware that the sights he was seeing were very similar to the descriptions noted in the Mormon *Journal of Discourse*. He said, "Their findings match everything that happened to me" (106).

His second NDE was less intimidating because his life review was not as unpleasant—he had improved his behavior since his first "death." Initially he refused the heart surgery recommended to him because he wanted to die, saying, "I've died before and it was really quite pleasant" (107). Later, skirting perilously close to endorsing euthanasia, he said, "I think it's important for people to avoid a painful death" (108).

In this second NDE he was given the power to forgive—was

even *compelled* to forgive—his fellowman. In the midst of this experience, he heard a chant that apparently was the heavenly mantra, "ALLAHOM!" This chant is remarkably similar to one of the names of God, Elohim, giving this mantra a counterfeit religious sound. He concluded by quoting one of his own statements given on Russian television: "There are many paths to righteousness, I said, and that is good news for all of us, since no one seems to be on the same path, as far as I can tell" (109).

In all of these descriptions, Brinkley revealed:

1. His Mormon leanings, comparing the cathedrals he saw to the beauty of the Mormon Tabernacle and his NDE to the NDEs of the Mormon *Journal of Discourse.*
2. His refusal to believe in a judgment for our actions on the earth.
3. His belief that humans are good and powerful spiritual beings, in contrast to the Bible, which says that all men are corrupt and fallen.
4. His profit motive by which he was to create clinics and promote "spiritual capitalism."
5. His lack of timeliness in revealing the future prophecy only *after* the events had occurred.
6. His leanings toward euthanasia.
7. His belief that all religions are equally valid (or invalid).

A dangerous book indeed!

3

MORE NDE RESEARCHERS

This Light's for You, Bud

Margaret can never forget her near-drowning when she was twelve years old. Now approaching the realm of "ancient history" for her because it occurred over forty years ago, it still burns in her memory as though it happened just yesterday—well, maybe the day before yesterday. But it remains the most vivid recollection of her childhood.

She always was a good swimmer, and she loved to dive. One Saturday her mother had taken her to the nearby lake, and she was practicing her dives from the dock. Not yet Olympic quality, Margaret nevertheless enjoyed her mother's attention and encouragement.

She dove from the same point off the dock for about the twentieth time, and she was improving, her confidence rising with every "Great job, Margaret!" Once again she dove into the lake, this time splitting the water so that she hardly caused a ripple. So good was this dive that she hurried to surface to hear her mother's affirmation. But she misjudged the distance back to the dock and was coming straight up when she suddenly realized that she was under the dock instead of next to it. Too late to slow down! Her head smashed against the bottom of the dock, at the water line. Immediately she felt that she would pass out and sank below the surface. Disoriented, still barely conscious, she tried to swim back up to the surface, but she couldn't tell up from down. She felt the water becoming colder, and the light was fading. That's when she realized she was in trouble. As she suddenly felt intensely cold, she also noted a strange peace. No panic. No fear of dying, even though she didn't know how far below the surface she was, or even which way was up.

Then everything went black. Her friends told her that she must have passed out, but she doesn't remember anything until she awakened as someone pulled her to the surface. All she remembers is that it was black and very peaceful before she lost consciousness.

As she coughed and choked lying on the dock, she remembers thinking that she could have died; but only then did the profound calm disintegrate into fear again. She still only rarely tells this story because of the intense emotions it elicits. She knows she had a brush with death, and death was cheated—at least for the time. She had lived through both a medical and emotional crisis.

But what about the rest of the story? What about the tunnel, the travel, the "being of light"? The rest of the story doesn't exist. She had no other images, no encounters. But she still has a next time. Can she be prepared?

KENNETH RING

Dr. Kenneth Ring is a psychologist and one of the foremost NDE proponents (1-3). His book, *Life at Death: A Scientific Investigation of the Near-Death Experience* (1), examines the NDE in more detail than previous authors.

Ring recognized in the late 1970s that most works on the NDE were far from scientific, and he set about to examine the NDE phenomenon in a more rigorous manner. He was the first to separate the major elements of the NDE—the "core experience"—from other less important features of the event. He proposed to answer four major questions in his book (4):

1. How often does the NDE occur in near-death episodes, and does the "core experience" remain independent of the condition that produced it?
2. Does the mode of near-death (accident, suicide, illness) influence the NDE?
3. Does the prior religion of the person influence the NDE?
4. Does the NDE have long-lasting effects on the person?

Let's examine these questions ourselves.

Ring established certain minimal entry criteria for his studies (5):

1. The patient had to have survived an episode that brought him close to death or to have been resuscitated from clinical death.
2. He had to recover from #1 sufficiently to be able to discuss it.
3. He had to speak English.
4. He had to be eighteen years old or older.

These are reasonable starting criteria. The author, however, admits that most of his patients were, in fact, not resuscitated from clinical death (absence of pulse and blood pressure), and so the ones most likely to have experienced a legitimate "near-death" experience were uncommon in his report. Patients resuscitated from a true "clinical death" episode have severe memory loss (see Section II), so the most valid patients are excluded. The requirement for English-speaking is simply a practical matter and cannot be criticized. It will eliminate the cultural differences in whatever phenomenon is being studied but is at times unavoidable. Requiring legal age of consent is also a standard practice, and the author might have been criticized had he *not* excluded minors.

Selection bias is a problem for the manner in which patients were recruited for the study: it depended on the identification and referral of patients by medical personnel, and so patients without the features of interest (the NDE in general) would be less likely to be referred. True, the author states that the NDE per se was not required, but I would be surprised if the referred patients were similar to the non-referred patients. Furthermore, the author later relied upon the responses to advertisements for patients, which gave him 21 percent of his patient population.

The population for his first study consisted of 102 patients, two of whom had experienced two near-death events. Approximately one-half had a medical event as the basis for the near-death, one-quarter an attempted suicide, and one-quarter an accident. About one-half were male, 97 percent white, and one-half married. One-third were Catholic, one-third Protestant, and one-third another religion or no religion. The educational profile was well balanced across all types, and the mean age was forty-three years (in a range eighteen to eighty-four). The mean age at the near-death episode was thirty-eight. Most patients were interviewed within two years of the near-death episode.

Ring devised a rather complex scale to quantify the NDE. He ascribed points to the various qualities of the NDE. The range of possible scores was from 0 to 29 (6):

RING'S NDE SCALE

ITEM	SCORE
Subjective sensation of being dead	1
Peace, painlessness, pleasantness	
Strong	4
Weak	2
Bodily separation	
Clearly out-of-body	4
Otherwise	2
Entering a dark region	
Movement present	4
No movement	2
Encountering a presence or hearing a voice	3
Taking stock of one's life	3
Seeing or being enveloped in light	2
Seeing beautiful colors	1
Entering into the light	4
Encountering visible spirits	3
MAXIMUM POSSIBLE SCORE	29

He arbitrarily declared that a score of less than 6 was insufficient to qualify the patient as a "core experiencer," meaning a person who had the basic NDE, as described by Moody. A person with a score of 6 to 9 was called a "moderate experiencer," and a score of 10 to 29 qualified as a "deep experiencer." In his study of 102 patients, 26 percent were "deep experiencers," 22 percent were "moderate experiencers," and 52 percent were "non-experiencers." The percentages for men and women were equal.

Ring then analyzed the characteristics of the experience. Of those who qualified as having at least the core experience, 60 percent described a feeling of peace, 37 percent described a body separation, 23 percent described entering a darkness, 16 percent saw a bright light, and 10 percent entered that bright light (7). He then compared the core experiencers with the non-experiencers, but, of course, such a comparison is circular reasoning. The core experiencers were defined by the qualities of the NDE described by Moody, so one would expect the non-experiencers to have a different level and degree of sensations of the NDE. They were classified *based upon* the absence of such features. Even his subjects who qualified with a core experience had a very low incidence of seeing the bright light or entering the light, two features that Moody emphasized so strongly. Ring evaluated the "ineffable" quality of the NDE and found that about one-half thought the experience was difficult to express in words. Because of the way the subjects were originally classified, his attempts to analyze the perceptions of dying or the process of dying were flawed. He concluded that the NDE experiencers had more of a sensation of dying than the non-experiencers, but they were put into these groups *because* of these qualities.

The patients' perceptions of body, time, and space were also quantified. Most patients had neither heavy nor light bodily sensations, and most had no sense that time was either accelerated or slowed. The sense of space was neither distorted, extended, nor infinite for most NDE experiencers. In fact, most patients thought that the concepts of time, space, and body either were absent or irrelevant during their experience. Only one-quarter of the patients felt they were approaching some sort of limit or border beyond which they were supposed to pass. Nevertheless, Ring concluded that the phenomena described by Moody were very similar to the events described by Ring's own patients.

Ring next addressed the events that precipitated the NDE. He found that males and females were different ages at the time of either accident or suicide, males being younger for both of these events, while the age ranges were similar for illnesses. The NDE was present in 56 percent of patients with serious illnesses as the basis for the event, 42 percent for accidents, and 33 percent for suicide attempts (8). There was also a difference in the male/female distribution of the NDE: men were more likely to have the NDE in conjunction with an accident or suicide attempt, while the NDE was more likely to occur in women with a illness.

Ring also attempted to classify the event by likelihood that the event would have led to death had there been no intervention (9):

0: the person was in no danger of dying;

1: it was unclear if the condition would have led to death without intervention;

2: the condition would probably have led to death without intervention;

3: the person would have died without intervention;

4: "resuscitated—*probably* was clinically dead" (emphasis mine).

The mean scores for males/females were 2.94/3.13 for illnesses, 2.66/2.52 for accidents, and 2.08/2.18 for suicide attempts (10). Persons with suicide attempts were further from death. Persons with illnesses were closest. Unfortunately, he did not tell us how many people were actually documented to have experienced "clinical death" by any criteria. More importantly, it is not clear that the ratings were made without the knowledge of the presence or absence of the NDE or of the qualities of the NDE, if present. That is, we don't know if these ratings were biased by the knowledge of the presence or absence of the NDE. It is clear, though, that most patients could not have been "clinically dead" with absence of pulse, blood pressure, and heartbeat.

Ring tried to find qualities of the respondents that correlated with the NDE. He reported that many factors were *unrelated* to the NDE: social class, race, marital status, age, and religious denomination. He then reported on the long-term effects of the NDE and noted that the medical or situational crisis itself, *not the NDE*, seemed to be the dominant factor in the life changes of the patients. Simply surviving a brush with death was what was important, not the sensory experiences of the tunnel, the light, etc., though there was a trend for those patients with the NDE to have a renewed sense of purpose in life, to be more loving, to appreciate life more fully, and to be stronger. Those with the NDE seemed to be "more religious"—a vague classification—after the event, while "belief in God" did not change. Said another way, God-based beliefs were unchanged, while *feelings* were stronger after the NDE.

Ring concluded the study of religion and the NDE by presenting data indicating that the NDE experiencers had a stronger belief in the afterlife than persons without the NDE. Unfortunately, simply a belief in the afterlife is useless unless it carries with it a positive imperative for action that alters our life course. The message of the NDE is exactly the opposite—virtually everyone attains the blissful state after death, and nothing we do in this life matters! Ring once said, "I can't recall any case of someone reporting being judged by God" (11). Moody (12-18) claims that hell either is nonexistent or that it almost never is the destination during the NDE. Sabom's early reports (19-23) were mostly pleasant NDEs, while Rawlings (24-26) cites alleged hellish experiences. However, the overwhelming bulk of literature—and certainly the popular recent literature—suggests that at death "all is well"—love and peace abound. The NDE generally denies the justice and the righteousness of God!

SUSAN BLACKMORE

Next we need to consider the most elegant analysis yet articulated for the vast literature of the NDE, the work by Susan Blackmore entitled *Dying to Live* (27). She began by reducing the discussion to a consideration of only two alternatives: (1) either the NDE is evidence for life after death, or (2) it is the product of a dying brain with hallucinations, vivid imagery, and complex mental constructions. Unfortunately, she considered no other evidence for life after death except the NDE. Had she combined the two alternatives with another twist to her hypothesis, she would have stated it correctly: there is life after death (but the NDE offers no proof for that premise) *and* the NDE is the product of the dying brain. But she didn't.

From the outset of her book, Blackmore's position is obvious—she does not believe in an afterlife. A proponent of Darwin who does not believe that the world has a purpose ordained by God, she expresses her nihilism in the preface:

> There is no future heaven towards which evolution progresses. And no ultimate purpose. It just goes along. Yet our minds have evolved to crave purposefulness and cling to the idea of a self because that will more efficiently keep alive the body and perpetuate its genes. In other words, our evolution makes it very hard for us to accept the idea of evolution and our own individual pointlessness. (28)

This point of view is emphasized in one of her papers where she says:

> The physiologically induced tunnel can be one way of realizing something important about ourselves, a realization that can change our lives: that is, that we are mental models and nothing more. (29)

Blackmore reviewed some of the ancient accounts that have been hyped as the NDE. Many aspects of these works do indeed resemble the NDE, at least superficially. The basic sensory description in all is similar. The difference lies in the *interpretations* of these sensory events. In India, for example, the person of Jesus Christ does not appear in the visions. More commonly the NDE in India reveals relatives (both alive and dead) and other religious persons. Blackmore concluded that the basic experience reported in the NDE was similar across time and cultures, differing only in the details and the interpretation of the event.

Blackmore reported the frequency with which the NDE occurs, and she concluded that the reported numbers are grossly inflated. The polls do not assess the likelihood that the positive respondents actually had a medical event that brought them near death. One study from Locke and Shontz (30) of 1,000 students had 107 persons who felt they had been near death at some time in their lives, but only thirty-two persons had even lost consciousness as a part of their medical emergency. Only seven of these thirty-two had an experience that would have been classified as an NDE on the Ring scale (≥ 6 points, 0.7 percent, not the 20 to 25 percent often quoted). Clearly less than 1 percent of this general population had an NDE-like event, though the population surveyed was quite young. An older population could have yielded different numbers.

She also addressed whether it is necessary to be close to death to have an NDE, concluding that many investigators have found patients who had a complete NDE in the absence of any physical illness, danger, or injury.

Blackmore then reviewed her hypothesis that the NDE is caused by the physical manifestations of the dying brain. Many conditions can cause a lack of oxygen to the brain—one of the causes of central nervous system dysfunction; carbon dioxide toxicity can also frequently mimic the sensations of the NDE. The appearance of the components of the NDE with simple decrease in blood flow to the brain with G-force experiments in pilots is evidence that the NDE is simply a physiologic phenomenon, explainable by human physiology without invoking any ethereal or cosmic forces. Granted, the full-blown NDE is usually not caused by G-force loss of consciousness, and many of the other aspects are often missing, such as the life-transforming qualities of the NDE. However, life changes with an NDE can be explained by simple exposure to a life-threatening event and the realization that a person could have died, whereas the G-force loss of consciousness is recognized by the pilots and volunteers to be a controlled situation that did not bring them near death.

Blackmore was particularly interested in the happiness, joy, and peacefulness reported with the NDE. One would expect that some persons would have a hellish experience, particularly if one believes in an afterlife that has the options of both heaven and hell. Nevertheless, peacefulness is an overriding theme in the NDE. Only two researchers have reported subjectively unpleasant experiences with the NDE—Rawlings (24-26) and Greyson (31-35). All of the other major authors—Moody (12-18), Sabom (19-23), Morse (36-43), and Ring (1-3)—report only peace and reassurance from the experience. Indeed, peace is one of the defining qualities in the numerical scales developed for the NDE.

When Blackmore evaluated the case for selective memory, she found it wanting. The theory goes like this: the longer after a person has the NDE, the less likely the person is to remember the bad components of the experience. However, it would seem unlikely that a hellish experience could be reported as a trip to heaven under any circumstances, even with a powerful selective memory. The descriptions of Rawlings and Greyson are so vivid that it is also difficult to imagine that a person would simply forget such an experience. Furthermore, it is possible that a person is more reluctant to report a bad experience for fear of ridicule or censure because his life was bad enough for him to be consigned to hell. This argument breaks down if one believes in the skill and honesty of the interviewers.

So she concluded that the unpleasant NDE simply is much less common than the pleasant one, perhaps because the body's own endorphins are active during the NDE, thereby turning it into a positive experience. Blackmore rejects any notion that the peace and joy of the NDE could come from a higher power, based upon her own belief system (actually *lack* of belief) (44):

> . . . NDES, mystical experiences and indeed everything encountered on the spiritual path—are products of a brain and the universe of which it is a part. For there is nothing else. It is our longing for something more that leads us astray. It is an illusion that we can find "true spirituality" by looking outside of ourselves. It is all here, now, in the creatures we are, as we are.

Blackmore then addressed the alleged paranormal powers exhibited by the NDEer:

1. The ability to see oneself from a distance.
2. The ability to travel elsewhere and to see things that could not have been otherwise known without remote vision.
3. The precognition reported with some NDEs.

Simply stated, there is no independent confirmation of such visionary powers. Specifically, there is no study that examined the remote vision of the participant in an NDE, and the descriptions of the nearby events can be explained by the persisting sensory functions of the direly ill, superimposed upon the detachment that protects the person from the unpleasant events of the serious illness or accident. A person beginning the voyage into the near-death event has knowledge of his surroundings, and he continues to receive input from his remaining senses (though it is at times distorted because of inadequate blood flow to the brain). He is still able to synthesize a story of his resuscitation that can be remarkably accurate. He simply tells it in a detached way, describing himself in the third person or telling the story as though from a distance—for example, from near the ceiling or from the edge of the room. The detachment is simply the psychologic defense mechanism he has used to protect himself and to enable himself to deal with this traumatic situation.

A person is able to synthesize a coherent story that sounds very reasonable. Indeed, to a listener who *wants* to believe the story, the account is not only believable, it is glorious! Note here that I did not say, nor does Blackmore suggest, that these stories are *fabricated*. There is not necessarily an *intent* to deceive. The person who has just gone through the experience is simply doing what is logical—attempting to synthesize a coherent sequence of events from the sensory input before, during, and after the medical emergency or accident. In addition, the brain will add memories to the event from the distant past, and the event will be told within the context of the cultural, psychological, and religious framework familiar to the person undergoing the traumatic event.

We will see later that some of the senses are persistent during many medical emergencies, even though the person may not have been aware of the selective addition and subtraction of senses during the course of the event. Furthermore, the most common scenario to produce the components of the NDE lie between the range of a simple loss of consciousness and a true cardiac arrest. That is, some blood flow to the brain persists in virtually all of the medical conditions in which the NDE has been reported.

Blackmore identified a condition in which the NDE would be more convincing—in a blind person (better yet in a person congenitally blind—blind from birth). Even in a congenitally blind person, such a description would be subject to influence from descriptions of visual images given to the blind person by sighted persons throughout the blind person's life. However, Blackmore was unable to find a single documented case of such a person who had an NDE. In addition, she documents the suspected "wishful thinking" of some proponents of the NDE (45). Dr. Larry Dossey reported a story of an NDE in a blind person with details that seemed to prove conclusively that the blind person gained sight during the NDE—an event that could occur only supernaturally. However, he later admitted that the story was an idealized composite—that the event never actually occurred.

This raises many questions about the veracity of many of the reports of the paranormal powers of the person during an NDE. In Chapter 2 of this book I mentioned the "researcher" who badgered my patient into agreeing that he had experienced an NDE. He had experienced nothing but is chronicled in the NDE literature as an example of a "typical" NDE. This same "researcher" has repeatedly touted the paranormal powers of persons during an NDE. So I personally question the reliability of all such descriptions.

That enthusiastic proponents of the NDE can lose their objectivity is seen in the accounts of Iverson in his book *In Search of the Dead: A Scientific Investigation of Evidence for Life After Death* (46). He claims that Melvin Morse, a pediatrician, found in his research that the origin of the NDE was the temporal lobe (actually Morse didn't; he quoted the work of Penfield and others and offered unproved hypotheses). Iverson also contended that Morse's team "took part in experiments to stimulate the brain electrically" (they didn't; they cited the neurosurgical work of others from the 1960s).

Finally, what can we say of Blackmore's assessment of the NDE? She correctly described the physical aspects of the NDE.

However, she begins with a flawed belief system, allowing this system to corrupt her conclusions. She started with disbelief in an afterlife: "There is no future heaven towards which evolution progresses. And no ultimate purpose" (47). She found no spirituality in the NDE. But she concludes that there can be no God nor afterlife because the NDE showed her none. She tragically concludes (48):

> We are biological organisms, evolved in fascinating ways for no purpose at all and with no end in any mind. We are simply here and this is how it is. I have no self and "I" own nothing. There is no one to die. There is just this moment, and now this and now this.

However, by definition faith cannot require absolute proof. Mankind must abandon the need to "know" about heaven from the NDE and accept the imperative to believe based on biblical principles.

MAURICE RAWLINGS

Maurice Rawlings is a Tennessee cardiologist who began as a skeptic of the NDE. Being trained in the medical world, he needed scientific proof before believing anything. After evaluating the NDE in his patients, however, he became a believer in the phenomenon, but with a difference. His research drew him to a belief in Jesus as Savior, contrary to most of the other writers who deal with the NDE. In his first book, *Beyond Death's Door* (25), he traced the changes in his thoughts about the NDE.

The first encounter that raised questions in his mind was that of a forty-eight-year-old male patient who worked as a mail carrier. The patient was being evaluated for chest pains with a stress test—an electrocardiogram recorded during exercise. The patient collapsed after developing heart block during the test. Heart block is a condition that causes the heart to stop or to slow dramatically, often causing loss of consciousness. But patients with heart block usually have some remaining cardiac output that results in at least some blood flow to the brain. In this condition the patient is likely to maintain some brain activity. Dr. Rawlings states that he had to continue cardiopulmonary resuscitation (CPR) until he could increase the heart rate from 35 to 80-100 with a pacemaker. Likely the heart rate was much slower at the onset of the collapse, but the heart probably pumped at least some blood flow to the brain throughout the episode.

As Dr. Rawlings performed CPR, the patient would awaken and scream that he was in hell. Rawlings would stop CPR, and the patient would lapse back into unconsciousness. CPR would then bring him back again, only to have him repeat that he was again in hell. He implored Dr. Rawlings to do something to keep him alive so he wouldn't remain in hell, asking Dr. Rawlings to pray for him, a technique with which Dr. Rawlings was not too familiar. The remainder of the sequence is a bit obscure. Dr. Rawlings prayed for the patient in a simple but completely appropriate way. There is no indication that the patient expressed a request for forgiveness of sin. The patient stabilized, and Dr. Rawlings later decided that he himself needed to read the Bible to see what it said about hell, heaven, and the afterlife.

Curiously, upon reflecting about this patient, Dr. Rawlings reported that the man could remember nothing about the hellish experience, but recalled a rather pleasant scene of colors, a narrow valley with beautiful vegetation, a bright light, and relatives, including his mother whom he had not seen since he was fifteen months old. He could describe her, though allegedly he had never seen any pictures of her, nor had anyone told him what she looked like. (Is it reasonable that he had never heard a description of his mother's appearance or had never seen pictures if they existed? I doubt it.) It seems that the man was describing both his impressions of heaven and hell. Could he have gone to both places? Not likely. Did he first go to hell, then receive salvation (during the CPR), then go to heaven? Or did he go to neither place, but his mind interpreted the experience in terms of what he already knew about life after death? That is probably a better explanation.

Rawlings's story is reminiscent of another in Lindley and coworkers' report (49). They cite a man with at least three NDEs, the second of which was a trip to hell sandwiched in between two trips to heaven. Not a likely possibility by most theological constructs. Furthermore, not only did the man go to hell on the second of his three NDEs, but the fiery journey was a mistake! They report (50):

> Respondent: The second experience was different, I went downstairs! Downstairs was dark, people were howling, (there was) fire, they wanted a drink of water. . . . Then somebody came to me, I don't know who it was, he pushed me aside and said, "You're not coming down here. You're going back upstairs."
>
> Interviewer: Did he actually use those words?
>
> Respondent: Yeah. "You're going back upstairs. We don't want you down here because you're not mean enough."

The Christian concept of salvation challenges these stories that include trips both to heaven and hell.

I am absolutely convinced that both heaven and hell exist and that what the Bible says about them is true. But we will see later that such near-death experiences often produce accounts that are at variance with the Bible's teachings. Some patients have a brush with death and see Buddha! So we cannot use the NDE as a representation of the afterlife. We must reject the theology of the NDE.

Nevertheless, the NDE reported by Rawlings had a very positive result. Both Rawlings and his patient were convinced that a place of torment exists. They both began to believe there was an afterlife, and not all of it was good, pleasant, peaceful, and loving. Both accepted Christ, and both lives were changed.

Rawlings reported that about 20 percent of all resuscitated patients had either blissful or hellish experiences after being resuscitated, a number much larger than that found by other researchers or my own experience in caring for these types of patients. He believes that the preponderance of good experiences is caused by the delay in interviewing patients. As a defense mechanism, patients will forget bad experiences. The patients who have a pleasant experience are able to recall the details, and thus the overwhelming majority of experiences reported are good, says Rawlings. On the other hand, if patients have both bad and good components to their NDE, they might remember only the good and suppress the bad aspects (an exceedingly unlikely possibility because no component of a trip to hell would be good or pleasant, nor would a trip to heaven include any unpleasant components).

Rawlings went on to study other paranormal experiences and wrote *Life Wish* (24) in response to the rising interest in reincarnation. Reincarnation has gained popularity as Eastern religions have begun to flourish in the West. Stories of the implausible make great reading, and many books have been sold by tickling unwary ears, playing to public interest and demand. Rawlings used valid Christian argument to debunk the notion of reincarnation. He exposed major proponents of both the NDE and reincarnation, Ian Stevenson and Raymond Moody, and noted that a major weakness of mankind is the need to see the miraculous, to have a religious *experience*, which has become the hallmark of major religious scams today. As humans we are unwilling to subject ourselves to the rigorous exercise of study and prayer for the answers to life's questions. We want a vision or we want to share the experience of someone who has had a vision to provide us with answers to our problems. Reincarnation and communication with the dead are prime examples of this deceptive theology. What could be more fascinating than the notion that we might have lived before? Or that we might live again in this world? Or that we could talk to the dead?

Eastern religions offer reincarnation as a solution to man's desire to remain immortal. We all have an innate need to remain alive, to defeat death, to overcome the inevitable. Reincarnation is part of the theology of Hinduism, Buddhism, Zoroastrianism, and Jainism. Hindu philosophy contends that you are reincarnated in a form consistent with your previous life. A good and holy life will yield a reincarnation into a higher form, a more privileged caste. An exceptionally bad or sinful life will cause reincarnation into a lower form of existence, even possibly transmigration—the return into a life-form of a different species—for example, a dog. The law of karma demands that retribution be exacted for the deeds of your life. In Hinduism there is no forgiveness. The ultimate goal of a Hindu, therefore, is to live a "good" life and ascend progressively from life to life until perfection, or nirvana, is achieved.

Herein lies a major difference in the teachings of Eastern religions and Christianity. Hinduism assumes that mankind is basically good and that we can ascend in reincarnated form until nirvana is reached. Other Eastern religions—Buddhism, Zoroastrianism, and Jainism—teach similar principles. Reincarnation is important to all of them as well. Christianity, however, teaches the concept of the fall of man in the Garden of Eden, which determined that man will always be intrinsically sinful; thus mankind needs a Savior for redemption from sins. It is not possible to work one's way into heaven, especially working through progressively more virtuous reincarnated lives. Christianity denies reincarnation: "The dust returns to the ground it came from, and the spirit returns to God who gave it"

(Ecclesiastes 12:7). Paul says, "For to me, to live is Christ and to die is gain. . . . I am torn between the two: I desire to depart and be with Christ, which is better by far; but it is more necessary for you that I remain in the body" (Philippians 1:21, 23-24). He knew that at death he would be with Christ. He denied any chance of return to this earth in another body or form.

Reincarnation is an invention of man to substitute—to counterfeit—for the atoning death of Christ, who made it possible for us to have eternal life. We must choose between the two. Jesus said, "I am the way and the truth and the life. No one comes to the Father except through me" (John 14:6). He made it unequivocal, but we must choose. Is it Jesus or not?

Rawlings's latest book is *To Hell and Back* (26). In it, he described his own pleasant NDE that occurred in the throes of a heart attack. In this experience he had a short, two-minute NDE that included an ecstatic component and a life review, although it did not have many of the other elements of the NDE, such as the tunnel and the "being of light." It is also uncertain from his description what medications he was receiving at that time. He then outlined the experiences of other people who have had unpleasant NDEs. He contrasted the pleasant and unpleasant NDEs, and he exposes the deception prevalent in the cult of the NDE—the concept that unconditional love awaits everyone at death.

CAROL ZALESKI

The most scholarly treatise of the historical and literary aspects of the NDE comes from Carol Zaleski (51-52), who traced the roots of the NDE from pre-Christian times to the present.

Recognizing that nearly all cultures have had a fascination with death and the afterlife, Zaleski reviews the role of the "otherworld journey" in cultural explanations of the hereafter. She outlined the relationship of the NDE to religion by reviewing the concept of the voyage to other worlds. Many, if not most, NDEs are steeped in the bizarre and occult, certainly not a domain for the Christian to embrace. Some of these voyages achieve a macabre effect on the traveler and reader alike:

> The legacy of the ancient Near East is rich in otherworld journey themes. One of the earliest known literary narratives of descent to the underworld belongs to the cult of Inanna, the Sumerian goddess of fertility. In the Descent of Inanna, she boldly seeks to storm the gates of Arallu, the land of the dead, ruled by her evil sister Ereshkigal; but her powers as queen of heaven do not avail Inanna in this shadowy, dust-choked realm. At each of the seven gates, she is forced by a guard to strip off one of her garments. When she arrives, naked and powerless, before the throne of death, a baleful glance from her sister is enough to reduce Inanna to a rotting piece of meat. The God Enki revives her by sending down water and food of life; in the end, however, Inanna purchases her freedom only by delivering her lover, the vegetation god Dumuzi, into the hands of death. (53)

This tale of celestial strip poker (in which the traveler is always the loser), degradation, and betrayal hardly glorifies God, edifies the spirit, or raises the hopes of man about life after death.

Zaleski traced the style of the NDE adventure, first with the traveler leaving his body to tour heaven or hell (or in some cases purgatory), only to return to live a transformed life. Later in the history of the NDE, the story more commonly involved a saintly person of the church who had repeated visions of the afterlife, but who often did not leave the body during physical duress to achieve the trip. Finally, the modern version of the NDE emerged, with the familiar exit from the body, travel (usually down a tunnel), encountering a "being of light," seeing a life review, and returning to life with new meaning and direction. Zaleski recognizes that the components of the NDE have changed over the centuries:

> . . . gone are the bad deaths, harsh judgment scenes, purgatorial torments, and infernal terrors of medieval visions; by comparison, the modern otherworld is a congenial place, a democracy, a school for continuing education, and a garden of unearthly delights. (54)

Zaleski wove the fabric of the NDE as a garment that protected the populace from the fears of death and the annihilation that might follow. In her view, even the evidence from the caveman suggests that mankind had an early fascination and concern with death. Men's visions both expanded and satisfied the imagination for images of the hereafter. The very fact that men have always had a concern with the remains of the dead and constructed elaborate burial rituals speaks to the wonderment and fear that death evoked. The Pharaohs of Egypt memorialized their passage in the most elaborate manner possible, with huge pyramids, burial trappings, and even guides and directions painted on the walls of their crypts. They had rudimentary concepts of judgment, though society seemed to dwell upon the destination of the rulers to the abandonment of a concern for the common man. *The Ancient Egyptian Book of the Dead* (55) and *The Tibetan Book of the Dead* (56) simply reinforced the need to address issues of the destination of the spirit after death.

Zaleski tracked the literature of death and dying through the biblical accounts of Enoch, though she combined an acceptance of both the pseudepigraphic works of Enoch (not recognized as Holy Scripture) and canonized Scripture (recognized by the Church generally as part of the Bible). Within Judaism, mysticism was found in both the writings of the Merkabah cults of the Gnostics and the Cabalistic writings. Often these additions to the Holy Scriptures appeared in the form of expanded stories of the patriarchs, granting to them the glory of travel to the heavenlies to witness sights that had been hereunto withheld from mortal man. The traditions of the Zoroastrians, Muslims, Hindus, and Buddhists include similar revelations.

Even Catholic tradition includes many otherworldly visions. *Dialogues* from Pope Gregory the Great in the sixth century (57-58) contain numerous accounts of departure from the body, visits to the heavenly realms, and return to earth with renewed purpose. A businessman named Stephen on the route to Constantinople died and was summoned to hell. He was granted another chance with his life because his "judge" declared that he had really wanted Stephen the blacksmith. Upon hearing about this mistake, Stephen the businessman awoke. Pope Gregory insisted that such errors in identification were not really mistakes, but were intended to be warnings to the returnees. Similarly, Saint Patrick reported accounts of purgatory, enticing holy living from his listeners. Such tales became widely influential when they were written in the *Treatise on the Purgatory of Saint Patrick* (about A.D. 445) and were later translated into many languages and dialects (52, 59).

Our own literary and artistic collections of visions and NDEs include many artists' images of Saint Stephen's gaze into heaven, Dante's look into hell in the *Inferno*, and the horrors of Van Eyck's painting of *The Last Judgment*. So the ancient NDE was a transforming influence on its hearers then, as now.

However, the proponents of the NDE seem to have major disagreements with both medical concepts and biblical truth.

Now let's look at some of the major questions about the NDE.

4

MAJOR ISSUES

Over My Dead Body . . .

John Paul McAllister had many opportunities to experience an NDE in one single day. But all fell short. Not even one NDE, though his heart stopped and required resuscitation 152 times during a single twenty-four-hour period. But who's counting when you're in the throes of repeated cardiac arrests, battling for your life? The nurses, that's who.

John's day had started without incident—a quiet breakfast with his wife and a leisurely review of the morning newspaper. He'd been retired on disability since his heart attack five years earlier. He had some mild "congestive heart failure," the doctors called it. To John, it simply meant that he had a little swelling of his feet at the end of the day, some limitation of his activity because of fatigue or shortness of breath, and occasional difficulty breathing at night when he would retire to bed.

As he finished the sports pages, he collapsed without warning facedown on the breakfast table. His wife, Ruth, could remember no antecedent symptoms, even later after the panic surrounding John's cardiac arrest had subsided. John had seemed entirely normal to her. No chest pain. No shortness of breath. No dizziness. Not even any palpitations. It was truly an unexpected "sudden death." But not death. Ruth immediately called the Medics, and they arrived at John and Ruth's home in only a few minutes. Ruth had attempted CPR, though she didn't know how successful it had been. The Medics quickly restarted John's heart, loaded him in the ambulance, and took him to Harborview Medical Center.

By the time John had arrived in the Coronary Care Unit, the Medics had needed to restart his heart three more times. And the ride took only five minutes. That's when the nurses and doctors knew he was going to be a problem. They called it an "electrical storm." His heart's electrical system was repeatedly malfunctioning, causing ventricular fibrillation—in layman's terms, cardiac arrest. And whatever was causing the storm didn't go away. Usually a person who has a cardiac arrest will stabilize rather quickly, with few if any recurrences of cardiac arrest in the next few days. The doctors suspected that he had experienced another heart attack with blockage of a coronary artery, but in the quiet time between cardiac arrests, CPR, and defibrillations (restarting the heart), his electrocardiogram looked remarkably unchanged from what it had been before that day's events.

Over the next twenty-four hours, the nurses counted 152 total cardiac arrests requiring electrical shocks to John's chest. It was very unusual for anyone to be counting, but once they started they seemed compelled to continue the tally. Many times during this horrendous day the medical team performing CPR could detect that John awakened with the CPR itself, even before his heart had been restarted with the defibrillation paddles. He would try to push the team away because the CPR hurt his chest, but as soon as the CPR was stopped, he would lapse back into unconsciousness until a normal heart rhythm was briefly restored. It is one of the most distressing sights for a doctor or nurse to witness—a patient fighting you as you are doing a procedure to keep him alive.

Medical personnel have their breaking points, too, and on more than one occasion a nurse would beg to stop—to let John die. However, between cardiac arrests John was perfectly conscious and alert, and he implored the team to continue to do their best to keep him alive. It was impossible for most of the team to quit when he clearly wanted them to continue. Furthermore, he didn't seem to be suffering any brain damage or further deterioration of his heart's pumping function with all of these arrests. It was just that the electrical storm wouldn't go away.

By the end of that gruesome twenty-four hours, John's chest looked like raw meat. The repeated CPR had broken many ribs, and the scores of electrical shocks to the same area of skin over the chest had burned it like a torch. Such trauma made it even more difficult for some of the medical team to continue, and a heated ethical debate ensued. Was this effort worthwhile? Wasn't John just going to die anyway? Why not admit defeat and let him slip away "with dignity"? The argument was compelling. But John still asked for help when he was conscious, and his wife wanted them to continue.

Just as mysteriously as it had started, the electrical storm passed out to sea. Like a hurricane, the beginning and the end of the winds were easily recognized. His rhythm stabilized, and he required only a few more shocks over the second twenty-four hours, and then none.

John remained in the hospital for another twenty-one days, recovering from the events of the first forty-eight hours, undergoing testing, and starting some medication to prevent a recurrence of this chaos. A drug to ward off any future hurricanes.

During his convalescence, John was profuse with his praises of the nurses and doctors who had stayed with him throughout his ordeal. He remembered almost the entire sequence of events because his heart never stopped for more than a few seconds or minutes at a time. He recalled the CPR, the fiery shocks to his chest, and the unmistakable warm sensation of the skin of his chest as it was repeatedly electrified with the defibrillation paddles. He even remembered fighting the team as they worked on his heart. But he never went to heaven or hell. He never saw a tunnel or a light. Though he was a devout Catholic, he never saw Jesus or the Virgin Mary.

His life was changed as a result of the experience, though. He now cherishes each day, fully ten years after he survived his record-breaking encounter with a cardiac defibrillator. And each time he comes to the outpatient clinic he also returns to the Coronary Care Unit to thank the nurses who saved his life. And to thank them for honoring his request to weather the storm.

How does John's experience compare with reports of the NDE?

ISN'T THE NDE DEEPLY ROOTED IN HISTORY? HAVEN'T ALL CULTURES IN ALL AGES RECOGNIZED THE NDE?

The Ancient Egyptian Book of the Dead (1), written about 2500 B.C., speaks about the afterlife and gives advice about prayers for guidance after death. It is an extensive catalog of prayers and spells for the dying and dead used to achieve favors for the afterlife. It mentions some of the qualities of the netherworld, but its descriptions in no way resemble modern-day NDEs. The Egyptians seemed to have had no problem adding one theology upon another, for as the spells accumulated, the gods they worshiped in the spells changed. Early spells recognized an astral afterlife. Later, glory and honor were due to the sun-god. Most recent editions expressed worship to Osiris. The Introductory Hymn to Osiris contains the following passage:

> Worship of Osiris Wennefer, the Great God who dwells in the Thinite nome, King of Eternity, Lord of Everlasting,

> who passes millions of years in his lifetime first-born son of Nut, begotten of Geb, Heir, Lord of the Wereret-crown, whose White Crown is tall, Sovereign of gods and men. . . . Hail to you, King of Kings, Lord of Lords, Ruler of Rulers, who took possession of Two Lands even in the womb of Nut; he rules the plains of the Silent Land, even he the golden of body, blue of head, on whose arms is turquoise. . . . May you grant power in the sky, might on earth and vindication in the realm of the dead, a journeying downstream to Busiris as a living soul and a journeying upstream to Abydos as a heron; to go in and out without hindrance at all the gates of the Netherworld. May there be given to me bread from the House of Cool Water and a table of offerings from Heliopolis, my toes being firm-planted in the Field of Rushes. (2)

This is a bit convoluted in wording, but the Egyptian concept of the afterlife seems to have conformed somewhat to the modern-day image of heaven.

Biblical accounts in the Old Testament attest to resuscitation of people thought to be dead—the widow's son in 1 Kings 17, the Shunammite boy in 2 Kings 4, the man raised by the bones of Elisha in 2 Kings 13.

Plato in *The Republic* speaks of Er who went to heaven and returned:

> Er, the son of Armenius, a native of Pamphylia . . . was killed in battle. When the dead were taken up for burial ten days later, his body alone was found undecayed. They carried him home, and two days afterwards were going to bury him, when he came to life again as he lay on the funeral pyre. He then told what he had seen in the other world. (3)

The Tibetan Book of the Dead (4), written from about A.D. 700-800, chronicles journeys that occurred at "death" in persons who subsequently returned to life in this world, though the references to the events at dying in no way parallel the events described for the currently popular NDE. The book, however, is primarily a guide to instruct people in the proper way to die. It preaches reincarnation in the tradition of Hinduism and Buddhism, wherein the mind-set of the dying person determines the status of the reincarnated new spirit in a new body:

> The message [of *The Tibetan Book of the Dead*] is, that the Art of Dying is quite as important as the Art of Living (or of Coming into Birth), of which it is the complement and summation; that the future of being is dependent, perhaps entirely, upon a rightly controlled death. (5)

Similar to the wording of Christian traditional writings, the translator of *The Tibetan Book of the Dead* says:

> By right practicing of a trustworthy Art of Dying, death will then, indeed, have lost its sting and been swallowed up in victory. (6)

The instructions contained in *The Tibetan Book of the Dead* are complex, and at times incomprehensible compared to the simplicity of the Christian message of salvation:

> When the expiration hath ceased, the vital-force will have sunk into the nerve-center of Wisdom and the Knower will be experiencing the Clear Light of the natural condition. Then, the vital-force, being thrown backwards and flying downwards through the right and left nerves, the Intermediate State momentarily dawns. . . . When the breathing is about to cease, it is best if the Transference hath been applied efficiently; if [the application] hath been inefficient, then [address the deceased] thus:

> O nobly-born (so and so by name), the time hath now come for thee to seek the Path [in reality]. Thy breathing is about to cease. Thy guru hath set thee face to face before with the Clear Light; and now thou art about to experience it in its Reality in the Bardo state, wherein all things are like the void and cloudless sky, and the naked, spotless intellect is like unto a transparent vacuum without circumference or centre. At this moment, know thou thyself; and abide in which state. I, too, at this time am setting thee face to face.
>
> Having read this, repeat it many times in the ear of the person dying, even before the expiration hath ceased, so as to impress it on the mind [of the dying one].
>
> If the expiration is about to cease, turn the dying one over on the right side, which posture is called the "Lying Posture of a Lion." The throbbing of the arteries [on the right and left side of the throat] is to be pressed. If the person dying be disposed to sleep, or if the sleeping state advances, that should be arrested, and the arteries pressed gently but firmly. Thereby the vital-force will not be able to return from the median nerve and will be sure to pass out through the Brahmanic aperture. Now the real setting-face-to-face is to be applied. At this moment, the first [glimpsing] of the Bardo of the Clear Light of Reality, which is the Infallible Mind of the Dharma-Kaya, is experienced by all sentient beings. (7)

These rituals are supposed to be conducted by the dying's personal guru to enable the dying to achieve a "correct" death. It is hardly reassuring to know that to die correctly, one needs to have the proper guru in attendance to assure correct disposition of your spirit! The stages of the journey for the dead include heavenly visions first, then hellish visions. Furthermore, the prescribed incantations include many chants that include confusing references, at least for the Christian (for example, an admonition to "Remember the Precious Trinity" [8]; the "Precious Trinity" here is the Buddha, the Dharma, and the Sangha).

Albert Heim, a Swiss mountain climber, chronicled the near-death experiences of himself and fellow climbers who had survived falls in the mountains. Heim's report in 1892 (9) details a profound sense of calm at a time when one would expect fear and panic. Some of these climbers had a panoramic review of their major life events during the few seconds of the fall. Heim himself was a climber who had experienced such an event, and he described the feeling as one of intense calm, peacefulness, acceptance, and mental clarity and quickness:

> We have reached the conclusion that death through falling is subjectively a very pleasant death. In the absence of preceding illness it ensues in clear consciousness, in heightened sensory and ideational activity, and without anxiety or pain. (10)

Emanuel Swedenborg, a Swede who lived in the eighteenth century, wrote popular accounts of visits to other-than-earthly realms and investigated mystical aspects of our existence (11-12).

Irving Hallowell reported the experiences of Saulteaux Indians who believed that death involved pleasant and ecstatic out-of-body experiences (13). They were led in their journey to the afterlife by spirit guides, and there they met deceased relatives.

Recent alleged near-death accounts even include one from none other than David Livingstone, the missionary to Africa. He experienced an unexplainable calm while being attacked by a lion (14-16). Dwight Moody, the famous evangelist, reportedly had a deathbed vision. He told his relatives just before he died that he could see heaven and that God was calling him (17-20). But these were not NDEs. They were quite different from the popular accounts circulating today.

So, while ancient and even more recent writers have chronicled instructions for death and accounts of near-death, they do not support recent accounts of the NDE.

IS THE METHODOLOGY FOR STUDYING THE NDE VALID?

Most NDE literature is simply the recounting of personal "experiences," so that it is difficult to confirm any of the NDE claims. While some authors have made valiant attempts to create a science out of experiential description, most works fall short of that goal. The most obvious example is the construction of the scales and questionnaires for the NDE. All are arbitrary and unverifiable, if not misleading and full of suggestion and bias. Consider Greyson's questionnaire (21). His items are worded in a way to *guarantee* that a person will respond affirmatively to the search for an NDE:

> "Did time seem to speed up?"
> "Were your thoughts speeded up?"
> "Did scenes from your past come back to you?"
> "Did you suddenly seem to understand everything?"
> "Did you have a feeling of peace or pleasantness?"
> "Did you have a feeling of joy?"
> "Did you feel a sense of harmony or unity with the universe?"
> "Did you see or feel surrounded by a brilliant light?"
> "Were your senses more vivid than usual?"
> "Did you seem to be aware of things going on elsewhere, as if by ESP?"
> "Did scenes from the future come to you?"
> "Did you feel separated from your physical body?"
> "Did you seem to enter some other, unearthly world?"

> "Did you seem to encounter a mystical being or presence?"
> "Did you see deceased spirits or religious figures?"
> "Did you come to a border or point of no return?"

Anyone reading these questions would have to be impervious to suggestion to be able to answer them without being biased. Indeed, other researchers acknowledge that such questionnaires are too misleading to be useful. Blackmore said (22):

> I did not wish to use one of the standard NDE questionnaires (e.g., Greyson, 1983), because these might too readily suggest to respondents what they ought to be describing.

We must not confuse personal testimony, opinion, and bias with science. Furthermore, the guise of "science" is promoted in the most unusual ways. Osis and Haraldsson claim five pieces of "scientific evidence" for afterlife (23):

1. Mediumship.
2. Apparitions, especially those seen by several observers.
3. Reincarnation memories.
4. Out-of-body experiences.
5. Deathbed observations.

These pieces of "evidence" simply are not "science."

Furthermore, many NDE "researchers" use other techniques that are questionable at best. Often they rely solely upon the reporting from the subjects, without any attempt to verify the truth of the report. For example, Lindley and coworkers reported upon the NDEs of residents of the Pacific Northwest (24), but they admitted:

> Because of the time constraints on our research our criteria for inclusion in this study were simply that a person had

> been in a life-threatening situation and *felt* he had actually died [emphasis mine]. It quickly became apparent, however, that we would not be taking our sample from the uninformed. The "contamination" of the near-death population is widespread due to the success of books by researchers such as Moody (1975) and Ring (1980).

So they uncritically believed the story from everyone who *felt* that he had died. Medical confirmation was not required. Further, they acknowledge that their data are contaminated by the popular press. What veracity is left?

IS THE NDE COMMON?

We have seen that popular writers claim that the NDE is quite common. Gallup polls conducted in the early 1980s (25) revealed some startling findings:

BELIEF	YES	NO	UNSURE
In heaven	71%	21%	8%
In hell	53%	37%	10%
In life after death	67%	27%	6%
In the devil	60%	35%	5%
In the NDE	15%	83%	2%
In communication with the dead	24%	69%	7%
In reincarnation	23%	67%	10%

However, these beliefs were not matched with any confidence that their religion was adequate to assure them heaven at death (26):

RELIGION	CHANCES OF GOING TO HEAVEN	
	Excellent	Good
Protestant	24%	42%
Catholic	41%	49%

Estimates from these polls suggest that 47 million people have had what they describe as some form of religious or mystical experience (27). Twenty-three million persons think they have had an event that was life-threatening or that brought them to the verge of death. Over 15 million have had some "other-worldly feeling of union with a divine being," and over 3 percent of the American population (or over 8,000,000 people in the United States alone) claim to have had some form of NDE or "mystical encounter." But these statistics are highly suspect. Blackmore (22, 28-30) reviewed the data and concluded that the NDE is much less common than popular accounts would lead us to believe. Probably less than 1 percent of all medically verified crises are associated with the prototypical NDE (31-32).

The rise in interest in the NDE certainly could have inflated the estimates of its frequency. Suggestion, embellishment, and fabrication must all be considered when analyzing the reports in the popular press. No adequate study has been performed to assess the frequency of the NDE. Barbara Harris, in her book *Full Circle* (33), points out that "when a phenomenon is experienced a certain number of times by a certain species, it becomes more common for other members of the species, even if they have not been previously exposed to it" (34).

A practical example of this phenomenon is the response I received from a pastor friend. This pastor had spent years as a hospital chaplain in a cancer ward where much of the NDE research was conducted in the 1970s. He had seen hundreds of people die and many thousands of others come near death. I asked him if he thought the NDE was common. His response was immediately an enthusiastic "Yes!" However, on further questioning for the details of his personal observations of patients with the NDE, he recalled that in his extensive experience he had seen only three persons he thought had an NDE. One man had what my pastor friend *presumed* to be a heavenly vision, but the patient would not talk about it. One woman saw Jesus as John Wayne. One woman simply saw a person rowing a boat across a lake.

The pastor, upon reflection, stated that his immediate response that he had seen many NDEs was actually his interpretation of the change in the facial expressions in people who were dying. He had assumed that the expressions reflected a heavenly experience because of all he had heard about the NDE from the researchers with whom he worked and from the popular press. Here was an overestimate of the incidence of the NDE created primarily from the perception of what he was *supposed* to see.

Schoonmaker (35) reported that many patients who initially had no memory of the near-death event later "remembered" the details of the experience. He said, "Only after repeated invitations and reassurances" did they recall the NDE. Could these memories have been fabricated to please the investigator? Could they have been feeling coercion to "remember" the event?

Proponents of the NDE argue that it is actually underreported, saying that many physicians and medical workers cause the patient to suppress the reporting of the experience because of the listener's attitude of unreceptiveness or even ridicule. That argument, of course, cannot be easily countered. It is like the surgeon who says other surgeons cannot attain his excellent results because the other surgeons are less skillful. The technique of the patient interview is, of course, a skill. Some are more skillful than others. It would seem that the discrepancy in the reporting of the frequency of the NDE must relate to factors in addition to the skill of the physician, however. In our population of documented cardiac arrest survivors in Seattle, the NDE is virtually nonexistent. I have *never* seen a patient who described such an event. And I have asked all of my patients for a history of the events before, during, and after the cardiac arrest. Does that mean I am a poor interviewer? Perhaps. But it could also mean that the NDE is simply not a valid phenomenon in the setting of documented cardiac arrest.

Lukoff and coworkers have emphasized the need to recognize the importance of the spiritual realm in our patients (36). We in medicine tend to ignore or demean a patient's spirituality. Commonly we associate the presence of the spiritual with psychopathology. A person with religious beliefs is just a bit off kilter—one pickle short of a full jar or not quite dealing with a full deck of cards. I would hope that as a Christian I do not fall into that category. But certainly many doctors could miss the description of the NDE because of their insensitivity to probing the spiritual aspects of the experience of someone who has come close to death. These are precisely the people who should be questioned closely for their concepts of the afterlife—they will certainly have a real death event in the future, perhaps the near future, and it is incumbent on us to witness to them about the power of Jesus before it is too late.

But more likely I am dealing with a patient population that has different characteristics than patients reported in other studies. I see almost entirely patients who are resuscitated on the street. Most other reports deal with patients resuscitated in the hospital. All of my patients have some degree of short-term memory loss. Most patients reported from other centers have little to no memory loss because they do not actually lose pulse and blood pressure. The physiology of the cardiac arrest and its effect on the brain must be different in the bona-fide cardiac arrest victim who has brief total loss of blood flow to the brain.

Negovsky (31, 37) claimed that any event resembling the NDE occurs in only about 0.3 to 0.5 percent of all patients who are resuscitated from a near-death event. He argued that the cerebral cortex is silent during near-death, and that people should neither be able to see nor hear during this event. He also claimed that anyone who survives a near-death event unscathed must have had only minor alteration in blood flow to the brain. Cardiac arrest for more than four to six minutes will result in permanent brain damage, including severe loss of memory for the event, which is consistent with my clinical experience.

Druss (38) and Dobson (32) also found the NDE to be very uncommon. Martens (39) concurs, stating that the NDE is extraordinarily uncommon in a person with a documented cardiac arrest, perhaps because the memory process is severely impaired with more than a few minutes of lack of blood flow to the brain. He emphasizes that the reports from Moody and others are never documented with the medical details of the "near-death" circumstances, nor with the duration of the medical crisis or the duration of cardiac arrest, if one is even claimed. Martens reminded us that the part of the brain most vulnerable to lack of oxygen is the hippocampus, the area responsible for memory processing. A cardiac arrest produces amnesia for the time immediately preceding the arrest, for the event itself, and for the time immediately after the event.

NDE proponents elicit an inflated assessment of the frequency of the NDE because of leading or suggestive questions asked of the patient. Furthermore, "copy-cat" experiences certainly could explain the rise in the incidence of the NDE today. It took only one person to "find" a needle and syringe in a Pepsi can to stimulate scores of other identical spurious reports.

Obviously to call an event an NDE requires one to define near-death. No investigator has adequately defined that term, and no one has prospectively evaluated a large population of patients who might fit that description. The fact that the NDE has been reported in virtually all physical crisis circumstances—near-death, cardiac arrest, hypotension, fright, concern for another person who is in a near-death situation, etc.—makes the analysis (and the believability) of the NDE suspect. For the assessment of near-death experiences to be valid, only those cases where clinical death (absence of pulse and blood pressure) is documented should be included in the NDE tally. No one has limited his research to that definition.

The frequency of the NDE thus remains unknown. We can say

that the unusual sensory experiences must be real in at least some patients, though they are probably not common. It will probably become more common in the future as the techniques of cardiopulmonary resuscitation improve and become more widely applied to the population.

IS THERE A DIFFERENCE BETWEEN THE OBE AND THE NDE?

The OBE, or out-of-body experience, is the sensation that the body and consciousness become detached. In it, the patient reports seeing himself from a distant position. It is a phenomenon that lacks all of the other stereotyped sequential aspects of the NDE, such as the tunnel, the life review, the travel, the encounter with the "being of light," and the life transformation. The OBE lacks many of the vivid features of the NDE. The OBE may even be more common than the NDE and has also been reported by the ancients. In 1974, Ehrenwald reported a summary of the OBE (40). He described it as a phenomenon in which a person senses "being outside his body and perceiving his environment from a vantage point other than where his physical body happens to be." It is different from dreaming because the person is not asleep during the event. It is not a delusion or hallucination, supposedly due to paranormal features associated with it, such as the ability to know another person's thoughts, see the future, or become aware of events that are occurring elsewhere.

OBEs have been reported in many other cultures, folklore, and religions, including Yoga, other mystic religions, and even in Judeo-Christian works. However, these experiences are subject to much interpretation. Ehrenwald thought that they represented the human's desire to deny death by depersonalizing disturbing thoughts or situations, all the while fighting the breakdown of the bodily image. He interpreted them to be a quest for immortality and an attempt to legitimatize the concept of the soul and eternal life.

He did not recognize a separate category of near-death experiences (NDEs) distinct from out-of-body experiences (OBEs), perhaps because the popular literature for the NDE had not yet surfaced.

In surveys of college students, Hart and Palmer (41) reported that the OBE had occurred in 10 to 25 percent, though the incidence of drug use in that same population was not reported. Tobacyk and Mitchell (42) surveyed 445 college students and found sixty-five who had experienced an OBE, though they also did not query the drug use in this population. They found that the OBE induced belief in the occult—"precognition, psi, spiritualism, and witchcraft." Otherwise, the psychiatric profiles of the experiencers and non-experiencers were similar, though the researchers did not evaluate other aspects of religious belief and spirituality. They acknowledged that the only valid measure, however, would be to administer their testing before the OBE. It is entirely possible that the differences in religious belief were caused by the experience itself and not that the belief made the person more likely to experience an OBE. It is also possible that many of these OBEs were drug-induced, particularly considering the population studied.

The OBE has often been associated with occultism, and it was formerly called "astral projection," a technique that could be performed at will by some people. It is a component of many Eastern religions, including Hinduism, Tibetan Buddhism, Taoism, and Cabalism (43). These sensations can involve the feeling of separation from the body, an ecstatic religious experience, and travel to other worlds or can even assume bizarre and terrifying components.

IS THE NDE OR THE OBE SUBJECT TO INDEPENDENT CONFIRMATION?

The NDE and OBE, by definition, are personal experiences impossible to corroborate. When studied, the OBE has proved to be unreliable.

Palmer (44-47) evaluated students who claimed to have the power to produce an OBE. He put a picture in a distant room and instructed the students to leave their body and "project" themselves into the distant room and study the picture. If the students were able to describe the picture accurately, he would have concluded that their spirits could indeed have been in the distant room. While many students claimed to have had an OBE, none could accurately describe the picture. The conclusion must be that the OBE is unreliable at best or a fraud at worst. Opponents, however, claim that a self-induced OBE is simply weaker than a spontaneous one.

Charles Tart (48) studied Robert Monroe, a mystic, to see if he could produce evidence for paranormal phenomena. He asked Monroe to produce an OBE and to enter another room to read a five digit number that had been placed in the locked room. Monroe was unable to do so, but he simply claimed that the experimental setting was stifling his paranormal powers.

So neither the NDE nor the OBE has been confirmed.

DOES EVERYONE WHO EXPERIENCES A BRUSH WITH DEATH EXPERIENCE THE NDE?

It is obvious that this question cannot be answered either. The definition of near-death is nebulous, at best. However, some studies have attempted to answer this issue. Sabom (49-51) said that 42 percent of patients who are near death have the NDE. Ring (52-54) reported 48 percent in one study and 47 percent in another. Vicchio (55) said that 40 percent of patients have the NDE as they approach death. However, all of these estimates may have been inflated because of the selection techniques and the interview or questionnaire process. My series is 0 percent, but it is difficult for a person to describe the NDE when he has total amnesia for the one or two hours before the cardiac arrest and for the one to two days after the event.

IS IT ACTUALLY NECESSARY TO BE NEAR DEATH TO EXPERIENCE THE NDE?

Researchers are keen to claim that a person had an NDE as a doctor "pronounced" or "declared" the patient to be dead. However, temporary loss of blood pressure or pulse is not equivalent to death. Death itself can be hard to diagnose; near-death is almost impossible to define.

Moody (56-61) reported cases of the NDE in patients who were not physically endangered, and Gabbard (62-64) described cases of the NDE in patients who only *thought* they were going through a life-threatening situation. Greyson (21, 65-70) emphasized that the NDE could be identical in the person actually near death as well as the person who only envisioned a physical danger but who was not physically ill or harmed.

Owens, Cook, and Stevenson (71) tried to study the importance of the medical crisis itself by evaluating the medical records of fifty-eight patients who believed themselves to be near death and who remembered an unusual set of sensory and mental experiences during the event. These records were selected from those of 130 patients who had been referred or self-selected for an NDE. Retrospective evaluation of a medical event can be quite difficult because the documentation will be variably complete and accurate. Furthermore, the authors were not blinded to the results of the reported NDE because they had previously interviewed these patients. The authors state, "The raters often knew the nature of a patient's experience or the patient's evaluation of his or her condition, because they had interviewed many of the patients or had earlier read their accounts or questionnaires." This methodological flaw renders their evaluation worthless. The review of medical records should have been performed independently and could have been easily done by an unbiased set of physicians. Nevertheless, they assessed that twenty-eight of these fifty-eight patients were actually experiencing a medical crisis that might have led to death had not medical intervention been applied.

The authors discovered that the NDE was possible without a person being near death, but that an "enhanced perception of light" and "enhanced cognitive function" seemed more common if the patient was actually near death. Seventy-five percent of the patients who were near death reported bright lights, whereas only 40 percent of patients not in physical danger had the sensation of a bright light. The assessment of "enhanced cognitive function" was, of course, a retrospective analysis performed by the patient himself, because testing of cognitive function would be impossible at the time of the medical crisis. Seventeen of thirty patients not at risk of death compared to twenty-five of twenty-eight near-death patients had reported enhanced thought processes. The report of improved thought processes correlated highly with the experience of enhanced light. The tunnel experience was also strongly correlated with the sensation of light, but the tunnel itself was no more common with near-death patients (twelve of twenty-eight, 43 percent) than the other patients (nine of thirty, 30 percent).

Diminished thought processes, positive emotions, negative emotions, the sense of leaving the body and viewing it from above, the belief that death was imminent, and the life review were no different in the patients close to death than in those not near death. This study, for all of its methodological problems, tells us with certainty only that a person does not need to be near death to experience the NDE. In fact, other studies show that a person may be fully conscious and clinically well but still have an NDE. It is perhaps relevant that objective testing of thought processes in patients under the influence of hallucinogenic drugs, who also reported enhanced—even miraculous—thought processes, failed to reveal any objective improvement of cognition during these experiences (which are remarkably similar to the NDE). In fact, their mental powers are decreased (72-78).

Indeed, some patients who allegedly experience the NDE and who have a well-documented clinical course are never near death. Walker (79) reported a patient who claimed to have had an NDE but whose vital signs were never at jeopardy. This patient claimed to have had an NDE "just like those of others who had almost died: I journeyed across a river, and saw my dead father's face on the other side. I heard beautiful singing and saw angels all around. Then I heard my husband calling me, journeyed back across, and woke up in his loving arms." The author believed that the very stylized description was gleaned from television or from published popular accounts of the NDE.

Barbara Harris in her book *Full Circle* (33) describes her experiences as a hospitalized patient with severe orthopedic problems. She was lying in a specialized circular bed that allowed the nurses to rotate her body from position to position. She needed to urinate, and the nurses were not immediately available to help her. Her "near-death experience" was caused by the need to urinate and the emotional trauma of wetting the bed. Though she was a patient in a hospital, her "near-death" event was certainly not life-threatening. Furthermore, she describes being sedated heavily with morphine, Valium, and Vistaril, and it is unclear if any of these drugs had been given *before* her "near-death" experience.

Thus, the concept of the NDE becomes muddled because the cardinal feature of the experience (nearness to death) may be absent in most cases. This discrepancy, of course, raises valid questions about the entire concept of the NDE. Dying is a process. Death is a concept (80). If nearness to death is not required, then what are we talking about? Formerly, the definition of death revolved primarily around the loss of pulse and blood pressure. Now it is brain death that is important. But as we will see in Section II, brain death is also a nebulous concept, and the definition is constantly changing. Death becomes the point beyond which a person cannot be retrieved. But is it even necessary to connect the NDE to death? Since near-death is, by definition, not death, is it reasonable to debate intermediate states?

CAN THE NDE BE PRODUCED BY MEANS OTHER THAN BEING NEAR DEATH?

Electrical stimulation of the temporal lobe in humans during brain surgery can cause a sequence of events that include an out-of-body sensation, bright lights, unusual noises, and even a life review. Changes in blood gases such as oxygen deprivation, high or low carbon dioxide, and low blood flow to the brain can produce a syndrome very similar to the NDE. Loss of consciousness produced by many means (G-forces in pilots or experiments in which the blood flow to the brain is decreased) can cause symptoms like the NDE. Sensory deprivation causes hallucinatory states similar to the NDE. Drugs (especially hallucinatory drugs such as LSD and hashish) can cause an NDE-like experience. Certain other anesthetic agents (for example, ketamine) cause an experience like the NDE, and the early experiments with ether gave us accounts very much like the NDE. Temporal lobe epilepsy especially produces the out-of-body sensations associated with the NDE and OBE.

DOES THE NDE CHANGE LIVES?

There seems to be no question among the NDE researchers that the NDE can have a profound effect on the subsequent life of the experiencer. NDE-experiencers have an enhanced belief in an afterlife. The person who has the NDE may be more affected than a person who undergoes a life-threatening event that does not include the NDE, though we should not minimize the power of a cardiac arrest by itself to transform a person's life. These changes are supposedly similar to the life changes seen following salvation: increased love for others, peacefulness, decrease in the fear of death, importance of family and loved ones, increased sense of purpose and direction, increased attention to God, decreased greed and materialism, and more acceptance and forgiveness of others—some of the fruits of the Spirit but without connection to the Vine.

NDE proponents also think that the NDE in itself has tremendous power. Kenneth Ring is quoted as saying:

> The increasing number of NDEs means humans may be approaching the "critical mass" necessary for significant evolutionary change. If more and more people develop a direct inner awareness of the "core" NDE—the sense of Cosmic Unity that empathetically transmits total unconditional love—the threat of planetary disaster can be overcome and a more compassionate world society of humans can celebrate life on the planet. (81)

Ring's wording seems strangely "New Age" and should be considered to be suspect on those grounds alone. However, similar powers have been attributed to other bizarre events such as unidentified flying object (UFO) sightings (82); so claims for such powers in unusual events should not be surprising.

IS THE NDE RELATED TO PERSONALITY TYPE?

The NDE apparently occurs with equal frequency in the young and old, male and female, rich and poor, married and unmarried, and the religious and the non-religious.

Twemlow and Gabbard (64) concluded that the NDE was not related to demographic or cultural variables. The authors found little evidence for psychopathology in the NDE group, and an interest in the occult or unusual phenomena seemed to be unimportant. The physical condition of the person mildly influenced the NDE, and the "cognitive/perceptual style" was different in the persons who experienced the NDE. This factor has been described as the ability to alter consciousness and has been related to the susceptibility to hypnotic suggestion, as well as other altered states of consciousness. However, these and other assessments have generally been obtained in western societies, and other characteristics seem closely related to the underlying culture of the population.

Some researchers (62, 64, 83) report that there seem to be no particular personality types that make a person more likely to have an NDE if a life-threatening event occurs. However, Greyson and Stevenson (66) reported that the NDE experiencer was more likely to have had a similar or mystical experience in the past. Kohr (84) also suggested that a prior tendency for paranormal experiences primed the person for the NDE. Many of their patients may have been influenced by prior knowledge of the NDE, but it is difficult today to believe that anyone in the informed world of multimedia has not had some exposure to the concept.

IS THE NDE IDENTICAL AROUND THE WORLD?

Kellehear (85-87) has evaluated the NDE cross-culturally and found distinctive variations in the expression of the NDE based upon the prevailing thoughts, concepts, and religions of the population. Though the NDE is not described extensively in other cultures or in the medical literature, he found that features of the NDE are strongly associated with the culture. In China, neither the life review, the tunnel experience, nor the sensation of being out of the body was prevalent in the NDE. However, encountering dead relatives (and living relatives as well), seeing religious persons, and entering a form of paradise are common. In Native American Indian tradition, the NDE has no life review or tunnel experience.

Buddhism has also influenced the visions reported in the NDE (88). Buddhists revere their ancestors, so it is not strange to learn that the NDE in Buddhist societies often emphasizes encounters with long-dead relatives. Jesus is never a part of their experience:

> Then he lay down for a moment, and in his dream he saw himself proceed through the void, (still) holding the candle, and he beheld the Buddha Amitabha, who took him up and placed him (or: the candle?) on the palm of his hand, and (in this position) he went through the whole (universe) in all directions (or: its light spread everywhere in all directions). Suddenly he woke up and told everything about his dream to those who nursed him, who were grieved (at this sign of approaching death) and yet consoled (at his vision). When he examined his own body, there were no (longer any signs of) disease and suffering whatsoever. (89)

Though the person thought himself to have been healed, he died the next day.

Becker (90-93) described the Buddhist handbook for dying, the *Meditation on Amitayus Sutra*, a text that describes the Bodhisattva Amida, the person who supposedly meets the dying on their deathbeds (92). Buddhists also believe that the thoughts at the moment of death influence the subsequent journey; so instructions on the "proper" method of dying are prescribed in detail. A good death might result in the Dharma-master Chu-Hung greeting the dying from the Pure Land:

> Imagine thyself to be born in the world of highest happiness in the western quarter, and to be seated cross-legged, on a lotus flower there. Then . . . thine eyes will be opened so as to see the Buddhas and bodhisattvas who fill the whole sky; thou wilt hear the sounds of waters and trees, the notes of birds and the voices of many Buddhas preaching the excellent Law in accordance with the twelve divisions of the scriptures. When thou hast ceased from that meditation, thou must surely remember the experience ever after. . . . The innumerable incarnate bodies of Amitayus, together with those of Avalokitesvara and Mahasthamaprapta, con-

> stantly come and appear before such devotees [who have achieved this state]. (94)

Other descriptions are similarly directly opposed to Christian principles:

> . . . when that son or daughter of a family comes to die, then that Amitayus, the Tathagata, surrounded by an assembly of disciples and followed by a host of Bodhisattvas, will stand before them at the hour of death, and they will depart this life with tranquil minds. After their deaths, they will be born in the world Sukhavati [The Pure Land], in the Buddha country of the same Amitayus. (95)

Some NDEs have involved combined "heavenly" and "hellish" visions. One monk allegedly died and later revived to tell of ". . . the Pure Land, Maitreya's Palace, Yama's hells, and a miraculous rescue by six figures of Jizo" (96). Others reported the experience of dying "badly" and going to the Buddhist equivalent of hell where Yama, the god of the dead, rules.

Indian NDEs are particularly illustrative. The NDE was studied in India in the 1970s by Pasricha and Stevenson (97-98). They claimed that the tunnel experience, out-of-body experience, and bright lights were much less common in India than in the NDE of other cultures, though a life review is often described. Blackmore (22, 28-30, 99), who believes that the tunnel and bright lights are representations of the cerebral stimulation occurring with oxygen deprivation of the brain, was disturbed by the findings of Pasricha and Stevenson because the absence of tunnels in their report challenged her theory. If the tunnels and bright lights were simply manifestations of an altered brain physiology, then they should occur in all cultures.

Blackmore (22) reported eight NDEs she collected from India (or six, depending on the criteria used to define the NDE) out of a group of nineteen persons who responded to a newspaper ad. She found that the tunnel, in fact, occurred in 38 percent of subjects. Blackmore concluded that Indians do indeed have tunnels as part of their NDE, and so her theory about altered brain physiology remained unshaken. Of interest, she described brief case reports of the six subjects with the most convincing NDEs. None were definitively at the point of death by the medical descriptions, though one required "cardioversion" and another had been "electrocuted." One suffered from "tension"; another was undergoing angiography without any complications described; one was in a coma; and the final patient had a "cardiac arrest" during an operation, though no treatments were described.

Most Indians with an NDE saw visions of dead relatives or religious figures. Heaven (called "Swarag" in Hindu culture) was reported in a way wholly consistent with the Indian concept of the afterlife:

> I then saw a big tree. On each leaf was written: Ram, Ram [name of the chief Indian deity]. (100)

> I was in a beautiful place. There were beautiful gardens and a temple with many gods residing in it. (101)

Heaven is dominated by visions of relatives, either living or dead, perhaps a reflection of the veneration of the Indian culture for family and elders (102). Females are less common in the visions of the NDE in India, 23 percent versus 61 percent in other cultures (103).

In the Indian NDE it was common to have a person or group of people come to the "dead" person to take him away. This practice mirrored the Indian belief in Yamdoots, the messengers of the dead, who by tradition escort the dead to meet with the Hindu god of the dead, Yamaraj (or Yama). The "deceased" in India are often taken before Yamaraj or some other deity or tribunal to have their worldly life reviewed from a book. Hinduism is the prevailing religion of India, and in Hindu tradition a reading of your life history occurs at death. Chitragupta is the god who reads from the book that details the events of your life. Thus it might be expected that an NDE in India would include a person reading the review of your life, and indeed such a phenomenon is usually included in the Indian NDE. Commonly the NDE journey is interrupted by the realization that the "wrong" person has been allowed to die, usually because of a confusion in names, the "dead" having a similar name to the person who was supposed to have died. Pasricha and Stevenson report some of these cases of mistaken identity:

> They took me and seated me near the god. . . . I was summoned. . . . One of the clerks said, "We don't need Chhajju Bania (trader). We had asked for Chhajju Kumhar (potter). Push him back and bring the other man. He [meaning Chhajju Bania] has some life remaining." (104)

> Two persons caught me and took me with them. . . . Then there was a man sitting up. He looked dreadful and was all black. He was not wearing any clothes. He said in a rage [to the attendants who had brought Vasudev] "I had asked you to bring Vasudev the gardener. Our garden is drying up. You have brought Vasudev the student." (105)

> He had been taken to another place by 10 people. He had tried to escape, but they had then cut off his legs at the knees to prevent his escape. He was taken to a place where there were tables and chairs and 40 or 50 people sitting. He recognized no one. They looked at his "papers," saw that his name was not on their list, and said, "Why have you brought him here? Take him back." (106)

> A man was there, and he reprimanded the men who had brought me: "Why have you brought the wrong person? Why have you not brought the man you had been sent for?" (107)

Osis and Haraldsson summarized their findings by saying:

> . . . the characteristics of these apparitions are strongly molded by cultural forces. . . . When identified, they were named according to the patient's religion, e.g., no Hindu reported seeing Jesus; no Christian a Hindu deity. (108)

Pasricha and Stevenson (109) also quoted Sandweiss, who describes one Indian's encounter with Sai Baba, an Indian holy man of the present day:

> The records of the patient's *previous* lives were called for; "armloads of scrolls" were brought and read at length [emphasis mine]. At the end of the reading Sai Baba asked the judge to allow the subject to continue living (under Sai Baba's aegis) in order "to complete my mission of spreading the truth."

So not only is Sai Baba in control (though not the judge himself), but past lives (reincarnation) are important in the decision to allow us to live or to die. Further, the message to be spread throughout the earth is the message of Sai Baba, not the message of Jesus. Should such stories be interpreted as guideposts for our spiritual journeys?

Mistaken identity is thus a strong component of the Indian NDE, given as the reason the person is sent back to the earth. In contrast, in the American NDE the person is often given a *choice* to return or is sent back because there is some unfinished business to accomplish. Often the person returns because of the need to be close to a loved one (such as a young child). Pasricha (98) concludes that the Indian NDE is dominated by the passivity of the Indian. The god of the dead makes the decision for the "dead" to return to life, while the assertiveness of the western culture dominates the reason for the dead to return in the American NDE. Apparently we in America can choose our fate, while the Indian is controlled by the Yamdoots and Yamaraj.

According to a description of his NDE by a Mapuche man from Chile, he journeyed into a volcano and encountered dead relatives and a German man who seemed to be in charge (110). He was told that he must return to the living. His destination, the volcano, was shaped by the imagery of the local landscape that was familiar to him—surrounded by volcanoes. The history of his people was dominated by the German colonizers who had come to the region many years ago. Thus his NDE was shaped by the familiar cultural and geographic aspects of his environment but was quite different from the NDEs of other cultures.

An aborigine of Australia with an NDE met traditional spirits (for example, the Turtle Man Spirit) rather than Jesus or any other Christian figure. This account included no tunnel experience nor life review.

Feng (111) reported NDEs among survivors of the earthquake in Tangshan, China, which occurred in 1976. He also concluded that the features of the NDE might be significantly influenced by the persons' "races, regions, psychological and cultural backgrounds, and kinds of event."

Therefore, distinct patterns are imprinted by the local culture. "Cerebral maps" or "blueprints" for the NDE originate from the belief systems of the culture.

NDE proponents tend to promote religious universalism—the concept that all religions are equally valid. The Buddhist does not encounter Jesus at the end of the tunnel, and the aborigine may not even see the tunnel. If the cardinal features of the NDE are so culture-bound, can they really represent the truth of our destiny after death? If Jesus is real and the *only* way to eternal life, why do some people encounter Turtle Spirits and others see Buddha in the NDE? Could it be that the NDE is some form of deception? Are we to believe this phenomenon is a message from God? Would God give some a vision of Jesus and others a vision of a turtle?

IS THE NDE CONSISTENT?

While most NDEs are actually quite vague, some have included detailed descriptions of the travel and destination. If the NDE is a valid report of the afterlife, then the reports should be similar, if not identical. God should transport us in a similar fashion to an identical location that would be described consistently.

However, the mode of travel and the destination are quite different. The NDE experience in India includes accompaniment of the dying person by messengers and readers from books or papers, both of which are aspects of the Indian Hindu belief system. In the United States, however, the dying travel alone, though they may meet relatives or friends (either living or deceased) along the way.

The trip itself has variations that are difficult to reconcile. Some people are held by the hand, some ride a beam of light to the destination, and some are aware of only voices during the trip. One person described riding in a "blue bubble"; another described a procession of angels that held hands and formed a ladder to heaven (112).

The identity of the "being of light" at the end of the trip is variable as well. Some people describe it as God the Father, some as Jesus, some as Buddha, some as the "higher self," and a wide variety of other identifications, usually based upon the religious beliefs of the person taking the trip. Hindus identify Rama, Shiva, Krishna, angels, or other religious figures.

The colors of the light in heaven or paradise are also variable. Some NDEers describe it as red, some as blue, some as green, some as blue-green. Variations on the description make it more likely that the NDE is a creation of the person's mind or imagination.

Alnor (113) has emphasized that the physical aspects of Jesus reported by those NDEers and visionaries who see Jesus are different. Man has always been interested in the appearance of Jesus, and the color of His hair is often described in the accounts of the

NDE. This feature should not change from person to person if the vision is really the physical countenance of Jesus. However, some say that the hair is brown; some say black; some report golden. However, John in Revelation said, "His head and hair were white like wool, as white as snow, and his eyes were like blazing fire" (1:14). So some (or all) of the NDE reports must be incorrect. How do we tell which (if any) are true?

In India, the reason given for the return to earth is often that a mistake has been made in the identity of the person who is supposed to die. Usually a person with a similar name is the one appointed to die, and the death messenger made a mistake in picking the wrong person. (I would not want to worship a god whose messengers made mistakes like that!) In the United States, the NDE is usually terminated when the "being of light" announces that the person has more work on earth to accomplish, and the person returns—sometimes reluctantly—to his body on earth. (Similarly, I would not want to worship a god who can't seem to make up his mind about issues of life and death!) On rare occasions, the dying person is given a choice whether to return to the earth to continue life. (Does God give us a choice in such matters? The Bible says no.)

WHAT IS THE CAUSE OF THE NDE?

The causes hypothesized for the NDE can be classified into three broad categories.

Physical

These include the broad range of drug effects, seizure disorders, lack of oxygen, lack or excess of carbon dioxide, low blood flow to the brain caused by any of a variety of conditions characterized by low blood pressure, and neurochemical changes, all of which will be discussed in Section II.

Psychological

These theories suggest that the NDE is a psychological response to protect the psyche from the fear of death. It can include dissociative reactions, which are protective mechanisms to isolate the person from the grave physical danger that is occurring when the event really is associated with physical danger. It is a form of denial of the event. It replaces the danger of the near-death experience with a pleasant set of physical sensations. This defense mechanism would explain the presence of the NDE in the absence of any real physical danger when there is the perception that danger or death is imminent.

Spiritual

The spiritual theory suggests that the NDE has given the experiencer a brief glimpse of heaven. It accommodates all cultures and religions: the Hindu sees relatives, the Buddhist sees Buddha, and the Christian sees Jesus or God. Even more specifically, the Catholic sees the Virgin Mary as well as Jesus, and the fundamentalist sees visions consistent with hymns sung during his religious upbringing.

The NDE does, indeed, cause lifestyle changes, but such changes are poor evidence for the validity of the NDE vision. Furthermore, born-again Christians can have the NDE as a part of a serious illness or accident, but the presence of the NDE in a Christian setting does not explain or validate the theology of the NDE seen in other cultures.

Many investigators have tried to use the NDE as evidence for an afterlife consisting of heaven or hell. However, because the NDE is both culture-bound and religion-bound, it is difficult to ascribe any particular significance to the visions reported during an NDE. If NDE visions have validity, then it is necessary to conclude that all religions are equally acceptable, a theologically untenable position for the Christian. One can only conclude that the NDE simply reflects the culture and belief system of the experiencer. It thus loses its meaning for mankind as a whole and is revealed as a deceptive reassurance. It is a conditioned response to one's past experiences. If that background is Mormonism, the NDE will have Mormon overtones. If the background is Catholic, the NDE will have Catholic overtones. If the background is Hindu, then Hinduism will emerge from the NDE.

The NDE could be the result of wishful thinking, but it could also be a fabrication or the embellishment of vague sensory experiences associated with the serious physical condition of the ill. It could be the result of the desire to please others—family, clergy, researchers, church, physicians, psychologists. The NDE could be the byproduct of a vivid imagination, could be self-induced, or (more recently, as the phenomenon has received media attention) the result of a type of mass hysteria. It may be the result of demonic activity. Most likely, it is the result of the synthesis of unfamiliar sensory experiences (supported by the maintenance of minimal perfusion of the brain) in the background of a particular religious framework, augmented by the memories of what has been heard about the process of dying and near-death from popular media.

ARE ALL NDES PLEASANT?

Most early accounts described NDEs as pleasant, if not glorious, experiences. It is often called the "radiant NDE." The overwhelming feature of the NDE is peace and tranquillity. The NDE contends that God is unconditional love and total acceptance, and He is never judgmental. In this view God never reveals His justice, and in the NDE He does not demand righteousness from anyone. This preponderance of positive aspects made it immediately acceptable to the listening public. Everyone fears death to some extent, if only because it represents the ultimate unknown. To be reassured that death is pleasant and that nothing is to be feared is what the world wants to hear.

However, therein lies the deception. By hearing that "I'm O.K., you're O.K." and that all mankind encounters love and peace at death, the world is lulled into the notion that nothing in one's belief system matters. Even the non-religious—the atheist—finds heaven. So why bother with making a decision about God? Why bother with the concept that Jesus is the way, the truth, and the life? Nothing matters, so just live your life as you want, because the end result will be the same for everyone. No matter that your life is corrupt and full of sin. Heaven, peace, and love await you on the other side. The NDE is a very dangerous notion!

Bias may cause the NDE to be reported as pleasant:

1. A person wants an enjoyable experience and the reassurance that all is well in the afterlife.
2. The popular accounts are written mostly about ecstatic experiences, and people tend to want to recount these happy journeys.
3. No one wants the world to know that they went to hell as a result of a bad life when the popular books write only about happy experiences, emphasizing that the person with a bad experience must really be an exceptionally wicked sinner.
4. The tools used for the recounting of the NDE (questionnaires, interview scripts) may be biased to record mostly pleasant, rather than bad, experiences.
5. Bad memories may be repressed, particularly as the time from the NDE elapses.
6. Researchers may be reluctant to report the bad experiences because they are at variance with the previously published accounts.

7. People may be unwilling to relive the fright and fear that accompanied the negative NDE.

Garfield (114) reported a small series of patients interviewed relatively early after the near-death event and noted that 22 percent had nightmarish experiences, and an additional 11 percent had a mixture of good and bad components to the NDE. Lindley and coworkers (24) studied fifty-five patients who claimed to have had an NDE and found 20 percent to have had unpleasant experiences. In the Gallup poll of the NDE (25), however, the negative NDE accounted for less than 1 percent of the estimated 8,000,000 NDEs claimed to have occurred in that population. Greyson and Bush (68) cited Grey (116) who reported that there was a typical sequence of the negative NDE that paralleled the positive experience reported by Ring:

POSITIVE NDE (RING) (52)	NEGATIVE NDE (GREY) (115)
1. Peace	1. Fear and panic
2. Out-of-body sensation	2. Out-of-body sensation
3. Tunnel Experience	3. Entering a black void
4. Seeing the light	4. Sensing an evil force
5. Entering heavenly realms	5. Entering hellish realms

So there are accounts of negative experiences from patients about to die (or at least thinking they are about to die). But the overwhelming message going to the public from the popular works is the abundance of love and light. We must remember that sometimes light deceives!

A further danger arising from the cult of the overwhelmingly pleasant NDE is the possibility that it could bring our society closer to euthanasia. If the dying process and the life after death are so pleasant for the vast majority of the population, then why allow anyone to suffer from any illness, particularly the final stages of a terminal illness? The enthusiasts for the NDE claim that death itself is really a fine experience and that virtually all people gain peace and love immediately upon the approach of death. Furthermore, regardless of your past, you enter into a garden of bliss that can only be described as paradise.

Almost all NDE cultists describe an unwillingness of their patients to "go back" to their lives on earth. Some suggest that we should tailor our therapy in a terminally ill patient so that the ecstatic experience of dying is not blunted or obliterated. One author said that if NDEs exist and if they prove a heavenly after-life, then "any medical efforts to postpone the joys of heaven would be misguided" (116). So the NDE may become rationalization to justify active euthanasia. Certainly if the popular description of the NDE is accurate—and the *interpretation* accurate—then some physicians might be led to hasten the death of someone in pain. God forbid! If we are deceived by this "light" of the NDE, then we are most gullible indeed!

DOES THE NDE MAKE A PERSON MORE "PSYCHIC" AFTER THE EXPERIENCE?

Morse and Sutherland both have made strong claims that the NDE has aftereffects manifested as increased psychic powers, as well as experiences suggesting some "electromagnetic powers" imparted by the NDE. None of these claims has been tested, let alone proven. Dannion Brinkley (117) claimed to have the power to predict the future, but his "predictions" conveniently appeared *after* the events occurred. Sutherland herself acknowledges the fatal deficiency of the methods of her "study" of the psychic powers of people who have experienced an NDE:

> No effort was made to verify the claims of psychic phenomena either before or since the NDE, apart from ask-

> ing for explanations and examples of reported phenomena. (118)

In other words, if a person *claimed* to be psychic, he *was* psychic. Not exactly strong positive confirmation!

Atwater (119) also suggested some rather fantastic effects that were present in over 50 percent of the people who had experienced an NDE, only some of them being:

> More rapid digestion.
> General improvement in health.
> Ability to become "at one" with other things.
> Ability to hear plants and animals speak to them.
> Hearing words not spoken.
> Ability to see things that aren't there.
> Awareness of "energy fields" and "movement of energy."
> Bodily interference with electrical devices.
> Ability to see the future.

Of course, none of these alleged newly found skills were objectively documented.

So there is no evidence whatsoever that psychic abilities proceed from the NDE.

CONCLUSIONS

So what can we conclude?

1. The NDE is probably a real physical phenomenon arising from disturbed sensory input.

2. The NDE is uncommon but not rare.

3. The NDE is more common now than in the past because of the advent of cardiopulmonary resuscitation and

other revival techniques and because of the popularity of the phenomenon.

4. The major characteristics of the NDE are:

   Inability to express the sensation in words.
   Hearing the report that "you have died."
   Peacefulness and quiet.
   Unusual noises.
   The tunnel.
   Out-of-body sensations.
   Meeting other people.
   Seeing a light or a "being of light."
   Entering the light.
   Life review.
   Reaching a limit or border that is impassable.
   Coming back to earth.
   Experiencing a long-lasting effect on subsequent beliefs and priorities.

5. The NDE is different from the OBE.

6. Techniques used to elicit NDE accounts are important. The manner in which one asks about the NDE can result in denial of the phenomenon, embellishment of the report, or even fabrication of an NDE for the approval of the interviewer.

7. The NDE is affected by culture. The NDE imagery will be formatted in the terms of the person's prior experience and religious beliefs. The interpretation of the NDE will thus be dependent upon the religious framework of the experiencer.

8. Differences in the reporting of the NDE are probably related to both the techniques of the interviewer and the clinical setting of the near-death event itself.

Next we will examine the medical explanations for the NDE.

SECTION TWO

■

Medicine and the Near-Death Experience

5

WHAT DOES MEDICINE SAY ABOUT THE NDE?

Life Is a Terminal Disease

Recently I asked Dr. John Adams, a colleague in cardiology, what he knew about the NDE. John has worked exclusively during the last twenty-two years with patients who have survived a cardiac arrest. He has treated thousands of patients who have "died" and been resuscitated. His response was typical of the many cardiologists whom I have surveyed. He said, "Yes, I once had a patient who had an unusual experience during the arrest. He described to me a sensation of brilliant lights that to him had some kind of religious significance. But I never saw any other patient with that kind of event. And he seemed a bit weird." Only one patient in a career of twenty-two years of treating patients with cardiac arrest who had been resuscitated! This seems amazing but is actually very typical of the experience of most of us who deal with these patients. Most cardiologists responded, "What is an NDE?"

Why this discrepancy between the tabloid reports and the medical community? Striking as it may seem, the medical community is sharply divided on the issue of the NDE (1-34). In one camp are the believers in such events—a small group of psychologists, psychiatrists, and others who deal more exclusively with the mind and emotions. (In the early years of the study of cardiac arrests, the NDE was absent even in the psychiatric reports.) In the other camp reside the cardiologists, pulmonologists, intensive care specialists, and neurologists who either are completely unfamiliar with the NDE phenomenon or believe it is an invention of very imaginative minds—not a subject worthy of serious thought or research efforts.

In general, the medical community simply ignores the publications—medical or popular—that describe the NDE. Most physicians view the NDE in the same way they view witchcraft. In fact, the publications of reports of the NDE themselves are tightly compartmentalized. They appear in obscure journals such as *Anabiosis*, the *Journal of Near-Death Studies*, *Omega*, or other journals that by their very nature tend to publish positive accounts of the NDE. When mentioned in the more mainstream journals such as *Lancet*, the *Journal of the American Medical Association*, or the *New England Journal of Medicine*, the flavors of the articles and the responses are much different, tending toward skepticism and disbelief, if not outright ridicule of those who report such experiences. The NDE remains more a subject to be discussed in the popular press and in books designed for general consumption than in the critical and analytical world of the medical journal.

Most physicians, and physician-researchers in particular, tend to scoff at any concept that smacks of the spiritual or that suggests a dimension outside the precisely measurable world of scientific medicine. The Christian physician or Christian physician-researcher is a rare bird indeed. At least, if a researcher has Christian beliefs he "keeps them to himself" and does not allow them to influence his research or reporting. Judeo-Christian teachings are almost never discussed in medical circles. All of medicine must be measurable, quantifiable, reproducible, they say. This approach is detrimental to any spiritual quest, be it the NDE or mainline religious doctrine. These topics are relegated to leisure-time activities that are not to be broached in the hospital, clinic, or university. Especially the university.

For example, I recently performed a literature search in the National Library of Medicine for the time period of January 1990 to December 1994. It yielded only eleven articles under a search heading of "Jesus Christ." Of these, only seven actually dealt with Jesus; four addressed the disease incidence and patterns among members of the Church of Jesus Christ of Latter Day Saints—the Mormons. Furthermore, four of the seven articles that actually dealt with the person of Jesus were negative; that is, they purported that the resurrection of Jesus was a hoax. In this same literature search there were only two articles under the heading of "Holy Bible." Contrast these numbers to the citations found for "AIDS" (25,407 articles) and "stroke" (13,797 articles) for the same time period.

Keeping these biases in mind, let's examine the medical literature that might be relevant to the explanation of the NDE. This section will be divided into two major parts—the central nervous system and the cardiovascular system—because these are the major areas relevant to the NDE. A study of the central nervous system can give us insights into the explanation of the nervous, mental, emotional, and, yes, spiritual aspects of the NDE. Knowledge of the cardiovascular system can explain many of the phenomena leading to the physical manifestations known as the NDE.

6

THE CENTRAL NERVOUS SYSTEM

Your Body Has a Lifetime Guarantee

Ethel Collins had lived a very full life. She was sixty-eight years old and had seen her share of joy and sadness while raising her five children. Her husband had died three years ago, but Ethel had continued to live by herself in their modest home in Seattle. Every Sunday her daughter Ruth would come from Federal Way, a nearby suburb, to Ethel's home for Sunday dinner, usually bringing the grandchildren.

This Sunday was no different. Ruth and her husband, Bob, and the children came to Ethel's home, where a dinner of turkey and dressing awaited them. But Ruth noted that her mother was not quite the same this week. Ethel was tired, occasionally breathing heavily. Ethel even mentioned the heart attack that she had experienced five years ago, but she said that today she felt very different. No, she was sure this was not another heart attack. No chest heaviness or crushing pains. Yes, her breathing was a bit more labored, but not nearly as bad as it had been during the heart attack. And, yes, the breathing had been a bit worse over the past few weeks, though Ethel had told no one. So there was no real acute change.

Dinner started with grace, as usual. But when everyone looked up, Ethel crashed facedown onto her plate. There was no other warning. Ruth and Bob rushed to her side and noted that she seemed to be taking short, irregular gasps for air, then no breathing at all. She was turning blue. Bob began cardiopulmonary resuscitation (CPR), and Ruth ran to call the Medics. The grandchildren began to scream. They knew Grandma was very sick; even though they were young, they could tell that something horrible was happening.

Fortunately, Ethel lived close to the fire station where the Medics were located. They arrived in just over three minutes, and they found Ruth and Bob continuing CPR. Bob had recently taken a CPR refresher course at his job at the Renton Boeing plant, and Ruth remembered a bit from the course given at the children's school a few years ago. The Medics took over. They continued CPR, attached an electrocardiogram, and found that Ruth was in ventricular fibrillation—cardiac arrest. There is only one treatment for this heart rhythm—an electric shock across the chest.

The first three shocks didn't work. Next they put a tube in her windpipe to breathe for her and started a central intravenous line, then gave her some medications. The next shock restored a reasonable heart rhythm. Slowly her blood pressure returned, and the Medics began to make preparations to load her into the ambulance to transport her to the hospital.

Ruth and Bob said they would quickly drop the grandchildren off at Ruth's sister's house and come to the hospital as soon as possible. By the time they arrived one hour later, the medical team had sprung into action. Ethel still had the tube in her windpipe to help her breathe, and she had three intravenous lines now. She also had an arterial line to help monitor her blood pressure. But it was the rhythmic pumping of the mechanical respirator that bothered Ruth the most. Ethel had told her daughter a few months ago that she did not want to live a life tied to a bunch of machines, and here she was in exactly that situation. Yes, Ethel had even signed an advance directive that outlined these requests, but the paper was locked in the safe deposit box at the bank, and it was Sunday. No chance to get it today. Ruth was horrified at the thought that her mom was being kept alive against her wishes.

But was she? Was this what she had meant when she said she didn't want to be plugged into machines? The doctors talked with Ruth and Bob gently, but Ruth still had difficulty understanding. This condition might be only temporary. Ethel had received good CPR at the onset of her cardiac arrest, and the Medics had been successful in restoring a pulse and blood pressure reasonably quickly. Except for the recent mild shortness of breath, Ethel had been very functional before today. In fact, she had told her family about two months ago that she was really enjoying the grandchildren for the first time since her husband had died.

The doctors pleaded with the family to understand that her condition might rapidly improve and that she might return to complete functional recovery without any residual brain or other organ damage. Initial tests indicated that while she had suffered a cardiac arrest, there was not yet any evidence for any significant long-term heart damage. On the other hand, there was a small chance that she indeed could emerge from this catastrophe with some brain damage, even to the extent of being comatose and needing long-term care, perhaps even a long-term respirator. But it was simply too early to tell.

Ruth and Bob reluctantly accepted the advice of the doctors to continue the present treatment, even the indignity of being hooked up to those machines, at least for a short time. How were they to know what Ethel really intended when she signed that document about life-sustaining treatment? Was this what she meant? Or did she really understand that "life-sustaining treatment" might mean only a brief exposure to these machines? It was too much for the family to comprehend, so they simply left the decisions up to the medical team.

The first twenty-four hours passed slowly. The family stayed and slept in the Intensive Care Unit waiting room. The doctors said that Ethel was beginning to show some signs of improvement, but Ruth wasn't so sure. The flailing motions of her mom's arms and legs were too disorganized for Ruth to understand how the doctors could think this was improvement. Ruth was more determined now. Mom wouldn't want these efforts to be continued. Ruth began imploring doctors to let her mother die with dignity.

But over the next twelve hours Ethel began to drift in and out of consciousness. She even recognized the family once and began to make motions to indicate that she wanted the tube removed from her throat. Soon the doctors determined that she was breathing well enough to have the tube and the respirator removed. It was taken out about thirty-six hours after the cardiac arrest, and Ethel seemed surprisingly alert, although confused. Her memory was clouded, and she asked Ruth why she hadn't come over for Sunday dinner. She didn't understand what had happened, but she knew that her chest was sore. When told that she had suffered a cardiac arrest, she refused to believe the news. No, she must have just fainted. As for this chest soreness and now a cough, she must just have had a "touch of pneumonia." That made sense, didn't it? The shortness of breath the past few days? Pneumonia, yes. A cardiac arrest just seemed too preposterous.

This story is just one of many with a happy ending. Ethel recovered completely. She needed some treatment for her cardiac condition to prevent any further recurrences of the cardiac arrest, but she consented to this treatment so she could get back home to enjoy her grandchildren. And the time on the life-support machines? "What machines?" she said to Ruth repeatedly. "I don't remember any machines. And why didn't you come to dinner that Sunday, anyway?"

Ethel never did remember the sequence of events from that Sunday morning to the next Friday afternoon. She was a bit "foggy" about the next few days as well. And, yes, she had heard of Betty Eadie. Betty actually lived just a few miles from Ethel. Ethel had seen Eadie's TV show a few months ago about the wonderful experience she had reported in her book. But Ethel had no such memory, except that her daughter had missed that wonderful Sunday turkey dinner.

Was her amnesia typical for a cardiac arrest victim? If so, how could anyone with a real cardiac arrest ever report those beautiful trips to heaven and back?

THE CENTRAL NERVOUS SYSTEM

The central nervous system consists of the brain and the spinal cord. Nervous impulses travel to and from the brain via the spinal cord and the peripheral nerves. Most of the phenomena described for the NDE relate to the brain itself. While some events that occur during loss of consciousness may originate primarily in the spinal cord, this section deals with the organization of the brain.

Normal Anatomy and Physiology of the Brain

The brain is divided into discrete sections both anatomically and physiologically, though the physiology of thought, memory, and emotions remains incompletely understood (1-5). Proceeding from the level of the spinal cord in the neck and moving upward into the head, the important anatomic segments are (1) the medulla, pons, and midbrain; (2) the hypothalamus and thalamus; (3) the cerebellum; and most importantly (4) the cerebrum (Figure 1, see next page).

The medulla, pons, and midbrain (generically referred to as the "brain stem") control the more "vegetative" or what we think of as "automatic" functions of the body, such as regulation of blood pressure, heart rate, and respiration. Furthermore, the cranial nerves arise in these sites, controlling the function of the face,

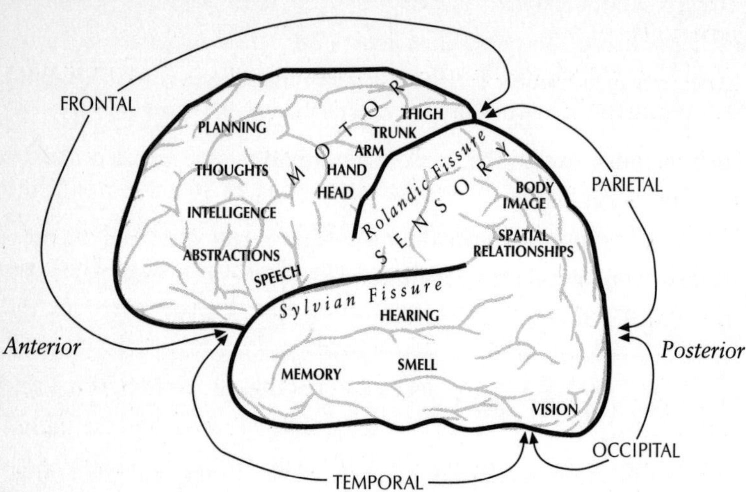

Figure 1. Brain anatomy and function. The anatomy of the human brain is depicted by this view of the lateral aspect of the left side of the brain. The major divisions are the frontal, parietal, temporal, and occipital lobes.

eyes, ears, nose, and throat. A specialized but poorly understood region of the brain stem is the reticular activating system. It is responsible for the maintenance of consciousness and is crucial when considering the responses to certain cardiovascular and neurological events that result in sleep, altered states of consciousness, stupor, and coma.

The thalamus serves as a "switching station" for sensory impulses, but more importantly for our purposes, it (with the reticular activating system) is a center for regulation of the state of consciousness, emotion, attentiveness, awareness, and the processing of sensory experiences. The hypothalamus is the site of control of temperature, salt and water balance, and the integration of the other portions of the nervous system. It aids in the control of the pituitary gland with all of its endocrine (hormone) functions. The hypothalamus also participates in the control of emotions.

The cerebellum controls a person's balance and coordination of motion and muscular activity. There is no direct contribution of the cerebellum to consciousness or thought.

The cerebrum is divided into the gray matter and the white matter. The gray matter is the cerebral cortex, or the outer layer of cerebral matter. The white matter is located more deeply. The cerebrum is further divided into the frontal lobes, the parietal lobes, the temporal lobes, and the occipital lobes.

The frontal lobes are the structures that, in large part, distinguish man from other animals. The frontal lobes in man are highly developed, and this region is where many conscious mental processes originate. Thought, reasoning, associative processes, intelligence, and some aspects of emotions are processed in the frontal lobes. However, many of these functions are also served by other portions of the brain because all of these functions can persist in patients who have lost all or part of their frontal lobes. The posterior portion of the frontal lobes, in front of the central fissure of Rolando (Figure 1), is the region that controls the motor function of the body over which we have conscious control. Specific regions of this strip of cortex are responsible for movement of certain parts of the body. For example, the lateral portion of the motor cortex controls the hand and arm, while the more midline part of the motor cortex controls the legs and feet. The representation of these areas in the brain is quite specific. Figure 2, on the next page, shows which regions of the brain control each part of the body. Speech control resides in the frontal lobe, usually on the dominant side—that is, the side opposite the handedness of the person (right-handed, left cortex dominant; left-handed, right cortex dominant).

Similarly, the brain tissue behind the fissure of Rolando receives the sensory impulses from corresponding parts of the body. This sensory cortex is located in the anterior part of the parietal

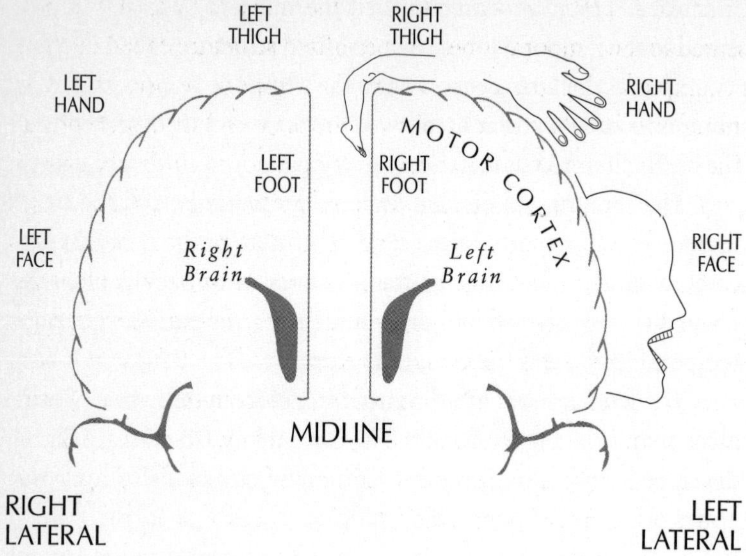

Figure 2. Representation of the motor function of the brain. The part of the brain responsible for motor activity is located anterior to the Fissure of Rolando in the frontal lobes. More area of the brain surface is allocated to the hand and the face than to other parts of the body.

cortex. The parietal lobes are also responsible for right-left orientation, certain abilities to write and calculate, and other spatial orientation.

Vision is represented in the posterior portions of the occipital cortex, and specific parts of the visual fields (upper and lower, left and right, central and peripheral) can be identified with accuracy.

The temporal lobes in man have an important function in the integration of memory, conscious awareness, and perception of the reality of surroundings. Visual and sensory integration are in part dependent upon the temporal lobes. Fibers carrying visual impulses course through the deeper portions of the temporal lobe. The sense of smell, hearing, and functions of the inner ear are also represented in the temporal lobes. A specialized structure called the hippocampus is located deep within the temporal lobes, and it is thought to have some control over memory and time perception. The ability to make associations is also contained in the regions of the temporal lobe. Complex emotions can be evoked by the stimulation of the temporal lobes, and mood changes have been associated with alterations here. Attitudes and social behavior can be affected by the temporal lobes, and the left temporal lobe, in particular, participates in language development. The temporal lobes, then, are where many of our inputs are molded into a sense of self-awareness. Is it any wonder, then, that many writers have identified the temporal lobes as potential sites of origin of the complex sequences that have been called NDEs?

Dependence Upon Oxygen and Nutrients

Blood flow to the brain is crucial to the maintenance of consciousness (6-7). God created us with amazing protective mechanisms that cause the body to preserve the blood flow to the brain and heart at the expense of blood flow to other parts of the body. When the blood pressure falls for any reason, arteries in the rest of the body constrict in an attempt to raise the blood pressure back to normal, while arteries in the heart and brain dilate (expand) to achieve as much blood flow there as possible (7). This mechanism is called "autoregulation" of blood flow. Over a wide range of blood pressures the blood flow to the brain remains constant. It is only at extremes of blood pressure that a change occurs in blood flow. During extreme hypertension (high blood pressure) the flow increases slightly, and under conditions of hypotension (low blood pressure) the flow decreases.

Blood flow will also increase as the metabolic activity of the brain increases. That is, the brain of a lethargic person will receive less blood flow than the brain of the same person performing complex mathematical calculations. A seizure places the highest metabolic demands on the brain and causes the highest blood flow.

Regional blood flow becomes very important within the brain itself (8). Portions of the brain furthest from a major brain artery become the most deprived of oxygen and glucose when blood pressure falls. The areas between major arteries are the most seriously affected, and their blood flow is often referred to as "watershed" areas. Decrease in blood flow creates a condition called ischemia—lack of oxygen and nutrients and buildup of waste products. Ischemic dysfunction or damage may be limited to the watershed zones if blood pressure is marginal, or the ischemic dysfunction or damage may be diffuse if the blood pressure is zero (as seen with a cardiac arrest due to ventricular fibrillation). Normal systolic blood pressure is 120-140 mm of mercury. (Blood pressure readings reflect the pressure in millimeters of mercury generated by the contraction of the heart, which forces blood through the body; for example, if the blood pressure is 120/78, the upper number—120—is the systolic pressure, and the lower number—78—is the diastolic blood pressure.) Blood flow to the brain is maintained at relatively normal levels until the systolic blood pressure is at about 50-60 mm of mercury (mean blood pressure about 30 mm of mercury), at which time the cerebral blood flow decreases from a mean of 50 ml/100 grams of brain/minute to 30 ml/100 gm/minute (3-4). That is, brain blood flow does not decrease until the blood pressure has dropped to a seriously low range. Furthermore, the occipital cortex (where the visual cortex is located) is particularly sensitive. The earliest ischemic dysfunction occurs in the parietal and occipital regions of the brain. It is well-known that the so-called "tunnel vision" can be produced by decreasing the blood flow to the occipital lobes. (See "The Eye and Vision," in Chapter 7.)

The brain is critically dependent upon continuous delivery of both oxygen and nutrients for its function (9). It can store neither, and it is the most sensitive organ in the body to changes of oxygen, glucose (sugar), and blood flow. Glucose is the major energy source for the brain. While the brain is only 2.5 percent of the total body mass, it uses 15 percent of the body's total supply of glucose and 20 percent of the body's supply of oxygen (10-11). The brain receives a large volume of blood, considering the relatively small size of this organ in relation to other regions of the body. Average blood flow to the brain is 50 ml/100 gm/minute, and that value remains fairly constant under many different circumstances. Comparatively, flow to the skin is 13 ml/100 gm/minute, to the heart is 84 ml/100 gm/minute, to skeletal muscle at rest is 3 ml/100 gm/minute, and to the body as a whole is 9 ml/100 gm/minute. Interrupt blood flow for only a few seconds and the brain will malfunction, causing unconsciousness, while the lungs, kidneys, stomach, and many other organs will continue to function and suffer no ill effects. Sudden cessation of blood flow to the head will cause symptoms in about five seconds, and unconsciousness will occur in about six seconds. Stated another way, the brain has an oxygen reserve of only about five to six seconds.

An experiment can be performed to demonstrate the importance of oxygen, compared to nutrients, for the brain (12). In this experiment, a patient breathes nitrogen in place of oxygen; therefore, the blood continues to flow and has all of the nutrients and is lacking only in oxygen. If a person suddenly begins to breathe pure nitrogen, thus removing oxygen from the lungs, loss of consciousness occurs in about seventeen to twenty seconds. In this experiment designed to cause unconsciousness, ten to fourteen of these seconds are necessary to free the lungs of oxygen and for the oxygen-deficient blood to travel to the brain and exert its effect. The remaining seconds use up the oxygen reserve of the brain. Lack of oxygen is called hypoxia; complete lack of oxygen is called anoxia. As the patient resumes breathing oxygen, the mental changes and loss of consciousness revert to normal as quickly as they appeared. More prolonged oxygen deprivation will, of course, cause malfunction and damage to other organs, as well as permanent brain damage.

A remarkable experiment was performed in 1944, a study that would probably never be allowed today because of changes in acceptable ethical standards. Rossen and coworkers (13) devised a technique that could suddenly interrupt the blood flow to the head in normal human volunteers. It was first tried in dogs and proved successful in those experiments. The apparatus was a pressure cuff placed around the neck of the animal that could be suddenly inflated to a pressure of 600 mm of mercury. This high pressure (a dog's blood pressure is similar to a human's) immediately interrupted blood flow to the brain, both the arterial inflow and venous outflow. The dog's corneal (eye) reflex (a measure of responsiveness) ceased in ten seconds, and the dog's breathing stopped in twenty to thirty seconds. They showed that the dog's brain could survive up to six minutes of total circulatory arrest without significant damage. Longer arrest produced permanent damage.

The authors then extended their experiments to man, studying eleven schizophrenic patients and 126 normal volunteer male subjects. (Children, do *not* try this experiment at home!) Because of the anatomy of a human's arterial blood supply to the brain, it is also possible to occlude (block) virtually all of the blood flow to the brain by external pressure on the neck, identical to the experiments on dogs noted above. The carotid arteries (both external and internal) are near the surface of the skin and are readily blocked with firm pressure over these arteries in the neck. Collateral branches provided by the subclavian arteries are also easily occluded by pressure in the same region of the neck. The vertebral arteries are more protected, but both the middle and proximal portions of the vertebral arteries can be occluded by similar high pressure over the lower portion of the neck. The neck cuff for the human experiments would inflate within one-eighth of a second, and both the subject and the experimenter had control of the mechanism that activated the release of the cuff, should emergency release be necessary. Either person could press a button that would deflate the neck cuff and restore blood flow in less than one second. Thus, the entire blood supply to the brain could be readily interrupted in man, just as in the dog.

The investigators wanted to study the effect of acute cessation of blood flow to the brain in man. They knew that the brain was quite sensitive to blood flow because of its high demand for oxygen and glucose, the high metabolic rate of the brain, and the lack of reserves of these nutrients within the brain. They found that their apparatus could successfully stop circulation to the brain without affecting the trachea, and so breathing itself was not influenced, except as altered by the lack of blood to the brain. They performed their studies without any complications, leaving the cuff inflated and stopping blood flow to the head for as long as 100 seconds. The early experiments were limited to the interruption of circulation for only the amount of time required for the subject to lose consciousness. All subjects recovered within one to two minutes without any aftereffects.

These were the findings of their study:

1. Cessation of circulation for five to ten seconds resulted in:

Fixation of the eyes. Subjects were instructed to follow a moving finger or a swinging pendulum with their eyes during the inflation of the neck cuff. In most subjects, the fixation of the eyes preceded the loss of consciousness. The time to fixation of the eyes after cessation of circulation to the brain averaged 5.5 seconds. It consisted of cessation of eye motion in the midline, though the subject was still conscious. He was not able to follow any moving object, even though he later reported that he could still see it moving. This part of the study demonstrated the exquisite sensitivity of that part of the brain responsible for ocular (eye) movement. It also showed that different aspects of consciousness can be dissociated—awareness persisting without responsiveness.

Blurred vision. Some saw bright or dark spots in front of their eyes, often progressing from the outer visual fields to the center of vision.

Constriction of the visual fields (tunnel vision or loss of peripheral vision—without any bright light at the end of the tunnel or any "being of light"). The ocular symptoms were quite consistent. The loss of peripheral vision came first, then blurring of vision, then total loss of vision.

Loss of consciousness. This effect was sometimes accompanied by turning the eyes upward immediately prior to a "seizure." Interestingly, the subjects again reported a dissociation of different levels of consciousness; some reported being unable to see while still being conscious and able to hear what was going on around them. Because subsequent unconsciousness was brief, all subjects were able to remember and report their experiences. None developed amnesia for the actual process of losing consciousness itself, though none could remember any events that occurred after they had passed out. A few subjects reported paresthesias (tingling) in the arms, hands, face, neck, or less commonly the legs. The time to loss of consciousness was six to 6.5 seconds.

What the investigators called "anoxic convulsions." (We now know that these bodily movements are not true convulsions like those seen with grand mal seizures.) The "convulsions" occurred during the unconscious period, and not a single subject recalled this part of the experiment. The "convulsions" appeared much like the tonic-clonic activity of a grand mal seizure, lasting only six to eight seconds, though Aminoff and coworkers later demonstrated in 1988 that the movements were not really seizures from the cerebral cortex (14). Rossen and his colleagues noted that the "seizures" usually occurred after the cuff was released, but the cuff was always released simultaneously with loss of consciousness, and the seizures may have simply represented the later stages of the lack of blood flow.

Of considerable interest were the reports of the subjects after regaining consciousness. Their demeanor was quite variable, ranging from "dazed" or "confused" to "excited" or "euphoric." Some insisted that they had not lost consciousness, even though they clearly had become unresponsive. Others said they had experienced no desire to stop the experiment, even though they knew they were losing consciousness. The electroencephalogram (brain wave test—EEG) did not show typical seizure activity, and the electrocardiogram (heart tracing—ECG) showed only some slight slowing of the heart rate. They noted no transcendental, out-of-body, or near-death experiences, though the purpose of the study was not necessarily to study those phenomena. However, we should expect that they would have reported an NDE had any subject experienced one.

2. More prolonged arrests of circulation to the head were performed in only the schizophrenic patients (studies also unlikely to be allowed today). These experiments lasted as long as 100 seconds, and the initial phases of the arrest were similar to the more brief experiments. However, the subjects developed cyanosis (blue color) to the face and head, and many had involuntary urination and defecation. The slowing of the heart was more profound, and the corneal (eye) reflex was tested and found to disappear after about ten seconds. The authors concluded that the centers in the brain responsible for heartbeat and respiration were more resistant to loss of blood flow than other regions because circulation and respiration were not much affected. They noted that the "seizures" were more prolonged and started with a tonic (stiff) phase, followed by a clonic (jerking) phase. On questioning the subjects, they noted no experiences that could be classified as an NDE (but remember, these were schizophrenic patients). Two previously

catatonic patients briefly lost their catatonia (relative unresponsiveness to external stimuli) and responded more normally only for a few minutes after the experiment.

Meduna and colleagues performed some other experiments, published in 1950, that evaluated the brain's response to increased carbon dioxide content (15). It was known that autoregulation of blood flow protects the brain at the peril of the blood flow to virtually all other organs. The blood vessels in the brain have a capacity to enlarge or dilate in response to an increased demand for oxygen and nutrients. The brain's blood flow responds dramatically to changes in the level of carbon dioxide content, while blood flow changes only slightly with changes in the oxygen level of the blood and fluid surrounding the brain. Blood flow increases with increasing carbon dioxide content, and it decreases with decreasing carbon dioxide content. Subjects were allowed to breathe increasingly higher concentrations of carbon dioxide.

The researchers noted that the body's response to elevated carbon dioxide in the blood was similar to the experiences reported by people who had an NDE, though it was less intense and less reproducible. They saw bright lights, felt a sense of detachment, occasionally had a panoramic recall of memories, and felt a sense of spiritual enlightenment or ecstasy. This technique of breathing elevated carbon dioxide levels was even used as a psychiatric treatment for a time, but later fell into disfavor because of lack of effectiveness for long-term therapy of psychiatric disorders.

While blood flow and delivery of oxygen are critical to the maintenance of consciousness, nutrient delivery is also important. The brain depends upon the presence of glucose for its metabolic activities, and it is unable to derive energy efficiently from other sources of energy that the other tissues of the body can use. The brain uses about sixty grams of glucose per minute (9-12). Thus, a person with hypoglycemia (low blood sugar) can begin to experience symptoms from the lack of energy delivery to the brain.

Furthermore, the brain, in contrast to other tissues, cannot store energy for future use. It is dependent upon the blood flow at any instant for the energy needed at that point in time. Processing of memory is also dependent upon energy delivery. If blood flow stops, it is impossible to store new memory because there is no energy source available. Different parts of the brain can have variable sensitivities to changes in glucose and oxygen delivery.

A common manifestation of this phenomenon is the response of a diabetic to an excess of administered insulin. I recently went to lunch with a diabetic friend of mine who seemed perfectly fine at the beginning of our meeting. He had taken his insulin as prescribed, but he had missed breakfast that day. The insulin caused his blood sugar to drop. I first noticed that he was beginning to speak in rather disjointed sentences, but we continued our discussion about plans for an upcoming project. After a few more minutes, he admitted that his mind was not processing the discussion too well, and he excused himself as he drank a couple of large glasses of orange juice (containing sugar and citric acid) to replenish the energy stores in his blood. He seemed to recover quickly, and we continued the conversation for nearly thirty minutes.

Later, as we returned to his office, it became evident that he remembered none of our conversation, even the part soon after he had taken his sugar load. Not only did he have trouble remembering the details of the conversation, the next day he could not even remember the meeting! It was as if he had awakened in his office and didn't remember the trip to lunch at all. He apologized for being so "spacey," but acknowledged that he had been trying to keep his blood sugar "on the low side" to prevent other diabetic complications. He had been able to preserve certain central nervous system functions (remaining conscious, talking, walking, listening, and at times even responding appropriately) while losing another function (the ability to process the memory of the entire event). Thus, not only is the brain critically dependent upon having the right amount of glucose available, but portions of the brain can function selectively at different blood sugar levels.

Consciousness and Alertness

Maintenance of consciousness is thus dependent upon adequate blood flow, oxygen, and glucose delivery. But what else is important? What are the neural requirements for the conscious state? What determines whether we are awake and alert, asleep, stuporous, or comatose? And what are the next stages in the process toward death?

Consciousness is a state of alertness or arousal in which the person can process external stimuli and respond to the environment (16-25). In man, consciousness is supported by the activation of the cerebral cortex by the reticular activating system and the thalamus. Diseases or lesions in these regions of the brain can cause an impairment of consciousness.

Niedermeyer divided the components of consciousness into (1) "vigilance," (2) "mental contents," and (3) "selective attention" (16). He emphasized that the term *consciousness* encompasses memory, thinking, emotion, and the will. "Vigilance" itself exists in varying degrees, and it is not an all-or-none phenomenon. It is dependent upon the interaction of the cortex of the brain with the reticular activating system. It is often considered to be the end-product of arousal or wakefulness. "Mental contents" implies the integration of the incoming sensory inputs and includes the concept of memory. "Selective attention" (as represented by awareness) suggests that the sensory inputs are processed and modulated (by the thalamus) to include some, and exclude other, incoming messages.

Emotions are modulating factors in this schema of consciousness, and the emotions originate mostly in the hypothalamus and the limbic system. (The limbic system is the part of the central nervous system that includes the temporal lobe and many of its structures; the term collectively describes the structures located at the edge—the limbus—of the medial portion of the cerebral hemispheres.) Consciousness is modified during sleep. The sleeping-waking cycles are dependent upon the integration of structures from the brain stem (hypothalamus, thalamus, and reticular activating system) through the cerebral cortex. Sleep comprises non-rapid-eye-movement (NREM) sleep (of which there are four stages) and rapid-eye-movement (REM) sleep. REM sleep actually resembles wakefulness in its electroencephalographic (EEG) manifestations and is the time during which dreaming occurs. The difference is that muscle tone is absent during REM sleep but present during wakefulness.

Other workers have divided consciousness into three states: wakefulness, REM sleep, and non-REM sleep (19, 26-28). Levels of consciousness can overlap, such as the mixture of wakefulness and REM sleep, which can produce states such as lucid dreaming and some out-of-body sensations. Included in this category are hallucinations, whether produced by drugs or not. These states may also be potentiated by sleep deprivation or alcohol.

Sleep is a state of relative inactivity of the cerebral cortex caused by a change in the activity of the reticular system. However, sleep differs from coma by the fact that during sleep the person is responsive to sensory stimuli. A loud noise, a bright light, or a touch to the shoulder can cause the reticular activating system to spring into action and stimulate the cortex into wakefulness. Varying stages of wakefulness can occur, to which any student of Shakespeare can attest. The more boring, repetitive, and quiet the external stimuli, the more likely that the student will lapse into dormant stages approaching sleep. The professor's loud question jolts the reticular activating system into business, usually to the delight of nearby fellow students.

STAGES OF CONSCIOUSNESS

NORMAL STATES	ABNORMAL STATES
Awake/alert	Seizures/post-seizure states
Lethargic/somnolent/drowsy	Hallucinations Detachment

Asleep	Depersonalization
	Amnesia
	  Recent/short-term
	  Remote/long-term
	Clouding of consciousness
	Delirium
	Obtundation/confusion
	Stupor
	Coma
	Clinical death
	Biologic death

Stupor and coma differ from lethargy because the lethargic person can respond to external stimuli and be restored to the state of alert wakefulness (though the process may be slow), whereas the stuporous person requires painful or noxious stimuli to increase awareness. When the stimuli cease, the person lapses back into stupor. The comatose person cannot respond to external stimuli.

Coma itself is a complex mixture of processes (16, 23-33). It includes the state of unarousal caused by the extensive damage to the cerebral cortex, a consequence of trauma, lack of oxygen or nutrients to the cortex, or toxic or metabolic causes. Coma usually denotes lack of electrical activity in the cerebral cortex. Many different forms of coma can be produced by conditions that bring a person near death, such as cardiac arrest. Virtually none of these states has ever been reported in association with any accounts of the NDE.

Anoxic Encephalopathy and Memory

Cardiac arrest, if brief, can cause transient metabolic derangements without any permanent structural damage (8, 13, 30, 32, 34). Quite limited interruption of circulation to the brain can cause only minor memory loss for the event itself, similar to a simple syncopal (loss of consciousness) episode. Very brief loss of consciousness produces amnesia only for the time of unconsciousness (7, 13, 30, 35-39). Extend the time without blood flow to the brain and the amnesia extends to include the actual loss of consciousness itself. Longer insult to the brain will cause amnesia for the time period before the loss of consciousness (retrograde amnesia); the ability of the brain to process memory after awakening may be impaired also (antegrade amnesia) (8, 35-37). The survivor of a cardiac arrest may suffer more serious brain damage that leaves permanent effects but does not result in coma. Such a condition is called anoxic encephalopathy (30-33, 35-36, 38-40). It is characterized by short-term memory loss with preservation of remote memory.

The amnesia in the anoxic encephalopathy syndrome can be quite variable, but these patients can usually recall events from years ago but cannot remember any of the events surrounding the cardiac arrest. Often the survivor of a cardiac arrest will be comatose for a period of hours to days, at which time it can be difficult to determine what the level of mental functioning will ultimately be (consider Ethel's case at the beginning of this chapter). Some patients will never recover and will remain in a coma. Others will recover minimally and remain in a persistent vegetative state, able to breathe and maintain cardiovascular function, retaining some sleep-wake cycles, but remaining unresponsive. Still others will have seizure disorders. Cortical blindness, spinal cord damage with paralysis, muscle jerking (myoclonus), and various impairments of memory and intellectual function have been reported.

Some will have brain death, and then the rest of the body will ultimately die.

Most often my patients have some degree of anoxic encephalopathy. They are the cause for my skepticism for the high incidence of the NDE reported in cardiac arrest. Virtually never have my patients with a documented out-of- hospital cardiac arrest due to ventricular fibrillation been able to remember the events surrounding the collapse, nor do they recall any event resembling an NDE whatsoever. Often they are very disappointed to have missed the wonderful experience reported in the popular press about the NDE. They suffer memory loss that obliterates the entire event from recall. Some even deny having had a serious medical emergency because they simply awake in a hospital with no hint in their memory that anything serious has happened.

Memory cannot precisely be localized anatomically in the brain. Memory is closely tied to the cerebral cortex, particularly the temporal lobes, and the hippocampus plays a pivotal role in the formation of memory. The hippocampus seems to be the main integrating structure for the memory process, though the actual memory is stored elsewhere. The hippocampus is located in a region where the processes of memory, emotions, and sensory events (especially vision) intersect, and the involvement of this region in the NDE has been suggested. The hippocampus is also the area of the brain most susceptible to the effects of loss of blood flow, oxygen, and nutrients (35). It begins to degenerate and die before any other structure of the brain following an anoxic or hypoxic insult. Cell death there can be recognized microscopically as evidence for lack of oxygen being a contributor to the cause of death. Pathologists examine the hippocampus to determine if suffocation or lack of oxygen occurred. The deposition of new memory is interrupted by even a brief loss of blood supply to this region. So it is not surprising that acute, short-term memory is affected so profoundly by a cardiac arrest.

The antegrade amnesia that includes the acquisition of new memories can extend into days, weeks, or even months after the cardiac arrest, causing memory problems for a time period far beyond the acute loss of circulation. For example, a patient who had a cardiac arrest in January and was successfully resuscitated may think he is recovering quite well in March. However, he may still have trouble in March remembering what he had for breakfast on any given day. He may forget meetings or conversations that occur in the months after the arrest, while retaining memory perfectly well for the years before the arrest. This memory deficit usually improves over the ensuing weeks or months, although the memory of the cardiac arrest event itself and the surrounding time (including the time when an NDE *would* have occurred—if one existed) will never return.

The memory loss is based on the damage to the critical structures responsible for memory that are exquisitely sensitive to interruption of blood flow—the hippocampus, thalamus, amygdala, and related structures.

Experiments on the Central Nervous System

Hughlings Jackson in the late 1800s recognized that visual and auditory hallucinations were sometimes part of the complex of seizures arising from lesions in the temporal lobe (41). He thought they might be related to the confusional or "dreamy states" that these patients sometimes described as part of their symptom complex.

In the 1930s Wilder Penfield, a visionary neurosurgeon, began some experiments that would change the thinking of the medical community about the functioning of the brain (42-44). In performing neurosurgery he noted that stimulation of certain areas of the brain would elicit specific responses. Because of the nature of neurosurgery and the fact that there are no specific nerves on the surface of the brain that record pain, he discovered that he could stimulate the brain with small electrical probes while the patient was fully conscious. Stimulation of certain areas of the motor cortex could cause virtually any part of the body to move.

For example, stimulation of the motor cortex responsible for movement of the hand would cause the hand to move, even though the patient had not tried consciously to move his hand. Similarly, stimulation of a part of the sensory cortex caused the patient to report a sensation as if it had come from that part of the body. A small electrical current applied to the area of the brain responsible for the sense of touch for the hand, for example, would cause the patient to say that something was touching that hand. Penfield and his many coworkers thus were able to "map" the brain and discover which areas were responsible for which functions.

Not only could Penfield cause the patient to move an area of the body if he stimulated the motor cortex or to experience sensory phenomena by stimulating the sensory cortex, but he could elicit more complex responses by stimulating other areas of the brain. Stimulation of the visual cortex could cause the patient to describe visual sensations, usually bright lights. More importantly, he found that stimulation of the temporal region caused the patient to describe much more complex sensations and even entire events from the past! It was as if the memory, or at least a handle on the memory, resided here. Temporal lobe stimulation caused the patient to "relive" certain experiences from his past as though they were occurring at that exact time. The patient even recalled events and complex memories that had been "forgotten." They were not forgotten, of course, but stored in an area from whence they could be recalled only with difficulty, even though the patient had lost all conscious memory of them. An individual memory was not confused with other memories, as though the complete sequence of the patient's entire past could be revived from the recesses of the brain. The time sequence of the memory always proceeded in the proper direction (though sometimes faster), as though the patient's life was recorded on film and the film had been intercepted at an exact point in time.

Penfield became fascinated by the variety of sensations that he could elicit from his patients by stimulating these areas of the temporal lobes. Some stimulation caused his patients to have a "life recall" in which many scenes passed into the patients' minds in vivid detail, so complete that the patients had difficulty separating the real from those produced in the operating room. Other phenomena included bright lights, a sense of detachment, a sensation of traveling down a tunnel, and an overwhelming sense of peace. Some patients entered a state akin to a mystical or ecstatic experience with stimulation in the region of the temporal lobe. Do these phenomena sound familiar? These are the components of what has been called the NDE. Listen to some quotes from patients during Penfield's sessions in the operating room:

> "It was a scary feeling. We are there, a world within that world, all of us were there. It was so real, yet so artificial." (45)

> "I seem to see someone—men and women. They seem to be sitting down and listening to someone but I do not see who that someone might be." (46)

> "I hear people coming in—I hear music now, a funny little piece." (47)

> "People's voices talking. . . . Now I hear them. . . . A little like in a dream." (48)

> "I hear singing. . . . Yes, a choir." (49)

> "Oh God! I am leaving my body." (50)

Furthermore, some patients described loud roaring or buzzing sounds, visual hallucinations, and even meeting with people long since dead. These were not real meetings, of course, but simply the memory of prior events. Often they were composite sketches of memories of encounters with people or memories of events with additions to what had actually happened (51). Stimulation of the temporal lobes can also cause altered perceptions of present circumstances.

Other authors—even in antiquity—have reported similar phenomena. Antonius Guainerius in the early 1400s said, "I myself have seen a certain choleric youth who said that in his paroxysms he always saw wonderful things, which he most ardently desired to set down in writing" (52). Mulder and Daly in 1952 said, "The hallucinatory phenomena were unusually vivid and complete, and, although these attacks might have been precipitated by tension, the content of the hallucination did not seem related to the emotional problems of the patient. Frequently, the patient described the sensation of viewing vivid past experience while retaining awareness of the present" (53). Halgren and colleagues in 1978 refined some of the classification of experiences elicited by stimulation of the hippocampus and amygdala and concluded that "the mental phenomena evoked by medial temporal lobe stimulation are idiosyncratic and variable, and are related to the personality of the patient stimulated" (54).

It would seem that any event that can be produced by stimulation of the brain is not really a vision of the afterlife or a trip to heaven. Such visions are simply a set of neural discharges coming from a complex area of the brain that integrates such functions as vision, emotion, hearing, memory, perception of time, language, moods, attitudes, and social behavior. This is not as romantic as the concept of the NDE but is probably a better explanation. A temporary condition—the stimulation of the brain—did not in the most remote stretch of the imagination represent the approach of death. But the stimulating electrode created images that were very similar to the entire "core experience" of the NDE. It is highly unlikely that God would give us a key to enter heaven through these operating-room experiences. Passage of an electric current through the brain simply does not allow us a glimpse into heaven and the eternity beyond. This "light" is from man, not God.

Transformed by the Light? No.

Embraced by the Light? Hardly.

Life After Life? No way.

To Hell and Back? Not enjoyable surgery, but hardly a trip to hell.

My Glimpse of Eternity? Certainly not what I want eternity to be.

Closer to the Light? Only as close as the surgeon's probe.

Deceived by the Light? Probably!

DETACHMENT AND DEPERSONALIZATION

Two defense mechanisms for dealing with a stressful situation that have been invoked as an explanation for the NDE are detachment and depersonalization (55-61). The human mind has a difficult time accepting the concept of its own death, so it must deal with death in a way that is less threatening, so the theory goes. By separating itself from the fatal or near-fatal circumstance, the mind can deal with the event. That is, the mind says that the event is happening to someone else and that the person in danger is simply looking at the scene from a distance in a dispassionate manner. The entire sequence may appear surreal to the person in danger because the mind has created an alternate existence exclusively for this brief period of time. In this dual existence, the mind inhabits a created alternate "person" who is not in danger, while the body remains the person about to die. This defense mechanism can successfully insulate the person from the pain of the death or near-death, both the physical and the mental or emotional pain.

Noyes and Kletti in 1976 described the essential features of depersonalization that occur with frightening—but not necessarily life-threatening—situations (56). They document the following characteristics: apparent slowing of time (though the thought processes seem to speed up), lack of emotion, absence of fear, calmness and peacefulness, feelings of strangeness or unreality, separation from reality, heightened attention that is narrowly focused, ability to perform feats that would otherwise be impossible, detachment, loss of control, retrieval of memories, ineffability of the experience, mystical consciousness, and a sense of unity or harmony with the universe. They concluded by agreeing with previous authors that depersonalization was present in many fear-provoking situations and could explain many of the phenomena described in the NDE.

Serdahely has commented upon the similarities between the NDE and the condition called the multiple personality disorder (57). Both have an out-of-body experience, often an encounter with "the higher self," and both have a transcendental quality. Serdahely also claims that both may arise in the temporal lobes, and both may be related to prior child abuse. But the multiple personality disorder certainly does not encompass the many aspects of the NDE.

Depersonalization and detachment thus have many attributes to recommend them as the explanation for the NDE, though these mechanisms do not explain some aspects of the NDE, such as the stylized content of the NDE from person to person.

DREAMS

Dreams are said to be an outlet for the mind. They often contain images that express our fears or desires. The NDE, however, is not often confused with a dream because of the circumstances of the near-death event and because the events in the NDE are so vivid. Though dreams are occasionally quite detailed and vivid, the person with the NDE will say that the experience is quite distinguishable from a dream.

ILLUSIONS AND DELUSIONS

Illusions are incorrect interpretations of real objects, events, or stimuli in the environment. A person simply misinterprets what is really there. Delusions are persistent misinterpretations that cannot be altered by evidence that the event or object is not what the person interprets it to be—illusions that cannot be removed. The NDE quite properly could be either an illusion or a delusion. The person misinterprets the sensory experiences that occur in a medical crisis, calling them heaven or hell (or whatever the person's religious background or exposure dictates for end-of-life events).

HALLUCINATIONS AND VISIONS

Hallucinations and visions are used at times as the explanation for the NDE. Hallucinations are often visual, though they can involve the other senses as well, such as auditory sensations—voices speaking to the person. Many NDEs, however, are characterized by the absence of speech, as though the communication between the person near death and the other persons described in the NDE occurs mysteriously, without spoken words.

Hallucinations usually are associated with other evidences of mental illness, while the survivor of an NDE often has no evidence of any mental disease. Furthermore, hallucinations often recur, while the NDE is usually a one-time event. Hallucinations can be caused by drug abuse, but as we will see later, many persons with an NDE have not been exposed to any mind-altering drugs, either self-administered or given by medical personnel. Hallucinations are frequently very personal and may be uninterpretable or convoluted, as opposed to the NDE, which is more or less stereotyped and understandable.

Blackmore emphasizes that hallucinations are synthesized from a combination of memories and imagination (62). While they may be intensely personal, they also contain common ingredients among different personalities and even cultures. They tend to have stereotyped imagery, especially including the visual elements of tunnels, spirals, and intense colors. People often incorporate the tunnel in hallucinations, with imagery symbolizing a trip or journey from one mental or emotional state to the next, often viewed as ascending planes of life or passage from one level of reality to another. The notion that a tunnel symbolizes the birth process, however, seems to have been debunked by the finding that people born by cesarean section have as many tunnel experiences as those born by natural labor and delivery (63).

Hallucinations can be confused with visions as well. Visions are less personal and more directed externally or toward the community in general or the religious community in particular. Objectively, however, visions and hallucinations are difficult to distinguish.

SEIZURES

In addition to the responses obtained from stimulation of the surfaces of the brain by Penfield, naturally-occurring abnormal cortical discharges can distort a person's immediate consciousness. These discharges are called seizures, and most of us have seen someone who is having a seizure. It is sometimes preceded by an aura—a sensation that for the individual patient might be quite characteristic (a visual disturbance, a feeling, a taste, a smell, for example). This aura heralds the attack and is a warning to the patient that a seizure is beginning, although not all patients experience an aura before the major part of the attack.

In a typical grand mal seizure, the motor components of the brain's electrical activity are the most obvious, and we observe prominent shaking of the patient, often with both stiffness and a rhythmical component—the tonic-clonic seizure. After the motor activity has subsided, the patient may have some transient paralysis and may be quite somnolent for up to a few hours. He may be fatigued for hours or even days. This type of seizure involves rapid erratic discharges that affect the motor cortex. Motor seizures that are localized can affect only specific parts of the body and are called focal motor seizures. An NDE would never be confused with these types of seizures.

A more subtle type of seizure is the petit mal attack. During this seizure the patient may still remain upright and appear conscious, but he has alteration of consciousness during which he seems unresponsive and has a staring expression on his face. The person is usually motionless, and he will not respond to external stimuli. However, he usually does not fall and may even continue to perform tasks such as walking. He awakens abruptly with no memory for the events that occurred during the seizure; thus the name "absence seizure."

All of these seizure disorders can be recorded on the EEG, and all have characteristic patterns (16, 26-27, 64-66). They can be caused by a variety of abnormal conditions in the brain, including tumors, infections, scarring from old injuries, acute injury, metabolic abnormalities, and drug effects.

Another type of seizure involves particularly the temporal lobes and is called a temporal lobe seizure or psychomotor seizure (42-45, 51, 54, 67-68). It can be complex and can even involve apparently purposeful actions. The most well-known features of temporal lobe seizures are "deja vu" phenomena, sensations that a person has previously experienced the event that is occurring now, often associated with a "dreamy state" (67). A subtle variation on the phenomenon is the "deja vecu" experience in which the person does not think he is reliving a previous event but that he has already done the thing that he currently is in the process of doing. Objects may appear unreal or distant ("jamais vu"). The patient may go about complex behavior, and it is only obvious that he is out of touch if someone tries to interact or communicate with him or her.

Complex visual hallucinations can occur with temporal lobe seizures, including the sensation that the patient is viewing himself from a distance (autoscopy). Temporal lobe seizures can also cause auditory hallucinations, particularly voices speaking to the patient. It is the temporal lobe seizure that could mimic the NDE. Penfield further classified these temporal lobe seizures into three types: experiential, interpretive, and amnestic.

The experiential seizure is a flashback from a previous experience, a dream from the past. Spontaneous seizures originating in the temporal lobe may produce descriptions of recall similar to the stimulation of the temporal lobe. One patient said during a seizure, "Someone call a doctor. Someone call a doctor. . . . It's all over, forget the doctor" (69). Another person said, reporting her seizure, "It would be as though I were two persons, one watching and another having this happen to them" (70), similar to the out-of-body component of the NDE. Music may be a common component of this type of seizure. Gloor reported that experiential seizures "create in the patient's mind experiences, usually from his personal past, that have a compelling immediacy similar to or sometimes even more vivid than those occurring in real life" (71). He noted that the reports from different patients in different cultures and living centuries apart may be strikingly similar. Memories occur, or "there may be a feeling of recognition, of familiarity or reminiscence" (72). Visual phenomena predominate.

These seizures can often be caused by the electrical stimulation of the temporal lobes, especially the right temporal lobe. Gloor also reported that the temporal lobes, which contain the hippocampal connections and the auditory and visual pathways as well as the amygdala, are perfectly suited for the recall of events that have the major components of memory, hearing, and vision.

The interpretive seizure is an illusion mixed with the components of the present time—the deja vu experience, for example. Bancaud and coworkers concluded that "the dreamy state probably depends upon a neuronal network that engages both medial and lateral aspects of the temporal lobe, and that the anterior hippocampus, amygdala and superior temporal gyrus have relatively privileged access to this circuit" (73). (The superior temporal gyrus is found in the upper portion of the temporal lobe, a gyrus being a rounded elevation caused by folds on the surface of the brain.)

An amnestic seizure is a complex state in which the person appears to be awake and alert, but he is actually in a state of automatic actions (automatisms) and seems to be creating no memories of the time; that is, he will not remember the events when the seizure is completed. He has "lost the capacity of making a permanent record of his stream of consciousness" (74).

If the NDE is a form of seizure, it is more likely that it represents a mixture of the experiential and the interpretive types of temporal lobe seizure (by Penfield's classification scheme). Both the memory components and the illusory nature of the event seem to be present. The experiential component deals with the past, and the interpretive deals with the present (45, 51). However, some authorities refuse to believe that the NDE is any form of seizure. They point out that a temporal lobe seizure is often unpleasant or distressing, has stereotyped features (such as lip smacking, automatic body motions, nausea, or pain), and is often perceived as unreal or lacking vividness, contrasted to the NDE, which is quite vivid. Furthermore, most temporal lobe seizures are associated with amnesia.

The components of temporal lobe seizures are often lumped into a category called the "limbic lobe syndrome" (45, 51, 75-76). This syndrome involves the hippocampus, the hypothalamus, the temporal lobes, and the amygdala—structures responsible for mood, memory, and emotion. This syndrome involves vivid and complex hallucinations, intense emotions, depersonalization, and life recall. But many experts also deny that the limbic lobe syndrome is the cause of the NDE.

SENSORY DEPRIVATION

Lack of sensory input can have profound effects upon our mental attitude and emotions, as well as the perception of the environment. Elaborate experiments have been performed to deprive a person of all sensory stimuli for prolonged periods of time (77). This sensory deprivation can cause the out-of-body experience and hallucinations similar to the NDE. In this setting, the mind creates an alternative existence to combat the lack of sensory input. This alternative existence is constructed by the mind recalling old memories and sensations and integrating them into a coherent amalgam of thought. These constructs rely heavily on past visual images, and they are often recalled with a striking vividness. Thus, they bear some resemblance to the NDE. But the NDE usually does not involve sensory deprivation.

SLEEP DEPRIVATION

Persistent lack of sleep, extending over a period of days, can produce unusual sensations that are similar to an out-of-body experience (18). Surroundings seem unreal. A person describes feeling detached from the objects and events occurring nearby. Even hallucinations can be a part of the experience. But most NDEs are described without any evidence of sleep deprivation, so this explanation is not plausible.

DRUGS

Many drugs have been implicated in the production of the NDE (78-83). Early in the history of anesthesia, physicians recognized the mind-altering qualities of various agents used during surgery. At the turn of the century, Dunbar noted:

> I have made a point of asking patients in the surgical wards how they felt when they were being anesthetized [with ether or chloroform]. The common experience (eighty per cent of cases) is that of rushing into a dark tunnel. There is singing in the ears and a flashing of lights in the eyes. (84)

So the neural connections required for the NDE are present in the human brain at all times and must simply be activated by agents that alter the usual neurological processes.

The NDE bears a striking resemblance to the "trips" of illicit pharmacologic agents, particularly LSD (lysergic acid diethylamide). These drug-induced hallucinatory experiences contain vivid images, sensations of travel, apparent improvement in mental capacity and speed of intellectual processes (though, in reality, the mental acuity and speed are decreased), and "religious" awareness. Other drugs that can cause hallucinations that could be confused with, or produce, the NDE are PCP (phencyclidine or "angel dust"), morphine, codeine, cocaine, amphetamines, and barbiturates.

Most people who experience the NDE, however, are not actively abusing drugs. Chemical tests can detect these agents in the blood or urine, and the physician does not have to rely upon the patient's honesty for an accurate history of drug use. Screening for these agents after a cardiac arrest, for example, rarely produces positive results. During the course of the resuscitation, the patient may be given morphine or a sedative or anesthetic agent to aid in the resuscitation or to make the patient more comfortable, but the NDE has been reported in many patients without any drugs on board. Furthermore, the drug-induced trips are often more frightening than the reported NDEs, which are calm and reassuring experiences for the most part. Hallucinations with LSD are more bizarre and are less stereotyped than the predictable events of the NDE.

So it would seem that while some of the findings seen with NDEs can be attributed to drugs, the majority cannot. We must look to other explanations for the cause.

NEUROTRANSMITTERS

In order for the brain to function, nerve cells must be able to transmit impulses from cell to cell. This connection is accomplished by means of neurotransmitters, complex chemicals that serve as cell-to-cell relay mechanisms. The neurotransmitters include many chemicals: acetylcholine, norepinephrine, serotonin, glycine, dopamine, N-methyl-D-aspartate (NMDA), gamma-aminobutyric acid, glutamate, aspartate, ketamine, and many others (85-91). The nerve cell delivering the impulse releases one of these chemicals, which activates the next nerve cell in line. The cellular release and uptake of these chemicals can be enhanced or blocked by various other chemicals, which often have physical structures similar to the native neurotransmitter.

Morse and colleagues believe that the NDE may be closely linked to the serotonin neurotransmitter (92). They base their theory on the concept that many of the chemical agents (LSD, PCP, ketamine, carbon dioxide) that can cause OBE-like or NDE-like experiences can cause imbalances in the distribution and disposition of serotonin and similar chemicals.

One particular class of chemical neurotransmitter receptor—

the NMDA receptor—has received much attention recently for its possible role in the NDE (78-80, 85-90, 93-95). NMDA stands for N-methyl-D-aspartate and is a neurotransmitter receptor that seems to have beneficial effects in the brain when stimulated in appropriate amounts, but detrimental effects when overstimulated, perhaps leading even to cell death. While the chemical NMDA itself probably does not exist in the human brain, this type of receptor is present and is probably stimulated by alternate types of chemical neurotransmitters—glutamate or aspartate. NMDA receptors likely have a function in brain development, learning, and memory. In fact, the part of the brain most often associated with learning and memory, the hippocampus, is predominantly affected by the activity of the NMDA receptor. The NMDA receptor plays a role in the processing of sensory information, especially visual information in some species.

It appears that the NMDA receptor must be activated and the downstream cell stimulated to allow calcium entry into the cell for memory to be developed. Too much stimulation and too much calcium entry into the cell can cause cell damage. Thus, researchers are developing compounds that might block the overactivity or overstimulation of the NMDA receptor and prevent cell death. Substances that bind to the NMDA receptor site are powerful hallucinogens. It is interesting that chemicals that could produce cellular protection can also produce profound mental changes and hallucinations.

Ketamine is a chemical that can also bind to and affect the NMDA receptor (78, 80, 82). Ketamine is an anesthetic agent whose action can produce symptoms exactly reproducing most—if not all—of the components of the NDE. About 30 percent of patients given a small dose of ketamine will have hallucinatory experiences that they insist are "even more real than reality." During such low-dose exposure, a patient continues to process sensory input, and the immediate environment alters the content of the hallucinatory experience. Ketamine is also a weak anticonvulsant that has a chemical structure similar to PCP, the hallucinogen, and that blocks the action of the NMDA receptor. By such blockage, it could have a role in cerebral protection during such traumatic events as cerebral ischemia.

The NMDA receptor is thus complex, and not all aspects of it are understood. There may even be different types of NMDA receptors. PCP and ketamine are active at similar sites. Furthermore, chemicals produced by the body itself, called endopsychosins (81, 86), can act at these sites. These endogenous chemicals may be produced at the approach of death and actually stimulate the sensory, memory, and mental changes that constitute the NDE, similar to ketamine, while actually protecting nerve cells from death. Furthermore, these chemicals may affect the memory processing that occurs at the time of the NDE, in addition to potentiating the recall of past memories. While these mechanisms still remain only an unproved hypothesis, they are intriguing for understanding the chemical basis of the NDE.

ENDORPHINS

Perhaps no other chemicals in the brain are better known to the general public than the endorphins (91, 96-98). Who among us is unaware that the body produces its own endorphins with exercise, accounting for the pleasurable sensations encountered by long-distance runners?

Endorphins and enkephalins are peptide chemicals (that is, chemical compounds including at least two amino acids) that have structural similarities to the opiates. Beta-endorphin is a relative of morphine, and it has a function in the modulation of pain by binding to the opiate receptors and blocking painful impulses. It is secreted by the pituitary gland and diffuses to all parts of the brain. But beyond their relationship to pain, beta endorphins are thought to be secreted in larger quantities during stressful situations and could be particularly active during a near-death event.

Endorphins also sensitize the brain to seizures and would tend to make a temporal lobe (or limbic system) seizure more likely. While the endorphins do not produce hallucinations, they may be responsible for some of the detachment, peace, joy, and lack of pain reported by many people as they approached death. Indeed, the endorphins have been cited as a chemical given by a "benevolent deity" to intervene in the throes of death (96-97, 99-103). No less than the missionary David Livingstone was said to have had a form of near-death experience when he was attacked by a lion in Africa in 1872:

> I heard a shout. Starting and looking half round, I saw the lion just in the act of springing upon me. I was on a little height; he caught my shoulder as he sprang and we both came to the ground below together. Growling horribly close to my ear, he shook me as a terrier does a rat. The shock produced a stupor similar to that which seems to be felt by a mouse after the first shake of a cat. It caused a sort of dreaminess in which there was no sense of pain or feeling of terror, though quite conscious of all that was happening. It was like what patients partially under the influence of chloroform describe, who see all the operation but feel not the knife. This singular condition was not the result of any mental process. The shake annihilated fear, and allowed no sense of horror in looking round at the beast. The peculiar state is probably produced in all animals killed by carnivora; and if so, is a merciful provision by our benevolent Creator for lessening the pain of death. (96, 102, 103)

Of course, Livingstone was spared not only the pain of death, but death itself, by the miracle of his Creator, and he lived to tell the story. Interestingly, he did not have an NDE.

Endorphins, acting on the limbic system with its rich supply of opiate receptors, could account for the inappropriate calm that is often noted to overcome animals as they are about to die. This "limbic lobe syndrome" has many of the other aspects of the NDE, including the dissociation, the hallucinations, and the life review. It could explain how patients who are not near death but who think they are could have a sequence of events triggered by the frightening event. Endorphins act on the limbic system to reproduce some of the features of the NDE, though bodily death never comes close.

However compelling these arguments seem, it is important to know that it has never been proved that the endorphin levels in man rise during the stages of dying. Therefore, such a mechanism must remain only a conjecture.

WHAT IS BRAIN DEATH?

Surprisingly, brain death is quite difficult to define (28). In centuries past, a person was considered to be dead when his heart stopped, the blood pressure disappeared, and he stopped breathing. Today the situation is more complex. We view death in terms of brain death more commonly than cardiovascular/pulmonary death. A person with brain death is a candidate to be an organ donor, even though his heart and lungs continue to work. In fact, a heart or lung donor must have *good* cardiovascular and pulmonary function.

On the other hand, a person who is awake and alert but whose heart stops can be kept "alive" (at least for a short period of time) by machines that simulate heart and lung action until a donor heart is found for transplantation. As far as the heart is concerned, *clinical* death is reached when the heart stops pumping and the blood pressure is zero. At this point, the brain may still be completely normal, however. Furthermore, the heart may die in stages, as happens from many small heart attacks, each time killing a part of the heart muscle until it is no longer able to pump effectively.

But the definition of brain death is more nebulous, and it has undergone repeated changes and updates as our knowledge has grown. Brain death may also develop piecemeal or occur in stages in the patient with recurrent strokes, each stroke destroying another part of the brain. Cortical brain death deprives the patient of all higher functions such as thought, intelligence, and consciousness, while the lower brain functions such as maintenance of heart rate, blood pressure, and respiration continue. This state is referred to as "the persistent vegetative state" (64). Lower functions are maintained, such as breathing and heart function, but consciousness is impaired, presumably permanently if no reversible causes (such as drug intoxication or hypothermia) can be identified. In this particular condition, the patient may intermittently open his eyes, though apparently not responsive to environmental stimuli. Total brain death is present when not only the higher functions (cortex) are destroyed, but brain stem functions (which control cardiovascular stability and respiration) are eliminated. This type of patient can be "kept alive" by respirators and other machines and drugs, but without any neurologic function.

In 1968 a definition of irreversible coma was proposed that included the following components (29):

1. Unreceptivity/unresponsivity.
2. No movements or breathing.
3. No reflexes.
4. Flat EEG.

This definition emphasized the permanence of these findings and the necessity to confirm all of them at a minimum of two examinations at least twenty-four hours apart.

Over the next few years this definition was generally accepted, and it established the primacy of neurologic findings, compared to the earlier definitions of death that used cardiovascular and respiratory findings. In the 1990s, neurologic criteria form the basis for the definition of "legally dead."

WHAT IS NEAR-DEATH?

If the definition of death is so complex, the definition of "near-death" is fraught with even more confusion. Is "near-death" referring to the cardiovascular system? Is it referring to the central nervous system? If so, which part? Near-death could refer to the transient, reversible loss of function of either the cardiovascular system or the nervous system. When referring to the cardiovascular system, it most often describes a cardiac rhythm disturbance (ventricular fibrillation or cardiac arrest) that can be reversed if treated rapidly. Less serious cardiac conditions (other cardiac rhythm disturbances such as ventricular tachycardia in which some pumping function of the heart persists) might not fall into the "near-death" category.

Similarly, conditions that cause the heart to slow dramatically (even to the range of five to ten beats per minute) would not be classified in the same category, although they could cause loss of consciousness. Clinical death would proceed to biologic death (cell death) in the cardiac arrest patient if resuscitative measures were not begun or if they were unsuccessful. It is at this time that the NDE is alleged to appear—at the junction between clinical death and biological death. Negovsky, however, denies the existence of any brain activity during clinical death (31, 104):

> Some survivors report that they have experienced "visions" during clinical death, i.e., "near-death experiences" such as dreams or hallucinations. Perception of the outer world is not possible during clinical death. The cortex is silent, the EEG tracings are isoelectric. These visions seem to occur exclusively during dying. They are the chaotic sensations of

> a malfunctioning brain, reflecting the patient's distorted perception of the environment. Auditory perceptions seem to be last to disappear, after the visual cortex has failed and apnea [cessation of breathing] begun.

The process of memory formation in the brain is an active process requiring energy. Cell metabolism is required to create the nerve connections that form the basis for memory, and these processes are unavailable to the brain if the blood flow has been interrupted. The brain that is not perfused cannot have the metabolic activity necessary to produce energy to form memory. Almost by definition, the person who has a memory of the "death process" was not, in fact, dead. Blood flow to the brain was not interrupted; otherwise there could have been no new memory formed of the events at that time. So Betty Eadie's story (105), if it is not a total fabrication, was a description of the series of sensory inputs that produced a memory *before* her heart stopped and the blood flow to the brain ceased (if indeed her heart ever stopped) or *after* the blood flow was restored. Her memories could not have been generated from the time when she was "dead," if such a time ever existed.

Biologic death means irreversible cell death. But we have also seen that cell death can be sporadic, either regional or diffuse. Some cells may have started to die at the beginning of resuscitation attempts, and thus even the concept of discrete biologic death again fails us. Some cells die, but others survive. Clinical death may have been present transiently, and biologic death destroyed some cells (in the brain, the heart, and other organs), but the person survived. This survival was bought at the price of permanent death and loss of function of some cells. This condition, when described for the brain, is what was described previously as anoxic encephalopathy. A patient, then, could have had "near-death," in which the heart stopped beating transiently, and had biologic death of some brain cells, but did not die!

So death is not an all-or-nothing phenomenon. The concept that brain death occurs within a finite amount of time after circulation stops is an outmoded principle. Portions of the brain die at different times and at different rates. The hippocampus is the most sensitive part of the brain to loss of blood flow, while portions of the brain stem are much more resistant to lack of oxygen. In most people, the brain stops functioning after ten to fifteen seconds of loss of blood flow, and unconsciousness appears. We ordinarily think the brain can survive four to six minutes without blood flow, and as a general rule, that is a good estimate. Some people can survive great lengths of time if CPR is performed effectively. But there are certainly many people who have survived longer periods of cardiac arrest. Extrinsic factors, such as temperature, can affect survival. Patients who fall into cold rivers or lakes can survive long periods of immersion because of the lowered body temperatures. Ultimately, however, loss of blood flow leads to biologic death.

Generally we reserve the term "biologic death" to refer to the whole person or the whole organism. Biologic death is the final stage when a person is "declared" dead, though only God can "declare" death. Only He knows when the state of the organism has advanced so far toward total cell death that it is impossible to revive the person as a whole, functioning organism. Man's feeble knowledge and appreciation of the death process is frequently incomplete or incorrect. Many times we physicians "declare" a person to be dead only to discover that person breathing again or the heart beginning to beat again. God in His omnipotence knows when this revival is going to happen, and I believe He does not let the spirit depart until the appropriate time.

Thus, while death and near-death have been presented by many writers as tidy, neat, simple concepts, they are amazingly complex. Boundaries are fuzzy. Clinical acumen is inaccurate. Our ability to diagnose is limited. Therefore, we must not presume to know more than we really understand.

7

THE CARDIOVASCULAR SYSTEM

Death Is God's Way of Telling You to Slow Down

Ann Brown and her husband Bill had just returned from a trip to Israel where they had visited many of the Christian sites. Like the usual tourists, they had taken many photos of the historic landmarks mentioned in the Bible. Friday night was supposed to be a dinner-travelogue slide show at their home for the youth pastor and his wife from their church in Seattle. It was just a simple evening, no stress, but Ann had been having headaches since their return from Israel, though they seemed minor. Just a need for some aspirin every few hours.

The evening started uneventfully. Steve and Sarah Lupe arrived at 6 P.M., and dinner started soon thereafter. All four of the Brown children were there, and everyone was enjoying the meal. Just before the dessert, though, Ann noticed the return of a mild headache, and then her nose started to run. She was not bothered but excused herself from the table and went into the kitchen. By the time she walked from the dining room to the kitchen, she knew something horrible was happening. Blood gushed from her nose in a way she had never seen happen to anyone, and with four active children, she knew what a routine nosebleed was like. She called for Bill to come to the kitchen quickly, but by the time he got there, he could see that blood was covering the entire bottom of the sink where Ann was leaning. He quickly got some towels and some ice, but it was obvious that Ann was having a major hemorrhage and needed to go to the hospital.

He was familiar with medical emergency rooms, being a cardiologist himself. He knew it would take about ten minutes to get to the emergency room, which was also about the response time for the ambulance to get to their house since the Brown family lived in the country, miles from the nearest medic station. It would be quicker to drive directly to the hospital. It was a "no-brainer" decision. They yelled into the dining room that they were going to the emergency room and would call when they could. Steve and Sarah agreed to stay and watch the children, but they were perplexed, not even realizing what the emergency was or that Ann was rapidly losing blood.

Bill and Ann brought a basin with them in the car to catch the blood, which was spurting with each heartbeat. Clearly this was an arterial bleed from somewhere in Ann's nose. She had lost about a liter of blood by the time they arrived at the emergency room. Ice and pressure to the nose was making no difference at all.

The team in the emergency room swung into action quickly. They could also see they were dealing with a very unusual circumstance. Ann's pulse by this time was 150, and her blood pressure—which was usually 120—was down to the low 90s. The nurse started an IV quickly and efficiently. Clearly she was very experienced at handling emergencies. The ear, nose, and throat doctor happened to be in the hospital, and he was quickly paged to the emergency room. He began with the typical maneuvers of anterior and posterior nasal packing with mounds of gauze, and in about fifteen minutes these were accomplished. But the bleeding continued. Now some of the blood went posteriorly, causing Ann to gag and swallow much of it. Though the blood seen externally was decreasing, it was clear that the bleeding was continuing because her pulse was rising and her blood pressure was falling.

Whole blood had arrived from the blood bank and was being infused rapidly, and the nurse had pumped in over two liters of saline solution, but they seemed to be losing ground. Pressure trousers were applied. Pressure trousers are similar to the G-suits pilots wear to avoid losing consciousness when diving in jet planes, experiencing severe gravitational forces that cause blood to pool in the legs. Squeezing blood from the legs provides more blood for the central circulation. The trousers were cumbersome and took about ten minutes to apply to Ann's lower extremities. But even when inflated, Ann's blood pressure continued to fall. Her pulse rose—150, 160, 170, 180. Then no blood pressure was obtainable. Next came unconsciousness. The nurse tilted the emergency room gurney backward, so Ann's head was below the rest of her body, and they pumped the blood and saline into her even faster. Within a minute or two, the nurse was able to feel a feeble pulse. Blood pressure was now up to 60. There was no need—at least for now—for CPR.

Ann stabilized over the next few minutes in the head-down position, with rapid administration of blood and other fluids and the lower-body pressure suit. But clearly the bleeding was not stopping. She needed surgery. Other diagnostic tests could not be performed in this small community hospital. Was this an aneurysm? An arterio-venous malformation? What was it? There were two choices. Perform surgery here and blindly tie off the arteries leading to this region, or transfer her to the University Hospital for an angiogram to try to define the precise site and cause of the bleed. It took little time to make the decision. She was not yet stable, and the transfer could be risky. Surgery here was the choice.

Quickly the operating room was made ready, and Ann was whisked into it. This was a bit disconcerting for her husband, who usually saw the doctor's side of a drama like this, not the patient's. But there was really no alternative. Bill called home to report to the children that Mom was going into surgery for bleeding from her nose and to ask them to pray for her. Steve and Sarah were good friends to be there. As youth pastor, Steve knew them all well, and Sarah, a nurse herself, was a calming influence. All seemed to be under control at home.

The wait was shorter than Bill had anticipated. After only an hour and a half, Doctor East returned to Bill to report that he had successfully tied off many arterial branches leading to the right side of Ann's nose and that the bleeding had stopped. He could not identify the pathology that had caused the bleed, but it seemed to be less important now to know the cause than to have restored Ann's stable vital signs. Blood pressure and pulse were returning to normal. So far she had received four units of blood and over two liters of saline.

Ann continued to recover, though she had to remain in the hospital for eight days. She looked like a lot of people who have had facial surgery—swollen and bruised, like she had been hit by a baseball bat. But she was recovering, and that was the important thing.

Over the next few weeks, Ann and Bill had lots of time to reflect on the event. Specifically, Ann thought that God had allowed this event to happen to give her a testimony about the fleeting quality of life and the importance of blood—our own *and* Jesus' redemptive blood. Ann had heard about radiant near-death stories, but though her medical crisis was associated with unconsciousness and documented unobtainable blood pressure in spite of all of the medical interventions, she had experienced no NDE. She remembered feeling lightheaded, dizzy, and having a floating sensation, but nothing out-of-body and certainly no tunnels, lights, or "beings of light." No life review. No decision to return. Just peacefulness that she was in God's hands and that if she died she knew with certainty that her ultimate destination would be heaven because she was trusting in the blood of Jesus to redeem her.

Is this story unusual? Shouldn't she have had an NDE? What happens when we lose consciousness? Isn't fainting the beginning of the journey to the bright light? Let's examine the cardiovascular aspects of loss of consciousness and dying.

NORMAL ANATOMY AND PHYSIOLOGY OF THE CARDIOVASCULAR SYSTEM

The brain is dependent upon the provision of blood (and hence oxygen and nutrients) by the heart. The normal cardiovascular system can be envisioned simply as a pump and many pipes. Most cardiovascular phenomena can be described in terms of flows and pressures. The heart, muscle tissue and valves arranged as a pump, is a relatively small organ weighing only about 500 grams (one pound). The vascular system consists of vessels taking blood away from the heart (arteries) and vessels taking blood back to the heart (veins). The average-sized human has about five to six liters of blood. The heart pumps about five to ten liters of blood per minute to the entire body, supplying about 50 ml of blood for every 100 grams of brain tissue every minute. With exercise, the cardiac output can rise to fifteen liters per minute. "Brain exercise"—thought—can also increase the blood flow to the brain, but not nearly so impressively.

When considering the factors related to the NDE, the maintenance of blood pressure is the most important function of the cardiovascular system. Put simply, there are three factors to consider when evaluating blood pressure: (1) the return of blood to the heart; (2) the pumping strength of the heart; and (3) the status of the vessels receiving the blood. Blood pressure is maintained as long as adequate return of blood to the heart continues, as long as the pumping function of the heart persists, and as long as the vessels receiving the blood provide adequate resistance. High blood pressure (hypertension) usually causes few, if any, acute symptoms in the short term, whereas low blood pressure (hypotension) can cause profound symptoms. Let's examine some of the causes for hypotension.

The pumping function of the heart is dependent upon the strength of the muscle and the rhythm of the heart. The rhythm is the periodic contraction and relaxation of the muscle generated by specialized cells in certain regions of the heart. Ordinarily the heart pumps at about 60-100 beats per minute, and the blood pressure is maintained at ninety to 150 mm of mercury during contraction (systole) and 60-90 mm of mercury during the relaxation of the heart muscle (diastole).

Disturbances of blood flow occur when the blood pressure is too low. A common cause of abrupt lowering of blood pressure is an abnormality of the rhythm of the heart. An abnormally low rate can cause the *average* blood pressure to be too low, even though the peak pressure with each slow heartbeat is normal. Rapid heart rates do not usually cause low blood pressure (for example, with exercise, when the blood pressure actually increases), unless the rapid rate is excessive and caused by specific types of abnormal rhythms. Ventricular fibrillation is the rapid rhythm most commonly producing a cardiac arrest, and it causes a disorganized quivering of the heart muscle that cannot pump any blood whatsoever. Most often this rhythm occurs without any acute warning, though patients will usually have known that they have some type of abnormality of the heart before the ventricular fibrillation causes a cardiac arrest.

Because the heart is a muscle that itself needs oxygen and nutrients, it has its own blood supply. This blood delivery occurs through the coronary arteries. These arteries can become blocked, causing a heart attack that causes chest pain and damage to the heart muscle. Such damage may also cause the rhythm disturbance called ventricular fibrillation, cardiac arrest. But in a previously damaged heart, the rhythm disturbance can occur alone without any acute blockage of a coronary artery. So a person who develops a cardiac arrest may or may not have any symptoms of chest pain before collapsing.

Less serious rhythm disturbances than ventricular fibrillation can cause the blood pressure to fall, though not to zero as happens with a cardiac arrest. Such more minor problems (such as ventricular tachycardia, atrial fibrillation, and seriously slow heart rates [bradycardias]) can lead to symptoms of low blood flow, even including loss of consciousness. But without degeneration to more serious rhythm disturbances such as ventricular fibrillation or complete cessation of the heartbeat (total asystole), these rhythm disturbances (arrhythmias) do not in themselves cause a cardiac arrest or death.

SYNCOPE

What are some of the common causes of hypotension, and what are the symptoms?

One familiar form of hypotension is the simple faint. In medical terms, this event is usually called syncope. Anything that causes low blood pressure (hypotension) can cause a person to faint or lose consciousness (1-2). Often syncope is related to events that are emotionally distressing or frightening. Seeing blood causes some people to faint. The body responds to this event by dilating blood vessels and pooling blood in the lower extremities and in the abdomen; because of this stagnation of blood, the heart has no blood to pump forward, causing hypotension. The pulse rate also slows paradoxically when it should be increasing. A person usually goes through the following sequence: first a queasy feeling, then dizzy, giddy, warm, weak, sighing respirations or yawning, sweaty, abdominal cramping (sometimes vomiting), blurred or double vision, dim and tunnel vision, and maybe even ringing in the ears. These symptoms usually last only a few seconds (but can last for minutes); then comes loss of consciousness.

Some patients may then have a few jerking movements of the extremities or other portions of the body, but these are brief, though they may be difficult to distinguish from the jerking motions of a seizure. The person awakes as soon as he falls because the horizontal position of the body allows blood to flow back to the heart and restores blood pressure. Upon awaking, the patient will usually remember most of the symptoms, though variable degrees of amnesia can occur, depending on the duration of the loss of consciousness and the seriousness of the low blood pressure. Usually there is no incontinence of urine or stool (contrasted to seizures, where incontinence occurs more often), and the patient awakens quite rapidly with full mental alertness (again contrasted to a seizure, which causes confusion, somnolence, disorientation, and even transient paralysis for minutes to hours) (3-6).

What are other common causes of syncope? Any condition that can cause the blood pressure to fall to about 70 mm of mercury systolic (or a mean of 30-40 mm Hg) for five to ten seconds can cause loss of consciousness. McHenry and coworkers studied syncope in the early 1960s and found that as mean blood pressure fell from an average of 101 to 26 mm Hg, the mean blood flow to the brain fell from 50 to 28 ml/100 grams/minute as the symptoms of syncope began (7). Such drops in blood pressure cause a decrease in the blood flow to the brain-stem area responsible for the maintenance of consciousness (the reticular activating formation). Many medical conditions can produce loss of consciousness in this manner.

CAUSES OF SYNCOPE
(TRANSIENT LOSS OF CONSCIOUSNESS)

- Blood loss
- Generalized loss of fluid
- Heart rhythm disturbances
  - Slow
  - Rapid
- Pooling of blood in the lower body
  - Reflex vagal vasodilatation (automatic enlargement of blood vessels mediated by the vagus nerve)
  - Varicose veins
- Loss of normal blood pressure regulatory processes
- Obstruction to outflow of blood from the heart
- Localized drop in blood flow to the brain
- Decrease in pumping capacity of the heart

Studies by Lempert and colleagues (8) were performed to evaluate the causes and effects of lowered blood pressure that produce syncope. They were able to produce syncope in fifty-six of fifty-nine subjects by a combination of maneuvers designed to lower the blood flow to the brain. Forty-two patients had complete loss of consciousness, while fourteen maintained some degree of awareness of the surroundings. The duration of the loss of consciousness was about twelve seconds, with a range from 4.5 to 21.7 seconds. Muscle jerking (myoclonus) was present in thirty-eight of the forty-two patients who had complete syncope. Other motor activity resembling brief seizure activity occurred in thirty-three patients.

Importantly for evaluation of the NDE, auditory and/or visual hallucinations occurred in 60 percent of the patients. All patients had a visual component, and some (36 percent) had auditory hallucinations. The visual sensations were often simply aberrations of color vision or bright lights, though some reported familiar scenes and four patients described out-of-body experiences. The experience was actually a positive feeling for 83 percent of the patients and negative in only 17 percent. In a later explanatory letter regarding this study, the authors said:

> Whilst studying motor phenomena of syncope we were impressed by similarities between syncopal hallucinations and near-death experiences. . . . Subjects reported visual hallucinations—perception of colors and lights that could intensify to a glaring brightness, or landscapes and familiar people, in some cases with no discernible faces; out-of-body experiences—scenes in which they were involved yet they observed them from above; and auditory hallucinations that ranged from roaring noises to screaming or unintelligible human voices. Most subjects described the emotional experience of syncope as pleasant, detached, and peaceful, making them unwilling to return [from the syncopal experience]. Some compared it to drug or meditation experiences. . . . One participant disclosed: "I thought that if I had to die in this very moment I would willingly agree." (9)

The authors then compared the components of the induced syncopal episodes with NDEs as reported by Moody (10) and found them to be nearly identical. The exceptions were that the life review was absent in subjects with induced syncope, and auditory hallucinations were more frequent. The authors suggested that rather than a transcendental explanation for these hallucinations, the cause may be a suppression of the higher centers of the brain (neocortex) and a release (disinhibition) of the limbic structures of the brain (8).

These findings again suggest that the components of the NDE can be explained on purely physiologic bases. The patients with induced syncope were never near death, and yet they had an experience nearly identical to the NDE. Induced syncope is a laboratory phenomenon controlled by man, and certainly not at all likely to confuse God into thinking that death has come and that it is time to take the spirit from the body. Sensory events and the memories are subject to rational explanation without necessarily invoking any spiritual component.

Another common cause of syncope is the experience of strong gravitational forces (G-forces) experienced by military jet pilots when pulling out of a dive (11-12). This faint or syncope is also caused by pooling of blood in the lower part of the body caused by these strong gravitational forces. Pilots wear G-suits to compress the lower part of the body to force blood back to the heart when pulling out of these steep dives. Nevertheless, the loss of consciousness produced by these G-forces without a G-suit (or in extreme dives with a G-suit) exactly mimic the sequence of the "spontaneous" faint, with perhaps the exception of some of the abdominal symptoms.

In experimental situations, research on G-force loss of consciousness simulates the events described in the NDE, except that it is not as detailed or prolonged, probably because the low blood pressure is less severe or more brief. In studies of pilots with induced loss of consciousness, the pleasant experiences were described as vivid and were thought to occur just as the pilot was awakening from the syncope.

Whinnery and Whinnery (11) reported 500 cases of such loss of consciousness. Most of these subjects had what they called "myoclonic convulsive episodes." The subjects also had a form of dreaming incorporated into the loss of consciousness episodes, and these dreams mixed memories from the past with sensory input from the blackout itself (such as the muscular motion accompanying the "release seizure"). The dreams or visions were positive emotions associated with the sensation of floating. Pilots experienced paralysis, while maintaining the ability to hear or even to see their surroundings. That is, selective aspects of consciousness were preserved. Withdrawal of G-forces and resumption of normal blood pressure allowed vision and hearing to return. In the midst of this experience, pilots often described tunnel vision as well.

Any other condition that causes the heart to function less efficiently as a pump can cause low blood pressure. Extremely low blood pressure is called shock, which is unfortunate because the general public also uses the term shock to mean emotional distress, which may or may not (usually not) be associated with severely low blood pressure. Conditions causing such serious low blood pressure and shock include rhythm disturbances, heart attacks with chest pain and blockage of a coronary artery, or diffuse weakening of the heart muscle due to some condition that weakens the muscle, called cardiomyopathy.

Finally, blood loss can cause the pressure to fall. Many NDEs are reported in the context of blood loss. While these conditions can be very serious or even fatal, most reported NDEs occurred during situations in which the blood pressure was not seriously low because the patients recovered with only minor medical interventions. Furthermore, virtually all reported NDEs occurred in a setting where the patient did not require cardiopulmonary resuscitation (CPR) or electric shock (defibrillation) to restore the circulation. A true cardiac arrest—a real near-death experience where "clinical death" occurs—requires CPR and defibrillation.

Two other very common diagnostic cardiac procedures involve stopping the heart during the routine course of medical treatment. One of these procedures is open-heart surgery; the other is the electrophysiologic study.

Open-Heart Surgery

During open-heart surgery, the heart is stopped by the application of a cold preservative solution. The heart is then restarted at the end of the operation, the circulation in the interim having been provided by the heart-lung machine. Though the heart is stopped for periods of up to several hours for these cardiac operations (over 300,000 of them are done each year in the United States alone), they do not cause NDEs in these patients—with the possible exceptions of rare patients in whom the anesthesia is insufficient to keep them asleep for the entire operation. That circumstance can result in memories of the procedure in which the patient may report the sensation of detachment from the body. These inadequately anesthetized patients may describe the events of the surgery in great detail, often with the fear or panic that one would expect from having to live through such an experience. Detachment may be a major defense mechanism to cope with such experiences.

It has been argued that patients adequately anesthetized during open-heart surgery should not be expected to have NDEs because they were receiving anesthesia, which blunted their memory. On the contrary, anesthesia can produce states similar to the NDE with its "dreamy state" and elicited memories. Anyone who has had a blood pressure of zero from *any* cause should have no memory because total brain ischemia (decrease of blood flow to the brain) is one of the most potent amnestic experiences possible. However, during open-heart surgery the blood pressure is supported by the heart-lung machine, and so there is no serious or prolonged drop in blood pressure. But during open-heart surgery the heart is unequivocally stopped, and certainly this condition might be thought to resemble death. But there is no NDE.

Diagnostic Cardiac Tests

Another medical procedure that purposely causes the heart to stop is called an electrophysiologic study. It is a cardiac catheterization procedure in which small electrode wires are threaded to the heart to record the heart rhythm and to attempt to trigger abnormal heart rhythms. Patients already prone to abnormal rhythms can have these abnormalities produced by this technique in the laboratory, while abnormal rhythms are much more difficult to induce in persons without a tendency toward rhythm disturbances. Tens of thousands of patients each year have these abnormal rhythms induced, causing "clinical death." Ventricular fibrillation is produced, the blood pressure is zero, and the sequence is then reversed with an electrical shock to the chest. The time that the heart is stopped is quite short, usually about ten seconds, but these patients frequently lose consciousness. They will often describe a dizziness, a giddiness, or a lightheadedness before their vision dims, sometimes with tunnel vision; but they never report anything like an NDE.

PROGRESSION FROM LIFE TO DEATH

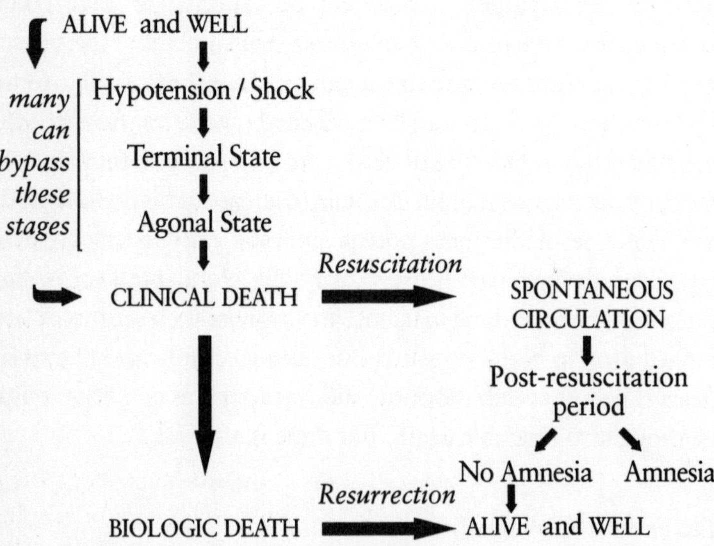

After losing consciousness they often have a stiffening of the muscles and bodily motions that can be misinterpreted as seizures. These patients then awaken with no memory of the shock or resuscitation procedure itself. In this circumstance the NDE *should* be the most common, if you believe the popular accounts, because (1) the patient was initially fully awake, (2) a documented "clinical death" rhythm was induced (that is, the heart actually stopped, and the blood pressure went to zero), (3) the patient lost consciousness, and (4) the patient was resuscitated without any drugs that could have clouded the memory of the event. On the contrary, these patients *never* have an NDE! Is this because they don't expect this testing to produce an NDE? This is like the movie *Flatliners*, in which medical students experiment to produce clinical death so they can see what happens after death. They arrange their experiment so they will awaken, of course. Contrary to movies, TV, and popular books, however, in real life when physicians do this same procedure—the production of clinical death—there is no NDE. Minor symptoms may occur, but they could never be confused with the reported NDE in completeness, intensity, or impact.

This medical simulation of clinical death occasionally also happens during another diagnostic test, the cardiac catheterization performed for angiography—the visualization of blood vessels in the heart by the injection of dye (contrast material). Uncommonly (less than 1 percent of cases), the heart will go into fibrillation during this procedure, and resuscitation is almost always successful. In these cases, the circumstances are the same—the patient is alert; the heart stops, the blood pressure goes to zero, the patient is resuscitated, and the patient awakens. Never is there an NDE in this sequence of events, at least in any of my patients.

The skeptic would say that in these circumstances the patient does not have enough time to "experience" the entire NDE, that the NDE is interrupted and does not have time to develop fully. However, most reports of the NDE remark on the rapidity of the travel and on the out-of-body aspect of the event, and some authors insist on the importance of the documentation of the "clinical death" of the patient. Here is another ideal circumstance where the exact events are known, the zero blood pressure is documented, the cardiac arrest is recorded, and there is no NDE! A temporary condition that causes a loss of consciousness near unto death. A temporary condition that can be easily created by man. A temporary condition that does not herald the inexorable progression to biologic death, although patients are unequivocally "clinically dead." A temporary condition that causes no NDE as described in the popular press. A temporary condition that does not illuminate the life beyond!

STAGES OF CARDIOVASCULAR INTEGRITY

MENTAL STATES	CARDIAC RHYTHM	STAGE
Awake/alert	Normal rhythm	
Dizzy/giddy	Minor bradycardias/tachycardias	
Near-syncope	Moderate bradycardias/tachycardias	
Syncope		
Bradycardias		ND
Tachycardias		
Ventricular tachycardia		ND
Ventricular fibrillation		CD
Cardiac arrest		
Asystole		CD/BD
Ventricular fibrillation		CD/BD

ND = near-death.

CD = clinical death; process is reversible, but vital signs (pulse, blood pressure) are lost.

BD = biologic death; process involves irreversible cell death, though patient may be resuscitated with loss of function resulting from the death of those cells that had progressed to biologic death.

CARDIOPULMONARY RESUSCITATION (CPR)

The technique of providing artificial circulation and respiration to a person who has collapsed with a cardiac arrest is called cardiopulmonary resuscitation or CPR. It is applied whenever a patient has no heartbeat, blood pressure, circulation, or respiration. CPR provides respiration by breathing into a person's mouth, causing expansion of the lungs. Pressing on the chest causes blood flow by expulsion of blood from the heart into the arteries.

The survival rate from cardiac arrest is dramatically improved if a bystander provides CPR while waiting for the medics to arrive to provide definitive resuscitative techniques (13). A true cardiac arrest requires electric shock across the chest from a defibrillator to restart the heart from its rapid, disorganized electrical activity, called ventricular fibrillation. Any collapse that does not require defibrillation to restore the heartbeat should not be classified as a cardiac arrest. The exception is asystole—complete cessation of the heartbeat from a slow heart rate that ultimately slows to zero. Ventricular fibrillation almost never ceases spontaneously. It almost always results in true death unless medical intervention including defibrillation causes the heart to resume its normal activity. That is why the medical aspects of many "near-death" experiences are not believable. The stories include no description of the medical condition of the patient and do not document the occurrence of defibrillation as part of the resuscitation process.

Many different conditions that simply lower the blood pressure can cause a person to collapse and pass out. A simple faint, caused by a transient drop in blood pressure, can cause a person to look like he or she has had a cardiac arrest, but the patient recovers quickly, often without any intervention from bystanders. Here is where the definition of "near-death" is important. "Near-death" to me means that the blood pressure was zero and the heart was fibrillating. Medical intervention short of defibrillation will not revive such a patient. So many of the popular accounts of "near-death" experiences are at best inaccurate, at worst fraudulent. While the patient may have been quite ill, usually blood pressure and pulse are preserved in the patients reported in these accounts. As long as at least *some* blood pressure is preserved, clinical cardiac death is not present, and the process of biologic death has not begun.

My work in Seattle has been conducted in conjunction with the Seattle city ambulance system, called Medic I. It is the most successful medical system in the world for reviving the cardiac arrest victim outside of the hospital. So we have seen thousands of patients resuscitated from cardiac arrest. Initially the success rates during the early years of CPR and defibrillation were poor, and some people even challenged the appropriateness of these attempts to revive patients who had collapsed outside the controlled environment of the hospital. But by the mid-1970s successes were clearly evident, and one-quarter to one-third of all patients who collapsed from a ventricular fibrillation cardiac arrest were successfully resuscitated to be discharged alive from the hospital.

This success gave us many people who should have been able to tell their stories of NDEs, if such experiences had occurred. But we found that anyone who had a true cardiac arrest had total amnesia for the event. In fact, this finding was so consistent that we were able to determine what the cardiac rhythm had been, simply from the patient's memory for the event, even before learning what rhythm the Medics had found on arrival at the scene. If the patient had any memory for the event, then the rhythm had *not* been a cardiac arrest (ventricular fibrillation). If the patient had no memory for the event, then it was at least possible that the rhythm had been ventricular fibrillation.

During CPR the blood flow to the body is dramatically decreased from normal levels. As good as CPR is, it remains very ineffective for restoring *normal* blood flow to all organs.

Furthermore, blood flow is naturally redirected to the critical regions of the body—the brain and the heart. God designed our bodies to respond to low blood pressure stress in this manner. When the blood pressure is low, the arteries in the body constrict in an attempt to raise the blood pressure. Constriction occurs most dramatically in the less essential organs, such as the skin and the muscles. In man, the body in general receives only 1 to 5 percent of normal flow during CPR, the heart receives only 5 to 10 percent, and the brain only 10 to 15 percent of its normal level (14-18). So CPR is actually very inefficient, compared to what the heart normally pumps.

Nevertheless, even this small amount of blood flow may be enough to provide some level of consciousness to the patient. It is not rare for the patient to exhibit some level of awareness during the CPR. However, it is unusual for a patient to have enough blood flow to the brain to awaken if ventricular fibrillation is really present. Distressingly, though, some patients do awaken enough to try to communicate with resuscitators during CPR. Rawlings describes such a patient in his book *Beyond Death's Door.* This patient awakened with CPR, then lapsed back into unconsciousness when CPR was stopped—an exceedingly distressing condition for both the patient and the medical team. More commonly, CPR can produce enough blood flow for the patient to process some sensory input during the resuscitation procedure, but not enough to be fully conscious.

During an episode of low blood pressure without cardiac arrest the patient can often hear things going on around him, even see things, but is often unable to move or talk. In the emergency room, the electrophysiology laboratory, the operating room, or the cardiac catheterization laboratory, where heart rhythms are often encountered that are causing low—but not zero—blood pressures, the doctors and nurses must be very careful what they do and say. Patients may appear to be unconscious because they do not respond to voice or even to pain, but they may actually be conscious enough to be hearing, seeing, and feeling the events around them. I frequently see patients who describe being in an emergency room with a heart rhythm problem that is causing a low blood pressure and being shocked with the defibrillator paddles in order to restore the rhythm to normal—and the patients remember the experience!

This is not an NDE. It is not a supernatural journey. It is simply that the blood pressure is low enough to make the person appear to be unconscious, but it is high enough for the person to be aware of the surroundings and to feel pain. Some have even described the fear of seeing the doctor coming to them with the paddles to shock them, wanting to say that they are awake but being unable to speak. The capacities to hear and think (and even the ability to see) were present, but the ability to talk was gone. So any description of an NDE must be analyzed with this physiology in mind. Some NDEs are clearly descriptions of such events.

A rare sequence may occur during CPR. Doctors and nurses decide that the resuscitation attempts on a patient are futile, and they cease their heroic measures. After a few minutes, the heart starts beating again, and the patient may actually survive long-term (19-26). While this occurs only in a tiny fraction of 1 percent of all CPR attempts, it is a real and disturbing phenomenon. Often the physicians have told the family that the patient has died, only to have to return to them to tell them that the patient revived spontaneously!

This phenomenon may represent the spontaneous correction of some metabolic abnormality (for example, alkalosis [excessive alkalinity] of the blood—a change in the acid-base balance of the blood in which the alkaline components predominate), and the sequence is termed the "Lazarus Phenomenon" or the "Lazarus Complex," named after the man raised by Jesus, as reported in the Bible (John 11). While the Lazarus Phenomenon in today's medicine is in reality a resuscitation, not a resurrection, the name has persisted. Often these patients are so sick that they do not ultimately survive more than a few minutes or hours, but some may recover to be discharged from the hospital.

With any of these scenarios, it is reasonable to ask: Was the person really near death? Was he simply selectively processing sensory input but was unable to communicate? Was ventricular fibrillation present? Was CPR producing enough blood flow to restore some of the sensory processing functions, but not fully reviving consciousness?

How can decreases in blood pressure and blood flow explain some of the experiences of people who are suffering from serious illnesses and hovering near death? A decrease in blood flow could have one of two effects: it could simply impair function of an organ, leading ultimately to cell death, or it could cause initial loss of inhibition of an area in the brain, followed later by nonfunction. There is good evidence for the latter sequence. Many portions of the brain operate as a balance between stimulatory and inhibitory forces. Loss of inhibition of certain brain cells could produce profound effects from any stimulation that might also be present. Let's examine each of the sensory functions to see how the reported events in the NDE can be explained medically.

The Ear and Hearing

One of the first sensory experiences described in the NDE is a loud noise, variably called a buzzing, a whirring, a rumble, a humming, or a ringing. Other descriptions have included roaring, clicking, hissing, or chirping. These sounds are remarkably similar to what is called "tinnitus" in other circumstances. It can be produced by the stimulation of various portions of the auditory apparatus, either in the ear or in the brain. Penfield's studies with electrical stimulation of the brain often produced such sounds, commonly by the stimulation of the temporal lobes (27-29). Furthermore, these sounds are characteristic of the noises described by people who lose consciousness by other mechanisms but are not close to death. The onset of fainting or syncope usually includes some sensation of ringing in the ears (1-7). The cochlear region of the ear responsible for hearing becomes "disinhibited," generating sounds that can be quite bizarre and unfamiliar.

Removal of inhibition has the same result as stimulation. Later, relative lack of stimulation or the unresponsiveness of the auditory apparatus is responsible for the quiet reported during some stages of the NDE. These sequences occur thousands of times each day in people who are not near death, and they can be produced at will by simple physiologic maneuvers. Any event that is so simple and common and can be triggered by man certainly cannot be unlocking views of heaven and conversations with God!

The Eye and Vision

Prominent to the NDE are visual phenomena. First the vision dims, then comes the tunnel vision, then the appearance of a bright light at the end of a tunnel, and finally a bright light that comes closer until the person is within or engulfed by the light. What do we know about the eye and visual mechanisms that could explain this fantastic voyage? Isn't an NDE the best explanation for such a sequence? Hardly.

The eye has layers, like an onion. The outer layer is called the sclera, the middle layer is the choroid, and the inner layer is the retina. The area at the back of the eye where the light rays are focused is called the macula, and the exact center of the macula is the fovea centralis. Vision is created by the interaction of light rays with specialized cells in the retina of the eye. The specialized cells in the retina are called rods and cones. Rods are responsible primarily for black and white vision, while the cones generate color vision. These cells initiate neural impulses that travel back to a specialized portion of the brain deep within the temporal lobe, and then to the back of the brain at the occipital cortex (30-31).

The retina has an abundant blood supply for the nourishment of the visual cells (the rods and the cones), and the middle layer of the eye, the choroid, is even more vascular (18, 31). The choroid is responsible for much of the supply of oxygen and nutrients to the retina where the visual cells are located. The central visual region of the retina near the macula is quite vascular, while the periphery of the retina is somewhat less vascular. In other words, the area of the eye responsible for central vision has more blood vessels than the area responsible for peripheral vision. The blood flow per gram of tissue is higher in the choroid than in any other tissue of the body. If one could imagine the representation of the density of blood vessels in the retina as being white where the vessels are abundant and darker where the vessels are more sparse, the representation of the retina would be a central bright white zone surrounded by an ever-decreasing brightness until the periphery of the retina would be a dark halo around the central visual region (31).

The blood pressure in the eye is lower than the pressure in many other regions of the body. Furthermore, as one moves from the macular region of the eye to the periphery, the pressure becomes even lower. Moderate drops in blood pressure are usually well tolerated by the eye. The retinal vessels are able to change flow efficiently (autoregulation of flow). With extreme drops in blood pressure, the periphery of the retina will become less well perfused than the macula, causing only the central portion of the visual fields to be preserved.

The visual cortex of the brain is also an area extremely sensitive to changes in blood pressure and loss of blood flow. Acute decreases in flow cause tunnel vision, and it is possible to create this tunnel vision in experimental subjects, such as astronauts routinely experiencing G-forces sufficient to cause visual symptoms. The high G-forces cause a drop in blood pressure, causing a graying of vision and then the production of tunnel vision (11-12). Any event that causes a similar drop in blood pressure will cause similar visual perceptions. All of us have had dimming of vision when we stand up abruptly after sitting or squatting for a prolonged period of time. The blood pressure does not fall enough to cause the second stage, which is the tunnel vision. But there are even other reasons that the tunnel vision might occur with prolonged decreases in blood pressure.

The blood supply to the visual cortex of the brain is crucial to the understanding of the tunnel experience and the bright light encountered during the NDE. The visual cortex where the images are sent for interpretation by the brain also has regional differences in blood flow. The region of the visual cortex connected to the macula in the retina is more vascular and better perfused than the rest of the visual cortex. The macular representation in the occipital lobes of the brain actually receives a dual blood supply—from the middle and posterior cerebral arteries. So it has a better chance of remaining perfused during periods of low blood pressure. The representation of the retina on the brain from the peripheral portions of the retina has only a single blood supply, so it is more vulnerable to a drop in blood pressure. So there are two major reasons why the blood supply of the eye and brain promotes tunnel vision during periods of low blood pressure:

1. The central portion of the retina is better perfused than the peripheral portions.
2. The representation of the macula on the surface of the occipital lobes of the brain is better perfused than other areas (32). Selective loss of vision in the periphery of the visual fields is likely to happen when blood pressure falls, even though the central vision may be preserved.

O.K., I have explained why the vision dims and why there is tunnel vision in a person during a medical crisis such as low blood pressure, but there are other aspects to the visual experience that can only be explained by passage into heaven and back, right? Wrong! The other visual phenomena are also understandable on a natural physiologic basis. The travel down a tunnel and the bright light have a basis in normal human physiology, and we do not need to invoke astral travel to understand them. What are the other reasons the tunnel vision and the bright lights appear? There are at least six other explanations:

1. Rods (black and white vision) are located in the area where the blood flow is the worst (18, 31).

2. Rods are more sensitive to lack of blood flow than cones (color vision) (33).

3. All retinal cells are more sensitive to light after a period of low blood flow (34).

4. Pupillary dilatation increases the effect of any stimulation (35).

5. The representation of vision on the occipital cortex is arranged in a fashion that promotes the visual imagery of tunnels and spirals (36-39).

6. Random firing of cells in the retina would lead to the image of a brilliant light because of the density and location of the light-sensing cells in the eye (18, 31, 38).

The lights described by those who have experienced a medical crisis with lowered blood pressure are usually described as colorful, if not brilliant. The rods are located more peripherally in the retina and serve the peripheral vision, while the cones are centrally placed in the macula where central vision is generated (18, 31). Thus, the cones that generate beautiful colors are sitting near the most abundant blood supply, while the rods in the periphery that generate the edges of our vision suffer from the ischemia of low blood pressure. The only signals going to the brain's visual cortex are coming from the "center of the tunnel" of adequately perfused tissues. And the best perfused portions of the visual cortex in the brain are receiving colorful signals from the eye! Hence, the appearance of a tunnel of beautifully colored lights!

Want another logical explanation for the beautifully colored lights? The cones themselves are more resistant to ischemia than the rods (33). So the cones not only have a better blood supply—they have a central location where they could produce a bright central light with surrounding darkness (the ischemic peripheral rods), and they are more resistant to ischemia, functioning better and longer under the presence of ischemia. A triple whammy! But there's more!

Gellhorn showed that the retinal cells respond to ischemia (decreased blood flow) and reperfusion (resumption of blood flow) in an unusual way (34). During anoxia, the inhibitory impulses are lost first, causing the equivalent of stimulation. Later the excitatory impulses disappear. With the resumption of more normal blood pressure and more normal blood flow to the eyes, the retina becomes *supersensitive* to light impulses. Blood flow in the retina actually rises above normal. That is, as blood pressure and flow improve or are restored, the retinal cells send *more* impulses to the brain than they would ordinarily send for the same stimulus, resulting in a heightened input to the visual cortex, at least partially accounting for the extreme brilliance of the lights described.

Next, the light of the NDE does not hurt the person's eyes. There are no aftereffects from the encounter with the "being of light." The "light" is not actually passing through the lens and the eye itself. The image probably resides entirely in the retina or the brain at the occipital cortex. It is not an actual external light; otherwise the retina would be damaged or at least stunned.

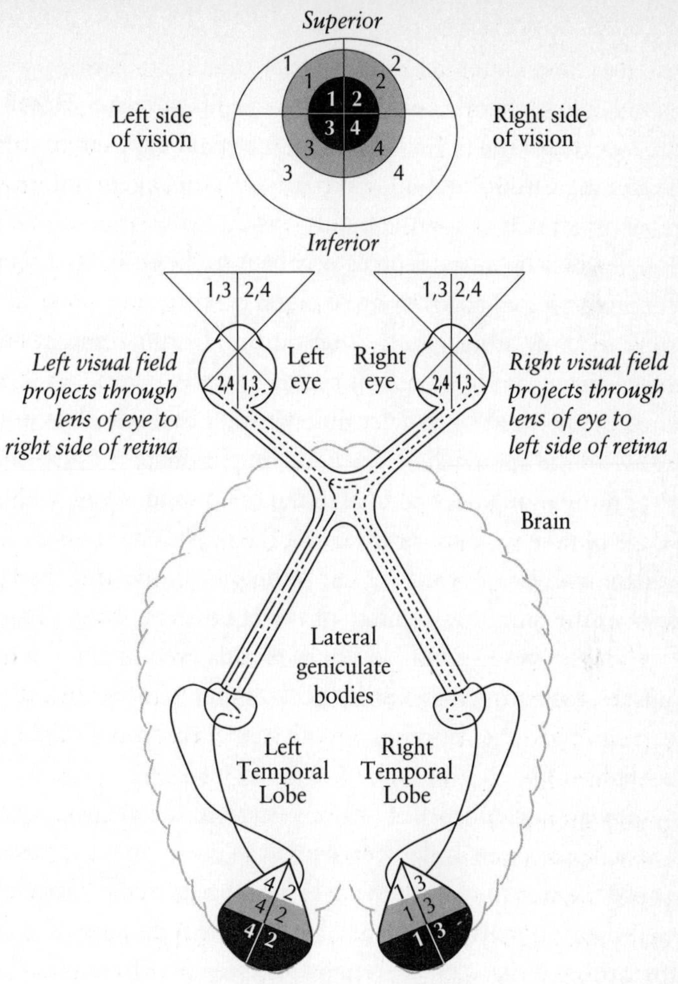

Figure 3. Visual pathways. Vision is dependent on intact connections from the eyes to the occipital cortex. The visual fields of both eyes are interconnected. An object to a person's left is projected to the right side of the retina of both eyes. This image is then transmitted to the region of the right temporal lobe, called the lateral geniculate body, where nerve connections continue the path to the right occipital lobe. Central portions of the visual field are represented more densely by nerve endings than peripheral portions, as illustrated by the shading in the figure. Loss of blood flow to the periphery of the retina or to selected portions of the occipital cortex will cause "tunnel vision."

Need any other reasons for the tunnel, followed by the brightly colored lights? Fear causes the pupils to dilate. This principle has been known for centuries. A person exposed to a life-threatening situation will have an outpouring of adrenalin (epinephrine) that causes the pupils (the central portion of the eye through which light passes on its way back to the retina) to enlarge. With more prolonged lowering of blood pressure, the pupils dilate further to allow more light to enter the eye. During resuscitations, doctors are always looking in a person's eyes to detect "fixed and dilated pupils" and so to determine whether brain death is beginning. With the approach of death, the pupils dilate because of the loss of normal pupillary control in the brain stem. Thus, with the passage of time (seconds or minutes), the pupils have two reasons to dilate: the early effects of fear and epinephrine and the later effects of the unresponsivenesss of the brain stem. These changes allow for excessive stimulation of the retina even by *normal* light exposure, enhancing the selective ocular input to the brain and further magnifying the sensation of both tunnel vision and bright colorful lights (35).

Cowan and colleagues (40) investigated the arrangement of the visual projection of the retinal input to the occipital cortex. He mapped the distribution of the eye's nerve cells to the back of the brain where vision is represented. He found that the pattern of concentric rings of vision on the retina are represented by straight lines on the occipital cortex. Thus, stimulation of linear regions of the cortex would produce spirals, concentric rings, or tunnels in the mind of the beholder. As these lines of stimulation move, the images would enlarge or shrink, giving the impression of motion to the visual images. Cowan hypothesized that the medical crisis produced disinhibition of linear regions of the occipital cortex and caused the tunnel sensation. This is complicated but sufficient to explain many of the reports of the NDE.

Furthermore, the density of the rods and cones decreases as

one moves from the center of the visual fields to the periphery (31). Random firing of these cells in the retina would tend to involve more of the cells in the center of the visual fields, creating an impression of central light and peripheral darkness. If the cones were mostly involved, the central light would assume brilliant colors. Ever-increasing intensity of this random firing of visual cells in the retina would give the sensation of moving toward the light and even entering the light. Random firing of the cells of the visual cortex of the brain would have the same effect. This "neural noise" could account for the light described almost universally in the NDE. Random firing of the cells of the occipital cortex would produce a central bright light because more cells in the brain correspond to the central visual axis than to the periphery.

This theory even accounts for the color reported for the light at the end of the tunnel in the NDE. If all cones in the retina (which respond to blue, green, and red light colors), or all of the occipital cortical cells representing them, were equally involved in this process of random firing or neural noise, then the light should be white. Because the cones for blue color vision are less dense than the cones for other colors, we might predict that the light would be yellow. Indeed, the light of the NDE is often described as white or yellow, much less often than the other colors.

Blackmore and Troscianko expanded this theory even a bit further (38-39). If the cells of the visual cortex progressively fired more rapidly (though randomly), the resulting sensation would be the impression of motion toward the center of the bright light, as though the person were actually traveling down the tunnel with the bright light at the end. The same would occur if the random firing were located in the retina instead of the brain.

Not convinced? Here is another medical fact. The stimulation studies of Penfield described above were able to reproduce all of the events we've discussed: the dim vision, the tunnel vision, the bright and colorful lights, and even the appearance of the people that survivors of medical catastrophes describe. It is possible to reproduce all of the NDE with temporal lobe stimulation, even without the low blood pressure and the ischemia we have been describing. But since the NDE has often (though not always) occurred in the context of a medical crisis, we will continue to explain the events based upon that physiology.

Other Senses

The senses of taste, touch, and smell are little affected during physiologic events associated with severe illness and near-death. Few NDE reports describe any major components of these senses. While some drug-induced states and seizures involving the temporal lobes have strong components of these sensory experiences, the NDE and the physical conditions that produce loss of consciousness from low blood pressure do not.

Integration of Sensory Input

How would a brain, which has as its duty the integration and interpretation of sensory inputs, handle the sequence of visual and auditory events? It would do it the way it had done it all of the patient's life—by trying to integrate all of the current and past information within a context of the person's belief system. So the person "interprets" the bright lights as a holy being, as God, as Buddha, as Mohammed, or whatever. Remember that the NDE has been described in all cultures, and the "being of light" can be almost any person imaginable. The patient "conjures up" a being consistent with his past experiences (often dead relatives) and belief system (a holy person). This explanation does not mean that the person is consciously deceiving us; his brain simply must "make sense" of all of these inputs on the basis of past experience.

That the sequence is so similar from person to person is not so surprising. The beginning of the experience is physiologic, "normal" if you will. It is dictated by the same bodily responses found in all of mankind. The interpretation of the later stages is what is left to the experience and beliefs of the person having the medical crisis. No one who previously had no knowledge of Christ has ever described seeing Him during a hypotensive experience! The encounters during the crisis are always at least within the realm of conscious experience for that person.

That some people have a hard time describing the experience is also not too difficult to understand. Because it is a unique experience, the synthesis of the sensory inputs by the human mind can be difficult to relate to conscious experience, or at least to describe. Of course it is indescribable. Our brains cannot integrate this new set of sensory inputs adequately to reconcile them completely with our past experience.

It is not as much fun to have a rational explanation for the NDE, is it? It's always more exciting to believe in supernatural events. That's the way we all think and behave. But you will see later that the supernatural explanation is not only a worse explanation for the physiology of the NDE, but it is completely contrary to Scripture!

WHAT IS CARDIAC DEATH?

Clinical cardiac death is usually described as the point in time at which the heart stops pumping blood altogether, either because of a slow rate that reaches zero or the fast disorganized rhythm called ventricular fibrillation. Either condition causes loss of consciousness and leads to *biologic* death—the actual destruction of cellular tissues—unless interventions restore blood pressure and flow. Clinical cardiac death can usually be reversed by resuscitative techniques. Biologic death is the condition in which the organism undergoes irreversible cell death. It cannot be reversed, even by advanced resuscitative techniques.

The progression from clinical to biologic death is a gradual process that occurs at different rates for different organs. The brain is the organ most vulnerable to the interruption of blood flow. The brain begins biologic death before other organs, and certain areas of the brain die before others. The "higher" functions in the cerebral cortex (consciousness and thought processes) are the most vulnerable to rapid biologic death. Biologic cardiac death usually comes next. Other organs (for example, the stomach, the liver, or the kidney) are more resistant to damage from ischemia.

WHAT IS NEAR-DEATH?

Near-death usually involves a rhythm disturbance that can be reversed by resuscitation techniques. Other types of heart disease processes that weaken the heart are not readily reversible. So near-death for the heart most commonly involves a slow heart rate (approaching zero) or a rapid heart rate (so fast that the heart no longer pumps blood). In both conditions, the blood pressure plummets to zero. Most cases of patients reported to have had NDEs have never had these conditions documented.

SUMMARY

So what, then, can we conclude from these discussions? Is near-death related to the NDE? Can we explain most, if not all, of the features of the NDE based on the physiologic events that occur in the critically ill patient?

First, near-death is a term that is frequently overused and almost always poorly defined. It should be restricted to those conditions in which there was really a "clinical death"—that is, loss of blood pressure and flow as well as documented cessation of the heartbeat. Virtually no NDE reports adequately document such conditions. Most "near-death" events in the NDE reports are simply medical illnesses that cause pain, low blood pressure, and perhaps some decreased perfusion (blood flow) to the brain. Rarely is a cardiac arrest documented, even in some reports from cardiologists and intensive care units.

Second, most explanations of the NDE—except poor perfusion of the brain—fall short in explaining all of the reported events:

Hallucinations. Most NDEs do not fit the pattern of hallucinations.

Drugs. Many people have never been exposed to any mind-altering drugs.

Neurotransmitters. Too little is known about them to implicate them in all NDEs.

Endorphins. Enticing, but never proved in the near-death patient.

Seizures. Some temporal lobe seizures may be similar to the NDE, but it is hard to believe that all NDEs are due to seizures from this selected region.

Depersonalization. Not likely to account for the stereotyped quality of the NDE.

Suggestion. Clearly most of the reported NDEs could have been (and probably are) suggested, fabricated, or invented by the person reporting the NDE, but some seem to be original and uninfluenced by popular reports.

Influence or coercion. Again, some NDEs are clearly reported in response to the examiner's leading questions and the patient's desire to give the medical personnel what they desire or are expecting. But this explanation does not cover all NDEs, and there seems to be a physiologic basis for some patients who report the phenomenon.

Finally, the brain perfusion hypothesis seems to be the most feasible explanation for the origin of the NDE. Many people who have serious medical conditions will have decreased blood flow to the brain, which triggers many of the sensations reported with the NDE. The brain must try to "make sense" of these unusual sensory inputs, and it does so in a way consistent with the background (particularly the religious background) of the person having the medical catastrophe. The person's concept of the afterlife will influence the interpretation of the bright lights, the tunnel, the noises, and the other sensations bombarding the person who knows that a life-threatening event is occurring. We are all familiar with pictures of bodies and angels hovering over a sick or recently deceased person. All of us have concepts of what heaven or hell might be like. All of us are familiar with stories of people taking a journey to heaven. This mental background forms the basis for the NDE. The recent explosion in the incidence of reported NDEs is due to the knowledge of the event reported in the popular media, for it is the rare person in our society who has not heard of the "light at the end of the tunnel."

Thus, a physical threat may trigger the NDE because the concept of what happens at death is already stored in the minds of most people from previous cultural and religious inputs. The brain simply interprets the strange sensations that occur near death in a way that "makes sense" to us, based on our memory, culture, and religious backgrounds.

Finally, it is also "trendy" (as well as potentially lucrative) to have had an NDE.

SECTION THREE

■

The Bible and the Near-Death Experience

8

DREAMS AND VISIONS IN THE BIBLE

There Is a God—You Aren't

Stu Graham had just experienced a devastating cardiac arrest. Fortunately, he had been resuscitated successfully, and he actually had very little neurologic damage from the event. He was one of the lucky ones, though his wife Joan refused to allow the use of the word "lucky." She believed that all events are a part of God's plan and that nothing should be called "luck." That approach to life reflected her religious beliefs. She knew that Jesus was Lord of her own life and Stu's as well.

But now the doctors wanted to do some testing to see if Stu was at risk for another cardiac arrest. Some patients have as high as a 40 percent chance of having another cardiac arrest in the year following survival from the first one. Joan and Stu thought such testing seemed appropriate. Though Stu was yearning for the day when he could see Jesus, he was not sure that his work on this earth was completed. He had experienced no NDE with his first cardiac arrest, so he was not influenced by any apparent messages from "the other side." Furthermore, he did not believe the NDE was a valid experience. He had talked with many people in his church, and their stories—all of which had been gleaned from the popular literature—just didn't seem to mesh with what he understood about Scripture's account of man's death. So he agreed to the tests.

The testing was not too difficult. Yes, there were many procedures over three days, but he tolerated them well. The cardiac angiogram had shown that his coronary vessels were clean. His exercise test had produced no rhythm problems. His echocardiogram showed that his valves were all functioning normally, though the heart muscle looked suspiciously weak. The radioisotope scan of his heart had also shown more definitively that he had some weakness of the heart muscle—a cardiomyopathy, his doctor had called it. His electrophysiologic test had produced some dangerous rhythm disturbances, and the drugs the doctors first used to try to suppress it had been unsuccessful. So his doctors told him that he had two choices—to use another drug that could have some serious side effects (especially in his lungs) or to have a device implanted to treat a cardiac arrest should he ever have another collapse.

Stu and Joan debated these options. Stu's lungs were already pretty badly damaged by thirty years of smoking. Any further damage from a drug could render him an invalid from his breathing. So the implantation of the device seemed like the right way to go. After all, his doctor had said that it was much like implanting a pacemaker and that the likelihood of complications was small. So after much discussion and prayer, they decided on the device—an automatic implantable defibrillator, the doctor called it. The surgery would be the next morning.

That night Joan had a horrible dream. She was not prone to remembering her dreams, though she knew that everyone dreams. Some people just remember the dreams better than others. This one she would never forget. She dreamed that Stu had encountered serious complications from the procedure. The device was difficult to position in the heart; Stu had two more cardiac arrests on the operating table, and he developed an infection a few days after the implantation. Not just any mild infection, but one that was life-threatening—"blood poisoning," as it used to be called. The doctors had to remove the device, and he almost died during the prolonged hospitalization. Was this dream from God? Was He telling Joan and Stu to forget about the device implantation?

Joan called the hospital immediately upon awakening that morning. She wanted to tell Stu to delay the operation until they had time to talk. It was a major inconvenience, but she was able to have the operation postponed for a few hours.

Joan and Stu talked, prayed, wept. What to do? Their doctor was a Christian, so they could openly express their concerns and he would not ridicule them. But he had no insights about Joan's dream. Yes, the complications that she saw in her dream were possible, but it still seemed most reasonable to proceed. But the decision was truly Stu's and Joan's.

They quickly consulted their pastor, but he also seemed to be of little help. How does one interpret a dream? Was it even possible that Satan was deceiving them into rejecting a procedure that would help Stu, one that would keep him alive to continue his strong Christian witness to their friends and coworkers? There seemed to be no easy answers.

Finally Joan and Stu decided to go ahead with the operation. They had serious misgivings, but they had to do something to try to keep Stu from dying from another cardiac arrest.

The operation seemed interminable. Joan paced the floor in the surgical waiting room for hours. Then the doctor appeared. It was obvious from the look on his face that the procedure had not gone well. He told her that Stu was O.K., but there had been some complications. It had been difficult to position the catheter in Stu's heart, and the mechanical irritation had caused his heart to stop twice during the operation. But the team had been able to restart it without difficulty, and Stu seemed to be doing all right at this point. Was this what Joan had dreamed? Was it all coming true? Was there more? She was afraid to consider the future. She was simply glad Stu was still alive.

His recovery seemed to progress well. Three days after the operation, he was really quite chipper. In just a few days he could go home. Did he ever relish that thought! He had been in the hospital now over two weeks, and he was ready for a break. It was so exciting that he began to have chills down his spine. But then the chills became worse. These were not chills of anticipation; they were the start of rigors—chills and shaking that accompany fevers from a serious infection! They lasted over two hours before the nurses and doctors had them under control. But the worst part was the thought that the device might be infected and have to be removed. Had Joan's dream been true from start to finish?

Over the next few days there were more tests. The fevers came and went, but Stu's temperature was never quite normal. No more of the shaking and high fevers, but he knew that something was wrong. He had been improving. His strength had been increasing. But now he was taking giant steps backwards. He was weak, tired, even depressed. And the device implanted under the skin was beginning to become red, puffy, and sore.

Then his doctor told him the news he had been dreading, but that he knew was coming. The device was infected. It had to be removed.

Joan's dream was now complete. Why had they not believed it? Does God still speak in dreams and visions? Ask Joan and Stu. They believe the answer is unequivocally yes!

We will now see what the Bible has to say about death and the NDE. These topics will also address dreams, visions, translations, healings, resuscitations, and resurrections.

DREAMS

Dreams are prevalent throughout the Bible, both in the Old Testament and the New Testament. Dreams were used by God to send messages to the patriarchs.

> *But God came to Abimelech in a dream one night. . . .*
>
> —*Genesis 20:3*

> *"The angel of God said to me in a dream, 'Jacob.' I answered, 'Here I am.'"*
>
> —*Genesis 31:11*

> *Then God came to Laban the Aramean in a dream at night. . . .*
>
> —*Genesis 31:24*

Dreams were prominent in the story of Joseph and the Pharaoh:

> *When two full years had passed, Pharaoh had a dream: He was standing by the Nile, when out of the river there came up seven cows, sleek and fat, and they grazed among the reeds. After them, seven other cows, ugly and gaunt, came up out of the Nile and stood beside those on the riverbank. And the cows that were ugly and gaunt ate up the seven sleek, fat cows. Then Pharaoh woke up.*
>
> *He fell asleep again and had a second dream: Seven heads of grain, healthy and good, were growing on a single stalk. After them, seven other heads of grain sprouted—thin and scorched by the east wind. The thin heads of grain swallowed up the seven healthy, full heads. Then Pharaoh woke up; it had been a dream.*
>
> *In the morning his mind was troubled, so he sent for all the magicians and wise men of Egypt. Pharaoh told them his dreams, but no one could interpret them for him. . . . So Pharaoh sent for Joseph. . . .*

> *Pharaoh said to Joseph, "I had a dream, and no one can interpret it. But I have heard it said of you that when you hear a dream you can interpret it."*
>
> *"I cannot do it," Joseph replied to Pharaoh, "but God will give Pharaoh the answer he desires. . . .*
>
> *"God has revealed to Pharaoh what he is about to do. The seven good cows are seven years, and the seven good heads of grain are seven years; it is one and the same dream. The seven lean, ugly cows that came up afterward are seven years, and so are the seven worthless heads of grain scorched by the east wind: They are seven years of famine.*
>
> *"It is just as I said to Pharaoh: God has shown Pharaoh what he is about to do. Seven years of great abundance are coming throughout the land of Egypt, but seven years of famine will follow them. Then all the abundance in Egypt will be forgotten, and the famine will ravage the land. The abundance in the land will not be remembered, because the famine that follows it will be so severe. The reason the dream was given to Pharaoh in two forms is that the matter has been firmly decided by God, and God will do it soon."*
>
> *—Genesis 41:1-8, 14-16, 25-32*

God had given a message to Pharaoh in a dream, and Joseph's interpretation established him in Pharaoh's court.

Dreams are usually considered to be the expressions of our fears or our hopes. Modern psychological theory states that dreams help us deal with the trials and stresses of our lives. Occasionally, though, our dreams will be messages sent from God. It can be difficult to discern which dreams come from God, which are simply internally generated, and which might be from Satan. It can be even more difficult to interpret these dreams correctly. What we do know is that dreams from God will never tell us something that is contrary to the Bible.

Dreams are less common in the New Testament, though they

still came as messages to God's children—for example, when Jesus' earthly father Joseph was told to go to Egypt:

> *. . . an angel of the Lord appeared to Joseph in a dream. "Get up," he said, "take the child and his mother and escape to Egypt. Stay there until I tell you, for Herod is going to search for the child to kill him."*
>
> —*Matthew* 2:13

In Acts 2:17 we read:

> *"'In the last days, God says, I will pour out my Spirit on all people. Your sons and daughters will prophesy, your young men will see visions, your old men will dream dreams.'"*

So prophetic dreams do occur in our times.

Are dreams the explanation for the NDE? Not according to the NDE proponents. The NDE is an experience usually associated with a traumatic event, often bringing the person to the brink of death. It does not occur during sleep. A dream is almost always clearly a dream. Rarely is it confused with any other state of consciousness. So dreams, which God still sometimes uses for our instruction and edification, do not explain the NDE.

VISIONS

Visions in the Old or New Testament refer to images or appearances that have the characteristics of sight but that are uniquely sent from God for our instruction. Often these experiences occurred in trances or in ecstatic states. They were usually visible only to the single recipient of the vision, not to others who may have been nearby. They could be prophetic or revelatory messages from God.

Visions abound in the Old Testament. Prophets frequently

spoke after receiving visions. The book of Isaiah is a good example, beginning with the statement that it is in fact a composite vision sent from God:

> *The vision concerning Judah and Jerusalem that Isaiah son of Amoz saw during the reigns of Uzziah, Jotham, Ahaz and Hezekiah, kings of Judah.*
>
> *—Isaiah 1:1*

Isaiah revealed to the people of Israel that both judgment and salvation were coming to the nation.

Visions were often detailed, such as one of Daniel's visions:

> *In the third year of King Belshazzar's reign, I, Daniel, had a vision, after the one that had already appeared to me. In my vision I saw myself in the citadel of Susa in the province of Elam; in the vision I was beside the Ulai Canal. I looked up, and there before me was a ram with two horns, standing beside the canal, and the horns were long. One of the horns was longer than the other but grew up later. I watched the ram as he charged toward the west and the north and the south. No animal could stand against him, and none could rescue from his power. He did as he pleased and became great.*
>
> *—Daniel 8:1-4*

The vision goes on in similar detail, each aspect of the vision very symbolic and known only to the recipient of the vision. This revelation was prophetic of the Medo-Persian empire and Greece—obscure to the casual listener or reader, but revealed by God to Daniel.

Though visions were common in the Old Testament, none relate directly to the proof or disproof of the NDE.

God in the New Testament also gave visions to communicate, to teach important concepts, to edify, to instruct, and to rebuke various acts. Peter, Paul, James, and John all had visions. Visions are usually intensely personal. Many theologians debate whether the granting of dreams and visions was only for the apostolic times or whether such events occur today. Certainly any dream or vision of today must be consistent with Scripture, and we are instructed to "test the spirits to see whether they are from God, because many false prophets have gone out into the world" (1 John 4:1). In the end-times there will be an increase in false prophets and sinfulness.

> *"At that time many will turn away from the faith and will betray and hate each other, and many false prophets will appear and deceive many people."*
>
> *—Matthew 24:10-11*

> *The Spirit clearly says that in later times some will abandon the faith and follow deceiving spirits and things taught by demons.*
>
> *—1 Timothy 4:1*

> *But mark this: There will be terrible times in the last days. People will be lovers of themselves, lovers of money, boastful, proud, abusive, disobedient to their parents, ungrateful, unholy, without love, unforgiving, slanderous, without self-control, brutal, not lovers of the good, treacherous, rash, conceited, lovers of pleasure rather than lovers of God—having a form of godliness but denying its power. Have nothing to do with them.*
>
> *—2 Timothy 3:1-5*

> *For the time will come when men will not put up with sound doctrine. Instead, to suit their own desires, they will gather around them a great number of teachers to say what their itching ears want to hear. They will turn their ears away from the truth and turn aside to myths. But*

you, keep your head in all situations, endure hardship, do the work of an evangelist, discharge all the duties of your ministry.

—*2 Timothy 4:3-5*

"For false Christs and false prophets will appear and perform great signs and miracles to deceive even the elect—if that were possible."

—*Matthew 24:24*

"Watch out for false prophets. They come to you in sheep's clothing, but inwardly they are ferocious wolves. By their fruit you will recognize them. Do people pick grapes from thornbushes, or figs from thistles? Likewise every good tree bears good fruit, but a bad tree bears bad fruit. A good tree cannot bear bad fruit, and a bad tree cannot bear good fruit. Every tree that does not bear good fruit is cut down and thrown into the fire. Thus, by their fruit you will recognize them. Not everyone who says to me, 'Lord, Lord,' will enter the kingdom of heaven, but only he who does the will of my Father who is in heaven. Many will say to me on that day, 'Lord, Lord, did we not prophesy in your name, and in your name drive out demons and perform many miracles?' Then I will tell them plainly, 'I never knew you. Away from me, you evildoers!'"

—*Matthew 7:15-23*

Don't let anyone deceive you in any way, for that day will not come until the rebellion occurs and the man of lawlessness is revealed, the man doomed to destruction. He opposes and exalts himself over everything that is called God or is worshiped, sets himself up in God's temple, proclaiming himself to be God. . . . And then the lawless one will be revealed, whom the Lord Jesus will overthrow with the breath of his mouth and destroy by the splendor of his coming. The coming of the lawless one will be in accor-

dance with the work of Satan displayed in all kinds of counterfeit miracles, signs, and wonders, *and in every sort of evil that deceives those who are perishing. They perish because they refused to love the truth and so be saved. For this reason God sends them a powerful delusion so that they will believe the lie and so that all will be condemned who have not believed the truth but have delighted in wickedness.*

—2 Thessalonians 2:3-4, 8-12, emphasis mine

Dear children, this is the last hour; and as you have heard that the antichrist is coming, even now many antichrists have come. This is how we know it is the last hour.

—1 John 2:18

These verses tell us that deception abounds on this earth and that we must be aware that Satan seeks to deceive us. The discernment of signs and wonders, of dreams and visions, will challenge even the elect. Often such dreams and visions will masquerade as Christian witness, with deceptive references to God, to Jesus, to the Holy Spirit. The language will be "right," it will have all of the expected Christian buzzwords ("sent from God," "anointed," etc.); but the message is not from God. The message will have just enough truth to deceive.

Acts 2:17 says, "'In the last days, God says, I will pour out my Spirit on all people. Your sons and daughters will prophesy, your young men will see visions, and your old men will dream dreams.'"

Acts 9:10-12 tells us about a disciple who was led by a vision:

In Damascus there was a disciple named Ananias. The Lord called to him in a vision, "Ananias!" "Yes, Lord," he answered. The Lord said to him, "Go to to the house of Judas on Straight Street and ask for a man from Tarsus named Saul, for he is praying. In a vision he has seen a man named Ananias come and place his hands on him to restore his sight."

Acts 10:3-6 reveals:

One day at about three in the afternoon [Cornelius] had a vision. He distinctly saw an angel of God, who came to him and said, "Cornelius!" Cornelius stared at him in fear. "What is it, Lord?" he asked. The angel answered, "Your prayers and gifts to the poor have come up as a remembrance before God. Now send men to Joppa to bring back a man named Simon who is called Peter. He is staying with Simon the tanner, whose house is by the sea."

The word "dream" or "dreams" occurs 123 times in eighty-seven verses in the *King James Version* of the Bible, while "vision" or "visions" (most of which came from God) occurs 103 times in ninety-six verses.

What is the difference between dreams and visions? On the surface the difference is obvious. Dreams occur when a person is asleep, while visions manifest themselves while one is awake. It may not be clear from some of the biblical descriptions whether a dream or vision occurred, and it is common for a person himself to declare that he was unsure whether the revelation occurred during sleep or wakefulness. The distinction is probably not important. What is important is the relation of the purported dream or vision to Scripture. If it is indeed from God, it will never contradict Scripture, and it must glorify God, not the man having the dream or vision. The Bible commands us to beware of false prophets and to measure dreams and visions by Scripture.

NDE proponents cite the visions of antiquity—alleged NDEs of mystics—and equate them with the visions recorded in the Bible. We must not be misled by excited descriptions of fantastic voyages that do not mesh with the Word of God. Today's Christian unfortunately is often misled by tales that will confuse "even the elect—if that were possible" (Mark 13:22). But let's examine some of the dreams and visions we *know* to be authentic.

MOSES

Moses desperately wanted to see God, but this prized experience was to be denied. Seeing God was impossible.

God appeared to Moses and the children of Israel as a cloud by day and a fire by night throughout the times recorded in Exodus, Leviticus, Numbers, and Deuteronomy. These manifestations are the only form of God that man can see apart from the Incarnation and pre-incarnate appearances of Christ, the Son. Even Moses, one of the greatest men recorded in the history of the world, was not righteous enough to be allowed to see God the Father. When Moses asked to be allowed to see God's glory, God responded with a plan by which Moses could only look at the retreating form of God. Thus God protected Moses from the certain death that would have occurred had Moses gazed directly on God's countenance. God shielded Moses with His hand as He passed by, and Moses was protected in the cleft in the rock from seeing God's face (see Exodus 33). This description of God's power certainly is at odds with the popular NDE accounts in which God is presented as being seen as a loving and benevolent friend, a chum with whom the traveler can discuss life in a very casual manner and then return to earth.

While the Bible speaks of Moses talking to God "face to face" (Deuteronomy 34:10), that expression means either that Moses talked directly to God ("face to face" being an expression of the closeness of the communication) or that Moses talked to that member of the Triune God—Jesus—whom man is allowed to see (1). Others—Enoch (Genesis 5:24), Noah (Genesis 6:9), Abram (Genesis 12:7; 17:1; 18:1), Isaac (Genesis 26:2), Jacob (Genesis

32:30)—spoke of seeing God or walking with God. But these expressions again mean that the Spirit of God or the Son of God spoke or walked with them. "The angel of the Lord" is often mentioned in the Old Testament as a person who spoke with the ancients (Gideon, Judges 6:22; the parents of Samson, Judges 13:21-22), and that angel is generally viewed as God the Son, Jesus. Job saw Jesus (Job 42:5). Jesus is "the image of the invisible God" (Colossians 1:15). "No one has ever seen God" (John 1:18). In the Incarnation—God become man—we see the God that man cannot see.

". . . you cannot see my face, for no one may see me and live" (Exodus 33:20) is a principle commonly violated in the NDE, the modern-day counterfeit of dreams and visions. Mankind can see visions of angels or of Jesus the Son, but we cannot behold the glory of God the Father and survive. Paul spoke similarly when writing to Timothy, saying:

> *God, the blessed and only Ruler, the King of kings and Lord of lords, who alone is immortal and who lives in unapproachable light, whom no one has seen or can see. To him be honor and might forever. Amen.*
>
> —*1 Timothy 6:15-16*

Many of the reported NDEs contain descriptions of a person traveling to heaven. A "being of light," often identified as God the Father, is beheld. Most of these descriptions portray the trip to heaven as a powerful experience in a brilliant light. The traveler then journeys to the side of God. These encounters are direct contradictions with the Bible. No man can encounter the glory, perfection, and power of God and remain alive, which, of course, all of the "returning pilgrims" from their near-death experiences claim to be.

Furthermore, in John 3:13 we see that "No one has ever gone

into heaven except the one who came from heaven—the Son of Man." And in John 6:46 Jesus says: "No one has seen the Father except the one who is from God; only he has seen the Father." This verse expressly says that the privilege of traveling to and from heaven is restricted to Jesus alone.

PETER

Peter in Acts 10 had a vision while in a trance in which he saw animals being let down from heaven on a sheet. All of these animals were declared fit to eat, confirming the purity of all food as part of the newly-established covenant between God and man. This dream at the time might have been interpreted as a message contrary to the law of the Jewish nation, but it was actually a manifestation of the grace imparted to man through Jesus. This revelation was clearly a vision:

> *He became hungry and wanted something to eat, and while the meal was being prepared, he fell into a trance. He saw heaven opened and something like a large sheet being let down to earth by its four corners. It contained all kinds of four-footed animals, as well as reptiles of the earth and birds of the air. Then a voice told him, "Get up, Peter. Kill and eat."*
>
> *"Surely not, Lord!" Peter replied. "I have never eaten anything impure or unclean."*
>
> *The voice spoke to him a second time, "Do not call anything impure that God has made clean."*
>
> *This happened three times, and immediately the sheet was taken back to heaven.*
>
> *While Peter was wondering about the meaning of the vision, the men sent by Cornelius found out where Simon's house was and stopped at the gate. They called out, asking if Simon who was known as Peter was staying there. While Peter was still thinking about the vision, the Spirit*

> *said to him, "Simon, three men are looking for you. So get up and go downstairs. Do not hesitate to go with them, for I have sent them."*
>
> —*Acts 10:10-20*

There was no bodily danger to Peter, no out-of-body experience, no bright lights, no tunnel experience. This was a vision, pure and simple.

STEPHEN

Stephen had a vision that is commonly misinterpreted by the NDE advocates as an example of a biblical report of an NDE. In Acts 7, Stephen was lecturing to the men of the synagogue and offended them. They were convicted of their wrongdoing by Stephen's faith and power, and they called the council (the Sanhedrin) to hear accusations against Stephen. Stephen gave his discourse about the history of Israel, and then he called the elders of the Sanhedrin "stiff-necked people, with uncircumcised hearts and ears" (Acts 7:51). Acts 7:54-60 records:

> *When they heard this, they were furious and gnashed their teeth at him. But Stephen, full of the Holy Spirit, looked up to heaven and saw the glory of God, and Jesus standing at the right hand of God. "Look," he said, "I see heaven open and the Son of Man standing at the right hand of God." At this they covered their ears and, yelling at the top of their voices, they all rushed at him, dragged him out of the city and began to stone him. Meanwhile, the witnesses laid their clothes at the feet of a young man named Saul. While they were stoning him, Stephen prayed, "Lord Jesus, receive my spirit." Then he fell on his knees and cried out, "Lord, do not hold this sin against them." When he had said this, he fell asleep.*

Here Stephen has a vision while awake, and he beholds the glory of the Lord, then dies. But, true to Scripture, he does not live after seeing the glory of God. The Greek word used here for "asleep" is *koimao*, which can be used interchangeably for "sleep" or "death." God knew the course of events before they happened, and He gave Stephen a view of heaven and God's glory on the way to his death. He knew that Stephen was leaving his body to ascend into heaven. This was no NDE. The vision actually occurred *before* he was stoned. Stephen did not die, see a vision, and then return to the earth to report about it. The vision was a *pre-death* experience. He was inside the city walls during the vision but was stoned after he had been taken outside the city walls, as was the Jewish law for such punishment. However, the Sanhedrin did not bother with the formality of a trial or sentencing; they had witnessed what they considered to be blasphemy and decided to exact punishment immediately upon their own judgment.

So Stephen's vision was not an NDE; it did not occur during the stages of dying. There was no sequence of typical physical manifestations reported (tunnel vision, bright lights, passage through a tunnel, etc.). He did not return after his eventual death, and he did not report any of the encounters or conversations typically described by those who claim to have had an NDE. He was not outside his body. He simply had a vision from God.

SAUL

Probably the most famous vision in the New Testament was Saul's encounter with Jesus on his trip on the road to Damascus (Acts 9:3-6):

> *As he neared Damascus on his journey, suddenly a light from heaven flashed around him. He fell to the ground and heard a voice say to him, "Saul, Saul, why do you perse-*

cute me?" "Who are you, Lord?" Saul asked. "I am Jesus, whom you are persecuting," he replied. "Now get up and go into the city, and you will be told what you must do."

Saul then later described the vision to King Agrippa:

"On one of these journeys I was going to Damascus with the authority and commission of the chief priests. About noon, O king, as I was on the road, I saw a light from heaven, brighter than the sun, blazing around me and my companions. We all fell to the ground, and I heard a voice saying to me in Aramaic, 'Saul, Saul, why do you persecute me? It is hard for you to kick against the goads.' Then I asked, 'Who are you, Lord?' 'I am Jesus, whom you are persecuting,' the Lord replied. 'Now get up and stand on your feet. I have appeared to you to appoint you as a servant and as a witness of what you have seen of me and what I will show you. I will rescue you from your own people and from the Gentiles. I am sending you to them to open their eyes and turn them from darkness to light, and from the power of Satan to God, so that they may receive forgiveness of sins and a place among those who are sanctified by faith in me.'"

—Acts 26:12-18

Saul was one of the most violent persecutors of new Christians of his day, and his Damascus road conversion was punctuated by a vision of none other than Jesus Christ. This vision is consistent with previous descriptions of encounters with Jesus and the principles of visions found in both the Old and New Testaments. Moody tries to make this experience into an NDE (2-4). However, this vision was not an NDE; there was no out-of-body experience, no tunnel, no life review, and certainly no physical danger that brought him near death. Saul was blinded; the NDE does not produce blindness, nor does the bright light of the NDE cause pain.

PAUL

Saul thus became Paul, who had other visions as well. In Acts 18 and Acts 22 Jesus gave Paul direction and encouragement through visions, but Paul's other major vision is also cited as a possible example of an NDE—his "trip" to "the third heaven." Second Corinthians 12:2-7 gives us the story:

> *I know a man in Christ who fourteen years ago was caught up to the third heaven. Whether it was in the body or out of the body I do not know—God knows. And I know that this man—whether in the body or apart from the body I do not know, but God knows—was caught up to Paradise. He heard inexpressible things, things that man is not permitted to tell. I will boast about a man like that, but I will not boast about myself, except about my weaknesses. Even if I should choose to boast, I would not be a fool, because I would be speaking the truth. But I refrain, so no one will think more of me than is warranted by what I do or say. To keep me from becoming conceited because of these surpassingly great revelations, there was given me a thorn in my flesh, a messenger of Satan, to torment me.*

Paul's description of what happened to him is quite obscure, and it is not even certain that he is talking about himself, though most commentators agree that he is describing an event in his own life (5-9). It is presumed that he is actually talking about a single event and that he is using the typical Jewish style of repetition to emphasize the description of the event. Otherwise, one must conclude that he experienced two events that transported him (1) to the third heaven and (2) to paradise. He is probably talking about a single experience, and he uses the terms "third heaven" and "paradise" interchangeably.

But what was "the third heaven" or "paradise" mentioned by Paul? To understand his references, we must know the prevailing opinions about the afterlife—about the concepts of heaven and paradise during Paul's lifetime.

Historically, Jewish religion dealt little with the afterlife. The Israelites were more concerned with the fate of the people as a nation. They paid little attention to the concept of individual salvation but were more concerned with redemption in national terms. The Old Testament contains little discussion about the fate of the soul or spirit. In fact, early Hebrew writing did not emphasize the concept of the divisibility of the body and soul. Later, however, as individuality became more prominent in the culture, the concern for personal destiny became more important.

The word translated "Paradise" was borrowed from the Persian language and was used in the Hebrew, Greek, and Aramaic (5). It meant "garden" or "a park surrounded by a wall." The original Hebrew used this word only with this meaning, while the Septuagint used the equivalent of "paradise" to translate four different Hebrew words. The earliest use of the word "paradise" was in the description of the Garden of Eden. The concept of an ultimate home for the righteous borrowed the same word. If there was a paradise in the beginning, and if a paradise would exist in the future for the godly, then it was reasonable to assume that an invisible paradise must exist for the times in between as well.

It was also logical to conclude that the dead would occupy this paradise until the final, eternal paradise was established. In the non-canonical Apocalypse of Moses (37:5), "paradise" and "the third heaven" were synonymous. The intertestamental writings were filled with such concepts, in contrast to the Old Testament, in which there was little discussion of any locations for the dead except for the mention of Sheol.

Sheol was an underground netherworld, a dark, cold place where the dead resided, a place of relative quiet, a semiconscious existence. Sheol was often used synonymously with "death" or "the grave." Apparently in the early concepts seen in the Old

Testament, all of the dead went to Sheol as entities called "shades." However, in no early descriptions of Sheol was it a place of punishment in itself. It was simply a place of waiting, of inactivity, until some later unspecified time or until (as some mistakenly believed) spirits simply faded into nonexistence. Sheol and hades probably represent the same place because some references to hades depict it as the dwelling place of both the righteous and the unrighteous. Furthermore, in the Septuagint the word "hades" was used extensively to translate the word "Sheol."

The word "hades" derives from the Greek name Hades, a mythological god of the underworld. Hades, the place, was initially envisioned as a neutral place where neither the saint nor the rogue would reside. Saints went to Elysian fields, while the darkest sinner was banished to Tartarus, which was also underground. Like Sheol, hades was a dark, quiet underworld destination that had little, if any, connotation of punishment or torment.

In Hellenistic times (about 300 B.C.), Sheol began to be described as a place divided into two regions, one (an upper region) for the righteous and one (a lower region) for the wicked. These two locations were similar to the paradise (Abraham's bosom) and hades described in the New Testament (10). These views persisted until the time of Christ. It has even been suggested that the resurrection of the saints that occurred with Jesus' death was the liberation of the dead from Abraham's bosom (perhaps Sheol?) to either paradise or hades. Then, of course, they must await the final Great White Throne Judgment for their final reward or punishment. However, early Christian thought was little concerned with concepts of paradise or hades because most attention was directed toward the *parousia*—the return of Jesus to establish His kingdom. This event was thought to be imminent. Only when Jesus' return didn't occur quickly did Christians begin to think about intermediate states between death and the soul's final destination.

In Paul's time, it was commonly believed that there were seven heavens. Most detailed references to the seven heavens occur in the apocalyptic literature called the pseudepigrapha. Three books of Enoch relate some of the character of the seven heavens (5). They relate "secrets" that Enoch saw after his transport to heaven (11). Generally considered to be written around the time of the other books of the New Testament, they are uniformly (with rare exception) considered to be uninspired and were thus excluded from the canon of Holy Scripture. Specifically, in Slavonic Enoch the stages that Enoch saw on his way to the heavenly throne are described:

1. A place where angels guard the ice, snow, and dew.
2. The location of fallen angels who are in torment awaiting their final doom.
3. A paradise of the righteous and a place of torment for the wicked—sort of a holding tank for the departed awaiting their final judgment (purgatory for the Catholic religion).
4. The location of the sun, moon, and stars and their attending angels.
5. Satan and angels who revolted against God.
6. Angels who rule the forces of nature.
7. The throne of God where the archangels and heavenly glory reside.

An alternative classification was common in Jewish theology at about the same time, in which three heavens were acknowledged:

1. The nearby atmosphere.
2. The stars and constellations (outer space).
3. The heaven beyond the visible constellations.

Whether Paul's concept of heaven included seven divisions or three is unknown. In fact, the third heaven of the first system above (seven heavens) corresponds well with the third heaven of the second system (three heavens); both are the dwelling place of man at death. Other systems cite five heavens, ten heavens, or even seventy-two heavens! The exact system is unimportant. In fact, the Bible is remarkably silent about these heavenly systems. There are references to "heaven," "the heavens," and the "heaven of heavens," but the makeup of these celestial spheres is not well described. Paul, in talking about "the third heaven," was simply speaking about his vision in terms that were current, relevant, and understood at his time in history.

Paradise is mentioned only three times in the New Testament. In the first (Luke 23:43), Jesus tells the thief on the cross that he will be in paradise on that very day. He is thus talking about a place where the dead go immediately upon death. The second is the use by Paul in the 2 Corinthians 12 text, and the third is in Revelation 2:7 where Jesus speaks of paradise as the final home of the believer, where the tree of life is the reward for the saved.

Paradise and hades were often considered to be the intermediate "holding stations" for the dead prior to Christ's return to earth and the Great White Throne Judgment, from whence people will be sent to heaven or hell—sort of like a narthex outside the sanctuary. Some feel only non-believers will be judged at the Great White Throne, believers—the saved—having been dealt with at "the judgment seat of Christ" at a prior time. At any rate, paradise and hades are repositories for the spirit but will not be for the resurrected bodies, which will be sent to either heaven or hell. Luke 16 may indicate that people in paradise can actually see those in hades, and vice versa, though travel between the two is impossible.

It has been suggested, however, that Jesus was speaking figuratively or in parables when He was telling the disciples about Lazarus and the rich man and the ability to see one dwelling place from the other. So the relationship of hades to paradise may be only illustrative. Hades in this context in Luke includes some of the punishments described in hell (fire, torment, thirst, and separation or punishment), though most theologians agree that the two are different places. Furthermore, as Christian attention changed, the intermediate state in paradise or hades subtly merged with the concepts of heaven and hell, so that hardly any distinction exists between paradise and heaven or between hades and hell in the minds of the twentieth-century Christian.

Hell and *Gehenna* probably describe the same place—the location of final punishment to which the unsaved will be banished at the Great White Throne Judgment. In all descriptions, they have the connotation of unbearable punishment—fire, thirst, separation, anguish, worms, torment. Gehenna, of course, refers to the place of fire at the outskirts of Jerusalem, in the Valley of Hinnom. Originally it was a place of child sacrifice for pagan religions. It later was a place where trash was burned continuously, and it was unequivocally identified by the people of the time as a place to be avoided. *Gehenna* was a term known to the ancients before Jesus' time, while the word *hell* was used more commonly by the early Christian church. In the eternal scheme, hell or Gehenna is the place of final judgment where both the body and spirit reside, whereas hades was a place for the spirit only. Of course, the Pharisees and Sadducees differed greatly in their concepts of the resurrection of the body—the Pharisees believed in it, but the Sadducees did not.

Heaven in itself was not always envisioned as a place of unchallenged joy, peace, and beauty. In Old Testament times, it was actually a site of turmoil and conflict between good and evil; witness the story of Job. However, the eternal heaven of the New Testament is indeed a blissful place of everlasting joy, peace, and rest.

Why be interested in the distinctions among the various destinations of the spirit? It is important for the understanding of the descriptions of the people who claim to have been to heaven or hell and back. If indeed there is an intermediate stage where the spirit passes awaiting the final resurrection of the body, then virtually all of the NDEs are incorrect in their eschatology. It thus would appear quite likely that the heaven reported in NDEs is not even theologically correct.

However, the order of eternal geography is not precisely delivered to us in the form of a road map. We cannot be certain about the relative positions of paradise, Abraham's bosom, and heaven, nor of Sheol, hades, hell, or Gehenna. We must accept God's justice with faith and believe that He has the ultimate knowledge of our travels, including the time that we are to depart from this body.

Did Paul's vision of paradise occur in the throes of a near-death event? If so, he certainly does not describe it as such. He saw no tunnels, and he described no bright lights. However, Paul had many occasions during which he may have been severely ill or beaten to the point of death. Indeed, he catalogs his experiences of beatings and torture later in 2 Corinthians 11:24-27:

> *Five times I received from the Jews the forty lashes minus one. Three times I was beaten with rods, once I was stoned, three times I was shipwrecked, I spent a night and a day in the open sea, I have been constantly on the move. I have been in danger from rivers, in danger from bandits, in danger from my own countrymen, in danger from Gentiles; in danger in the city, in danger in the country, in danger at sea; and in danger from false brothers. I have labored and toiled and have often gone without sleep; I have known hunger and thirst and have often gone without food; I have been cold and naked.*

So he had many opportunities to have had an NDE, if it exists. But the fact is that he does not describe this experience as the result of being near death. It has been suggested that it could have occurred with one of his stonings at Lystra described in Acts 14:19:

> *Then some Jews came from Antioch and Iconium and won the crowd over. They stoned Paul and dragged him outside the city, thinking he was dead.*

This passage does not describe any NDE or vision, however, and it is only speculation whether it is the event to which Paul refers in 2 Corinthians.

Modern scholars have tried to set a date for the visionary event in paradise that Paul describes and/or to place it at Lystra (6-7). Fourteen years before his writing about the event would place it at about A.D. 44, the range of times accepted by most experts being from A.D. 41-44. This date would not match any of the dates known for the major illnesses, beatings, floggings, stonings, or shipwrecks mentioned by Paul. P. E. Hughes (7) points out that Paul was not at all reluctant to speak about his Damascus road experience (which occurred years *before* 44 A.D.), nor was he silent about his trance and vision in Jerusalem (Acts 22:17) a few years after his Damascus road conversion. But this particular experience could not be expressed in words.

Paul also talked freely about his vision on the second trip to Jerusalem (Acts 11:30; Galatians 2:2), which probably occurred too late to be confused with the 44 A.D. experience. Likewise, other visions both are different in character and later in time than 44 A.D. (the Macedonian vision, Acts 16:9; the Corinthian vision, Acts 18:9). His trip to Arabia (Galatians 1:17) was before 44 A.D., and the stoning at Lystra (Acts 14:19) was after 44 A.D. Thus, scholars tend to think that the vision described by Paul occurred during his stay at Antioch (Acts 11:26), during which time he had no known serious trauma or illnesses.

Furthermore, Paul does not relate to us any of the other features of an NDE, and he specifically states that the things that he saw were "inexpressible" and things he was "not permitted to tell." Paul was perhaps the greatest Christian ever to live and one of the most verbal and prolific writers of the New Testament (a man never accused of being quiet or at a loss for words). But he was not able or was not allowed to describe what he saw in his vision. This contrasts sharply with those who allege to have experienced the NDE.

But what happened during Paul's vision? We will never know because he said that it was not proper for him to elaborate on its features. Paul was living during a time in which the Gnostic view held that a *true* believer was *always* blessed with ecstatic visions. Mystical sightings abounded. Many writings of the time report the transport of the believer to paradise or heaven. Indeed, the extensive system of heavens was no doubt an attempt to reconcile the many reports generated by the faithful. All Gnostic religious experience indeed required a mystical encounter, and it was usually gladly shared with other believers.

Paul's ministry had been challenged in Corinth, but he refrained from boasting about any visions he may have seen. The Corinthians wanted to hear that their leaders had mystical experiences as evidence for the authenticity for their leadership. Paul could have told them of many miraculous events and visions, but he chose to leave the question open—his experience may have been in the body or out of the body. Whatever his location, Paul was satisfied to give the glory to God and to avoid talking about his trip to paradise. His vision was not the means of authenticating his ministry, nor should any NDE be used for that purpose today.

Certainly Paul's vision could have been a physiologic event during one of the times he was near death; but if so, he interpreted it as a true revelation from God. So that he would not boast about it, though, he was given a "thorn in my flesh," variably thought to possibly be (6-7):

1. A disorder of his eyes (he was blinded for three days after his Damascus vision and may have had some resid-

ual eye disorder; in Galatians 6:11 he speaks of writing in large letters; in Galatians 4:15 he refers to the desire of the Galatians to give their eyes to him; in Acts 23:5 he does not recognize the high priest who is standing before him).

2. Epilepsy (some see Paul's falling down on the Damascus road as a seizure).
3. Malaria.
4. Or other less likely physical conditions such as a speech impediment, gastritis, lice, deafness, toothaches, etc.

Paul kept his thorn, whatever it may have been, to himself.

Apocryphal literature—the "Vision of Paul," variably titled the "Revelation of Paul" and the "Apocalypse of the Apostle Paul"—allegedly contains descriptions of the journey that Paul took to paradise (9). This revelation was actually a description written and contained in a marble box supposedly hidden under the foundation of his house in Tarsus in Cilicia, along with some shoes worn by Paul on his travels. The box was purportedly unearthed in about A.D. 388, though the earliest authenticated manuscript now available regarding this report seems to be from the thirteenth century A.D. It describes a vision of the gathering of souls at death by the angels of either paradise or hades. At a person's death, both groups of angels would meet at the body, and the appropriate team of angels would take possession of the person's soul to carry it from this earthly life.

Paul allegedly first saw the city of righteousness, which was a city with a golden gate, golden pillars at the entrance, and golden plates with inscriptions of the eternal inhabitants along with their deeds listed at the portals. Paul described the City of God as a place of great light. He later was escorted to the place of punishment where he saw many church people who had been hypocrites during their lives on earth. Ironically, for Paul's sake, the wicked were given a day of rest from their torment. He then saw paradise and was given the opportunity to meet with many patriarchs—Abraham, Isaac, Jacob, Joseph, Moses, Isaiah, Jeremiah, Noah, and others.

While this description is entertaining, it has no authenticity. Paul himself said that the mysteries he saw in paradise were "inexpressible," and he told us that it was unlawful for man to repeat the wonders that he saw in his vision. For this reason, Saint Augustine thought this "Revelation of Paul" was not authentic. The church fathers evaluated it and also rejected it as unauthentic, beginning at the Council of Carthage in A.D. 397 (12). But even if it were authentic, it was nevertheless not an NDE.

The end result of Paul's experience in the third heaven typifies the Christian's ever-present struggle—whether to wish for paradise and heaven to come soon or to persevere and complete the appointed work here on earth. Paul's summary statement in Philippians 1:21 was: "For to me, to live is Christ and to die is gain."

OTHERS

The book of Revelation, of course, is the most extensive vision recorded in the Bible. It was a vision given to St. John over an unspecified time period and covering many aspects of the last days. John was an old man when he received the vision, though there is no suggestion that any of his vision was associated with an illness or injury that brought him close to death. It contains no features of an NDE, though in the vision John did see Jesus.

What is the difference between a vision and a hallucination? A vision is the appearance of an image that has no physical correlate, but which usually does not connote any mental instability. A hallucination also has no physical correlate, but on the other hand it denotes mental illness. So the difference resides in the mental state of the person having the experience. The difference can be hard to distinguish. There are no hallucinations as such recorded in the Bible, though persons are described who were mentally ill. However, today we must assiduously guard against interpreting hallucinations as godly visions from people who report unusual experiences.

The descriptions of the NDE seem to fall in the category of visions, if NDEs exist at all, and if we are to believe what has been written. Visions, like NDEs, are often bound to the era and culture. The NDE should be evaluated with caution when we assess its descriptions of heaven and hell. The NDE is an exclusive and personal event that cannot be validated by an outside observer. Such can also be said of dreams, visions, or hallucinations. Too often today it seems that the report of a vision or an NDE is an attempt to gain fame or money or both for the storyteller. We should beware of those visions or NDEs that serve as a principal basis for a ministry or life experience. Visions should point the way toward God, not to the messenger or the messenger's bank account.

As we assess the physical explanations for the components of the NDE, we must accept the possibility that they could be simply the brain's synthesis of the physical input from cells deprived of oxygen. Thus, the NDE would fall into the category of illusions—the incorrect interpretations of real sensations.

9

TRANSLATIONS AND HEALINGS IN THE BIBLE

You Only Go Around Once in This Life

Emily Carter was not prepared for her diagnosis. She was only in her early fifties, and she had so much living to do. Her fourth grade class was only part of her life. She had a wonderful husband. One daughter was about to graduate from medical school, and the other was finishing college. But she had been feeling weak and tired recently, and she had gone to the doctor thinking that she must have a mild anemia or some long-lasting virus. But not cancer! How could she have cancer? She had no other symptoms. And ovarian cancer, at that. Her doctor told her that it was far advanced, in her lungs and liver at the very least, perhaps elsewhere. Chemotherapy could shrink the size of the tumors, but it would probably not cure her in such an advanced condition. She knew she had to agree to the chemotherapy. It was her only medical hope.

Of course, her real hope was in God. Her faith was strong, and her support system in the church would help her cope with this crisis. She mobilized all of her friends to pray for her, and pray they did.

Her spirit was strong, and because the children she taught in her elementary school class had heard that she was sick, she decided to tell them about her diagnosis and impending treatment. They seemed to take it well, and they also prayed for her. It was a Christian school, so prayer—even very specific prayer—was encouraged.

But over the weeks she sensed that the children were uncomfortable. One boy even asked her what he was supposed to do if she collapsed in class. Was he supposed to call Medic I? Was he supposed to do CPR? Or was he supposed to let her die to go to be with Jesus? The children were being unnecessarily burdened by her illness and chemotherapy, so she decided to take a leave of absence and let a substitute complete the year for her. She knew she probably wouldn't be able to complete the school year anyway.

The news media caught wind of her plight, and a television station ran a special report about her, her family, and the school class. It was supposed to be a human interest story about coping with cancer, but the talk show hostess was clearly moved by the story of how Emily's faith in God was sustaining her through this illness. It wasn't exactly politically correct to be speaking about God on television, but the station ran it anyway because the story was so compelling. Emily wanted to see her children graduate, but she understood that God's will might be otherwise. Her husband seemed to have more difficulty accepting her illness. After all, it was Emily who was going to her reward, and he would have to deal with the absence and loneliness left behind.

Emily fell out of the public view for a few months as she endured the chemotherapy. A few weeks after the last treatment, she went back for her checkup, expecting to find that the tumors had shrunk slightly. To her surprise (but not her students' because their childlike faith was strong), she was told there was no evidence of any remaining cancer anywhere! It was a cure! Or was it?

Should she wait a few years before declaring that she indeed had been healed? Maybe the tumors were just smaller and couldn't be seen. Maybe they would grow again. Or maybe the original diagnosis was wrong.

But Emily knew she had been healed. She wanted to tell the world. The television station ran another special about her, in prime time now. It was a bigger story and allowed them to feature the issue of miraculous healing. This topic had become more politically correct with all of the recent interest in angels sweeping the country. Do miracles happen? Are they to be believed? Was this the work of faith or of chemotherapy? But more importantly, underlying the whole story, was the question, does God control our lives and direct the time of our death?

TRANSLATIONS

There are at least two examples of a person being taken to heaven without tasting death, though neither returned to tell any story. Elijah was taken to heaven directly. Elijah and Elisha were walking together at the River Jordan, and from a distance fifty witnesses watched them. Elijah was transported to heaven in a fiery chariot and a whirlwind, as recorded in 2 Kings 2:11:

> *As they were walking along and talking together, suddenly a chariot of fire and horses of fire appeared and separated the two of them, and Elijah went up to heaven in a whirlwind.*

No mention is made of any return to earth at that time, though anticipation of Elijah's return is an integral part of Jewish tradition and ceremony.

Enoch also escaped death and traveled directly to heaven. In Genesis 5:24 we see that "Enoch walked with God; then he was no more, because God took him away." The reference here is a bit obscure and depends upon the preceding descriptions of life and death of other men of the Old Testament. The wording given to the end of life for Adam (Genesis 5:5), Seth (Genesis 5:8), Enosh (Genesis 5:11), Kenan (Genesis 5:14), Mahalalel (Genesis 5:17), Jared (Genesis 5:20), Methuselah (Genesis 5:27), and Lamech (Genesis 5:31) is "and he died." No such description was given for Enoch. In Hebrews 11:5 the event is clarified:

> *By faith Enoch was taken from this life, so that he did not experience death; he could not be found, because God had taken him away. For before he was taken, he was commended as one who pleased God.*

In the Canonized Scriptures, there is no mention of any return to the earth by Enoch to relate what he saw in heaven. However, the pseudepigrapha, thought to have been written or discovered sometime between 200 B.C. and A.D. 100, contains extensive writings about Enoch's visions. The pseudepigrapha include three distinct works: I Enoch (Ethiopian Enoch, probably written about 165-54 B.C. and divided into five sections that were written individually, making it a composite work); II Enoch (Slavonic Enoch); and III Enoch (Hebrew Enoch) (1). In II Enoch there is a story of Enoch's return to earth and a description of the secret sights that he saw in heaven, the end-times, the coming Kingdom of God, and the secrets of the present life. Sheol was described here in more detail than in previous works as a place where the good and the bad were separated.

But precisely the reason that this book was not included in the Bible is the reason that we must look askance at its believability; it has been judged to be unauthentic and uninspired. It was supposedly written before the great flood, and it is uncertain how—or if—it could have survived. It was discovered in about the first century B.C., the time during which reports of ecstatic visions flourished. It was during this time frame that many stories were fabricated about the ancient patriarchs. It was commonplace for true stories to be embellished to make a specific point or to illustrate a principle. Thus its original authenticity simply cannot be documented.

Furthermore, the descriptions of heaven are quite vague and obscure, and the vision—even if true—has nothing to do with a near-death experience. The sequence of recorded events is different from the stereotyped NDE, and critical factors of the NDE are missing, such as the tunnel experience and the command to return to the earth as a "revived" human. Some theologians accept the veracity of I Enoch because it is quoted in Jude 14-15, but simple quotation of this short passage from I Enoch in Jude does not authenticate the entire book:

> *Enoch, the seventh from Adam, prophesied about these men: "See, the Lord is coming with thousands upon thousands of his holy ones to judge everyone, and to convict all the ungodly of all the ungodly acts they have done in the ungodly way, and of all the harsh words ungodly sinners have spoken against him."*

Other biblical passages refer to non-canonical works and do not imply acceptance of divine inspiration for these works. So we cannot rely upon Enoch's alleged "experience" as evidence to support the concept of the NDE because it is (1) not an NDE and (2) probably not an authentic description. In fact, scholars in the Christian church have recently had occasion to renounce I Enoch as false, related to its propagation by Elizabeth Clare Prophet in her book *Forbidden Mysteries of Enoch—The Untold Story of Men and Angels* (2). She claims that the book was suppressed by authorities centuries ago and that it contains secrets about angels and heavens that are crucial to our existence and happiness. Most theologians deny this claim.

PHILIP

Other less dramatic examples of translation have been cited as evidence for the NDE. Philip was talking with the Ethiopian eunuch about salvation in Acts 8. After the eunuch accepted Christ as Savior and was baptized, Philip disappeared (Acts 8:39): "When they came up out of the water, the Spirit of the Lord suddenly took Philip away, and the eunuch did not see him again, but went on his way rejoicing." Philip then reappeared at Azotus (Acts 8:40), but there is no mention of any encounters with God or trips to heaven. This translation of Philip could simply have been a normal journey to Azotus by earthly means. It is possible that the description given in Acts simply means that Philip was obeying the Holy Spirit to go to Azotus and that he accomplished this trip by non-miraculous means of transportation, much as we do today when we feel the pull of the Holy Spirit to do something.

On the other hand, it could indeed mean that his trip to Azotus was accomplished by supernatural means. In either case, there was no near-death, no NDE, and no description of what happened to Philip between Jerusalem and Gaza and his destination in Azotus.

SUPERNATURAL HEALINGS

The New Testament is full of accounts of Jesus healing the people with whom He came in contact. The healings include all manner of illnesses, including some that are not specifically identified:

Blindness	*Matthew 20; Mark 10; Luke 18*
	Mark 8
	John 9
	Matthew 9

Demon possession	*Matthew 9*
	Matthew 12; Luke 11
	Matthew 17; Mark 9; Luke 9
	Mark 1; Luke 4
	Matthew 8; Mark 5; Luke 8
	Matthew 15; Mark 7
Muteness	*Matthew 9*
	Matthew 12; Luke 11
	Mark 7
Deafness	*Mark 7*
Leprosy	*Matthew 8; Mark 1; Luke 5*
	Luke 17
Paralysis/crippled or shriveled extremities	*Matthew 9; Mark 2; Luke 5*
	Matthew 12; Mark 3; Luke 6
	Luke 13
	John 5
	Matthew 8; Luke 7
Uterine bleeding	*Matthew 9; Mark 5; Luke 8*
Dropsy (fluid retention)	*Luke 14*
Fevers	*Matthew 8; Mark 1; Luke 4*
	John 4
Traumatic severing of an ear	*Luke 22*

As we read these accounts, we see that most of these would not have been expected to have had any NDE associated with them, except perhaps the demon possession and the fevers, some of which were described as serious illnesses approaching death. But the NDE was simply not a part of the ministry and theology of our

Lord. Had it been important, He had numerous opportunities to reveal what could happen at the edge of death; but that was not a part of His teachings. In fact, it says in the story of the beggar Lazarus (Luke 16:19-31) that the return of a person from the dead—from hell or heaven—would have no effect on man's commitment on earth. Man has the stories of the ancients, the prophets in the Bible, and other biblical accounts to convince him that Jesus is the Way.

The Bible specifically addresses this issue and declares the NDE to be a worthless form of religious inducement.

> *"'No, father Abraham,' [the rich man] said, 'but if someone from the dead goes to them, they will repent.' He said to them, 'If they do not listen to Moses and the Prophets, they will not be convinced even if someone rises from the dead.'"*
>
> —*Luke 16:30-31*

In no case did any of the healed people claim an experience other than an encounter with Jesus in His earthly form. And no one expected otherwise.

10

RESUSCITATIONS AND RESURRECTIONS IN THE BIBLE

Death Is Life's Last Test, But You Can't Rehearse for It

Sally Carson had always been a devout Christian. But she was gullible. She would believe anything that came down the road. Discernment certainly was not one of her gifts. So it was not too unusual for her to believe the story that her friend, Margaret Singer, told her.

Margaret's husband Alan was fifty years old and in excellent health. He was always thankful that he had been blessed with freedom from all of the ailments many of his friends were beginning to complain about—arthritis, lung problems (usually from smoking), even some with heart pains, and a next-door neighbor who recently needed a coronary bypass operation. But Alan was a Christian, too, and he knew where he was headed for eternity. He had also heard the stories from friends at Overlake Christian Church about people who had died and gone to heaven—or to hell.

Then came that fateful Monday. Alan was getting ready for work when the chest pains struck. After only a few minutes of pain, everything went dim, and then he collapsed to the floor. He drifted in and out of consciousness, but always with that horrendous sensation of an elephant sitting on his chest. He remembers the Medics arriving and talking about the "PVC's" and the "VT." He didn't know what these letters meant, but they must be bad because the Medics seemed distressed, and his pain was unrelenting. Alan even remembered the Medics pumping on his chest briefly. He thought CPR was only used after you had died, and he fought them intermittently until they gave him some medicine that forced unconsciousness upon him for the rest of the day.

When he awoke, he could remember little of the events that Monday morning. Oh, yes, the pain, of course. But not much else. Except the drifting in and out of consciousness—or was it in and out of his body? And those sounds and lights! What were they? Were they the trip to paradise that he had heard about? Certainly! That's what it had to be! And by the time Sally came to visit him on Wednesday, he had it all figured out. The light was the vision of Jesus, just like he had heard from his friends. And so the story grew.

Sally was enthralled. Alan had seen Jesus! Her friend Margaret's husband had seen the Savior! That confirmed all that Sally had read. She had so many questions. What was Jesus like? What color hair did He have? Was He tall? So many questions, and Alan tried to answer them to the best of his memory. His memory wasn't fabricated, but it was affected—because he'd had a heavenly experience, given to him (he thought) by God.

Sally took it all in. And she could not be dissuaded in her belief that a friend of hers had actually been to heaven and back. Or had he? What does the Bible say about such events?

RESUSCITATIONS

The accounts of resuscitation and resurrection that we find scattered throughout the Bible in both the Old and New Testaments could shed light upon the NDE.

The difference between resuscitation and resurrection is no

less important in the Bible than in modern medicine. Resuscitation is the revival of a person who is "clinically dead," usually meaning having no vital signs—no pulse or blood pressure and not breathing. Resuscitation, which reverses more than mere unconsciousness, must occur before "biologic death" supervenes—before the body begins to decompose by cell death. Resurrection, on the other hand, is the restoration of life to someone in whom the process of decomposition has begun.

Resuscitation is a process that must begin early, within a few minutes of collapse; resurrection can occur anytime later, but it must be clear that death has been established for a considerable length of time for it to be called a resurrection. The time frames of the two processes can be difficult to distinguish and can even be arbitrary. After a few minutes with no blood flow, brain cells begin to die, though other brain cells can recover if resuscitation of the cardiovascular system is successful. Death is *not* an instantaneous, all-or-none phenomenon.

The Widow's Son from Zarephath

The first reported resuscitation is the account of the widow's son from Zarephath in 1 Kings 17:17-23:

> *Some time later the son of the woman who owned the house became ill. He grew worse and worse, and finally stopped breathing. She said to Elijah, "What do you have against me, man of God? Did you come to remind me of my sin and kill my son?"*
>
> *"Give me your son," Elijah replied. He took him from her arms, carried him to the upper room where he was staying, and laid him on his bed. Then he cried out to the LORD, "O LORD my God, have you brought tragedy also upon this widow I am staying with, by causing her son to die?" Then he stretched himself out on the boy three times*

> *and cried to the LORD, "O LORD my God, let this boy's life return to him!"*
>
> *The LORD heard Elijah's cry, and the boy's life was returned to him, and he lived. Elijah picked up the child and carried him down from the room into the house. He gave him to his mother and said, "Look, your son is alive!"*

This story recounts the first report of cardiopulmonary resuscitation (CPR) in the Bible. The child was ill (Hebrew *chalah*, meaning "sick" or "afflicted"), and the sickness was so bad that there was no breath left in him. Clearly the child was clinically dead because he was not breathing. The widow blamed Elijah for bringing this catastrophe upon her, though she thought the sickness was possibly punishment for her sins. She states that she feared Elijah had come to "kill" or "slay" her son (Hebrew *muwth*, meaning "to die" or "to put to death"). Here is a fatal illness, not just a serious one.

Elijah stretched himself upon the child, a maneuver thought to be similar in effect to the chest compression of CPR. The child revived (Hebrew *chayah*, meaning "to live," "to recover," or "to restore to life"). This event clearly is a resuscitation, not a resurrection. The child, nevertheless, was not reported to have described any visions or revelations after travel to another realm or heaven. Here would have been an opportunity to record such an event if it had been in God's plan, but it is conspicuous by its absence. The NDE as described in the popular press is simply not a part of God's design.

The Shunammite Woman's Son

The next example of a resuscitation is found in 2 Kings 4:18-37. It is the resuscitation of a child by Elisha:

> *The child grew, and one day he went out to his father, who was with the reapers. "My head! My head!" he said to his father.*

His father told a servant, "Carry him to his mother." After the servant had lifted him up and carried him to his mother, the boy sat on her lap until noon, and then he died. She went up and laid him on the bed of the man of God, then shut the door and went out.

She called her husband and said, "Please send me one of of the servants and a donkey so I can go to the man of God quickly and return."

"Why go to him today?" he asked. "It's not the New Moon or the Sabbath."

"It's all right," she said.

She saddled the donkey and said to her servant, "Lead on; don't slow down for me unless I tell you." So she set out and came to the man of God at Mount Carmel.

When he saw her in the distance, the man of God said to his servant Gehazi, "Look! There's the Shunammite! Run to meet her and ask her, 'Are you all right? Is your husband all right? Is your child all right?'"

"Everything is all right," she said.

When she reached the man of God at the mountain, she took hold of his feet. Gehazi came over to push her away, but the man of God said, "Leave her alone! She is in bitter distress, but the LORD has hidden it from me and has not told me why."

"Did I ask you for a son, my lord?" she said. "Didn't I tell you, 'Don't raise my hopes'?"

Elisha said to Gehazi, "Tuck your cloak into your belt, take my staff in your hand and run. If you meet anyone, do not greet him, and if anyone greets you, do not answer. Lay my staff on the boy's face."

But the child's mother said, "As surely as the LORD lives and as you live, I will not leave you." So he got up and followed her.

Gehazi went on ahead and laid the staff on the boy's face, but there was no sound or response. So Gehazi went back to meet Elisha and told him, "The boy has not awakened."

> *When Elisha reached the house, there was the boy lying dead on his couch. He went in, shut the door on the two of them and prayed to the LORD. Then he got on the bed and lay upon the boy, mouth to mouth, eyes to eyes, hands to hands. As he stretched himself out upon him, the boy's body grew warm. Elisha turned away and walked back and forth in the room and then got on the bed and stretched out upon him once more. The boy sneezed seven times and opened his eyes.*
>
> *Elisha summoned Gehazi and said, "Call the Shunammite." And he did. When she came, he said, "Take your son." She came in, fell at his feet and bowed to the ground. Then she took her son and went out.*

Elisha successfully revived the Shunammite woman's son, starting appropriately with prayer. It is conjectured that the child had suffered some type of intracerebral catastrophe, such as a ruptured intracranial aneurysm, because of the statement, "My head, my head!" (verse 19), followed immediately by his collapse and soon thereafter by his death. Though some writers have suggested that the boy had sunstroke (1), such a diagnosis is unlikely. There is no question in the original text that the son was dead; the writer uses the Hebrew word *muwth*, which means "to die." Gehazi attempted to "awaken" the lad by putting Elisha's staff on his face, to no avail. Verse 32 again states that the boy was "*muwth*"—"dead."

Elisha then performed a series of maneuvers also reminiscent of today's CPR: lying on the child, putting mouth to mouth, eyes to eyes, hands to hands, and stretching himself on the boy. The flesh of the child became warm, and the child revived. In the process of this resuscitation, the child sneezed seven times. It was widely thought at that time that sneezing represented the passage of the soul into or out of a body, and the number seven is always associated with perfection or completeness.

Thus the child was restored to life—a resuscitation, not a resurrection because not enough time had elapsed to be certain of the beginning of bodily decay.

There is no mention of the child relating any visions or revelations after returning from his near-death experience. Of course, absence of proof of evidence is not proof of absence of evidence, but it would have seemed to have been an ideal opportunity to reveal such visions if they were a part of God's plan. But the book of 2 Kings is silent on the matter. Suspiciously silent.

The New Testament contains two accounts of apparent resuscitation (Jairus' daughter and Eutychus) and five descriptions of resurrection (the man at Nain, Jesus' friend Lazarus, Tabitha, the resurrection of the saints, and Jesus Himself).

Jairus' Daughter

The story of the raising of Jairus' daughter is reported in Matthew, Mark, and Luke. We read in Matthew 9:

> *While [Jesus] was saying this, a ruler came and knelt before him and said, "My daughter has just died. But come and put your hand on her, and she will live." Jesus got up and went with him, and so did his disciples. . . .*
>
> *When Jesus entered the ruler's house and saw the flute players and the noisy crowd, he said, "Go away. The girl is not dead but asleep." But they laughed at him. After the crowd had been put outside, he went in and took the girl by the hand, and she got up.*
>
> —*verses 18, 19, 23-25*

Here the Greek clarifies the sequence of events, though the interpretation of this passage is by no means unanimous. Most commentators state outright that the girl was dead. Indeed, the father thought that she was dead. He used the word *teleutao* to describe her, which means "to finish life, expire, die, be dead." The father believed that she was indeed dead. However, Jesus said that the maid was "*not* dead," using the Greek *apothnesko* ("to die or be dead") in the negative. He continued, "but asleep" (verse 24). Here he used the word *katheudo*, which means "to lie down," "rest," or "fall asleep." It is not a word that can be used interchangeably for either sleep or death. Often writers of Jesus' time (as today) used the euphemism "sleep" to mean "death." But when using such a construction, the Greek writers would use the word *koimao*, which can mean either "to put to sleep or slumber," "to sleep," or "to be dead." Contrast this use with the use found in 1 Corinthians 15:6, where we find the description of the 500 people who saw Jesus after His resurrection:

> *After that, [Jesus] appeared to more than five hundred of the brothers at the same time, most of whom are still living, though some have fallen* asleep. *(emphasis mine)*

Here Paul says that some of the brethren have died, and he uses *koimao*, used interchangeably for sleep and death. Also, in Acts 7:60 we see another use of "sleep" where the writer Luke actually means death when he is describing Stephen:

> *Then he fell on his knees and cried out, "Lord, do not hold this sin against them." When he had said this, he fell* asleep. *(emphasis mine)*

Luke writes according to the custom of the time and uses *koimao* (translated "asleep"). Jesus in describing Jairus' daughter did not use *koimao*, the word with dual meanings. He said plainly that she was "*asleep*," using *katheudo*, which can only mean "slumber." Thus the crowd mocked Him because they thought her to be dead. He simply took her by the hand, and she arose. What could have been her condition in this sleep? Other passages give us clues.

In Mark 5:22-24, 35-43, a parallel account to that in Matthew's Gospel, we read:

> *One of the synagogue rulers, named Jairus, came there. Seeing Jesus, he fell at his feet and pleaded earnestly with him, "My little daughter is dying. Please come and put your hands on her so that she will be healed and live." So Jesus went with him.*
>
> *A large crowd followed and pressed around him. . . .*
>
> *While Jesus was still speaking, some men came from the house of Jairus, the synagogue ruler. "Your daughter is dead," they said. "Why bother the teacher any more?"*
>
> *Ignoring what they said, Jesus told the synagogue ruler, "Don't be afraid; just believe."*
>
> *He did not let anyone follow him except Peter, James and John the brother of James. When they came to the home of the synagogue ruler, Jesus saw a commotion, with people crying and wailing loudly. He went in and said to them, "Why all this commotion and wailing? The child is not dead but asleep." But they laughed at him.*
>
> *After he put them all out, he took the child's father and mother and the disciples who were with him, and went in where the child was. He took her by the hand and said to her, "Talitha koum!" (which means, "Little girl, I say to you, get up!"). Immediately the girl stood up and walked around (she was twelve years old). At this they were completely astonished. He gave strict orders not to let anyone know about this, and told them to give her something to eat.*

Here the father again expressed his belief that his daughter was about to die, then that she was dead. He used *eschatos* to mean that she was at "the extremity of life" or at "the point of death" in verse 23. The news then came from the ruler's home that the child was dead—*apothnesko*—in verse 35. Here too we see that Jesus said she was not *apothnesko* but *katheudo*, meaning unequivocally that He was speaking about sleep. He did not use *koimao*. He later told her to arise, using *egeiro*, which means to waken or rouse *from sleep*. Then He did something that was not recorded in Matthew—

He commanded that they give her something to eat. The word here is *phago*, which means "to eat" or "to eat meat."

In a third account of this miracle by our Lord—Luke 8:41-42, 49-56—we see an even more specific account, this time from a physician who was accustomed to making detailed observations:

> *Just then a man named Jairus, a ruler of the synagogue, came and fell at Jesus' feet, pleading with him to come to his house because his only daughter, a girl of about twelve, was dying.*
>
> *As Jesus was on his way, the crowds almost crushed him. . . .*
>
> *While Jesus was still speaking, someone came from the house of Jairus, the synagogue ruler. "Your daughter is dead," he said. "Don't bother the teacher any more."*
>
> *Hearing this, Jesus said to Jairus, "Don't be afraid; just believe, and she will be healed."*
>
> *When he arrived at the house of Jairus, he did not let anyone go in with him except Peter, John and James, and the child's father and mother. Meanwhile, all the people were wailing and mourning for her. "Stop wailing," Jesus said. "She is not dead but asleep."*
>
> *They laughed at him, knowing that she was dead. But he took her by the hand and said, "My child, get up!" Her spirit returned, and at once she stood up. Then Jesus told them to give her something to eat. Her parents were astonished, but he ordered them not to tell anyone what had happened.*

Again the same words are used. *Apothnesko* for the crowd's description of the daughter's state: "to die." *Thnesko* for the later report: "dead." But Jesus said she was not dead but slept: *katheudo*. He then raised her and commanded that she be given something to eat. The *King James Version* says, "he commanded to give her *meat*" [emphasis mine]. We know now that a person suffering from hypoglycemia (low blood sugar) can lapse into a coma and be unresponsive. Jesus recognized this condition and assured the family that she was simply in a coma—"asleep" as opposed to being dead. After raising her, He told them to give her meat. Protein is good for a person with hypoglycemia because it causes a more effective rise in blood sugar, more controlled and sustained than with carbohydrates. Protein avoids the sudden rise in blood sugar that is frequently followed by a dramatic rebound fall in blood sugar that could cause the condition of hypoglycemic coma to return. This was good medical advice before anyone even knew about hypoglycemia! And there was no report of any NDE!

This story emphasizes the difficulty that can sometimes be present in diagnosing death. Many conditions can slow the bodily processes enough to make the patient appear to be dead. Hypoglycemia is just one. Anything that causes a lowering of body temperature (hypothermia) can also mimic death. Furthermore, it is well-known that patients "declared" dead by a physician can return to life, even after resuscitation efforts have been discontinued—the so-called "Lazarus syndrome" (2-9).

Eutychus

Paul has had attributed to him a healing that may have been a resuscitation, though the details are not as clear. In Acts 20:9-12 we read:

> *Seated in a window was a young man named Eutychus, who was sinking into a deep sleep as Paul talked on and on. When he was sound asleep, he fell to the ground from the third story and was picked up dead. Paul went down, threw himself on the young man and put his arms around him. "Don't be alarmed," he said. "He's alive!" Then he went upstairs again and broke bread and ate. After talking until daylight, he left. The people took the young man home alive and were greatly comforted.*

Paul was a long-winded preacher! How embarrassing to have a listener fall into a deep sleep, let alone fall from a windowsill. It is unclear what the bystanders thought his injuries to be. Nevertheless, those around him took him for dead. Here is where the confusion arises. The wording seems to suggest that Paul was telling them that even though they thought Eutychus was dead, he was actually alive. The word used here is *nekros*, meaning "dead." But Paul was quoting what the bystanders were thinking, not necessarily the actual medical condition as Paul himself saw it. He said, "Don't be alarmed. He's alive!" But that statement was made *after* Paul embraced him. So it is possible that Paul had revived Eutychus before telling the crowd everything was O.K. Nevertheless, the fact is that Eutychus was alive. Eutychus gave no account himself about the incident, and he is mentioned nowhere else in the Bible. For sure, we have no story told by Eutychus to his friends about any NDE.

RESURRECTIONS

The concept of resurrection has not always been an integral part of the Jewish tradition, and it was relatively new for the early Christians as well. In the Old Testament there were some examples of men being raised from the dead (mostly resuscitations, though the distinction was unknown at the time). But resurrection was not an important part of religious belief until the intertestamental period. Jewish religious leaders demonstrated little interest in the afterlife, and most of their teachings had to do with the present existence and the corporate destiny of the nation of Israel. Many pagan religions emphasized life after death, individual experience, and personal destiny, but the Jewish religion downplayed this aspect of theology. Mixing Judaism with pagan concepts was so repugnant to the Jews that these subjects received little attention until forced into the discussion both by debates between the Pharisees and the Sadducees and by Jesus' teachings and later His own resurrection. The Sadducees were particularly opposed to the concept of a bodily resurrection.

The Old Testament spoke of Sheol as the destination of the dead; however, detailed descriptions of Sheol in the Old Testament were lacking. It was only during the intertestamental period, in the time of Jesus, and in the few hundred years thereafter that the concepts of paradise, heaven, hell, hades, Sheol, and Gehenna were discussed and more widely accepted. After Jesus' ministry, the power of God was thus described more in individual terms and less in global and national terms. The detailed concept of individual resurrection was described earliest in 2 Maccabees (written about 70 B.C.), and one early notion of individual destiny—reward or punishment after death—was articulated in 4 Ezra (written about A.D. 70). So resuscitation and resurrection were emerging concepts as Jesus began His teachings. Let's look at the resurrections described in the Bible.

An Unidentified Dead Man

In 2 Kings 13:20-21 Elisha raised a man from death—a resurrection—after Elisha himself had already died!

> *Elisha died and was buried. Now Moabite raiders used to enter the country every spring. Once while some Israelites were burying a man, suddenly they saw a band of raiders; so they threw the man's body into Elisha's tomb. When the body touched Elisha's bones, the man came to life and stood up on his feet.*

It was customary at this time to use tombs repeatedly because of the scarcity of adequate burial plots in the rocky ground of Israel (10). The sites for initial burial were large and were one of two types. A loculus was a carved receptacle in a tomb that was dug perpendicular to the wall of the tomb; an arcosolium was a flat shelf-like repository dug parallel to the side of the wall of the tomb.

A person's remains after decomposition consisted only of bones that could be buried in a much smaller location, usually in a small box called an ossuary, often in the same tomb but removed from the loculus or arcosolium. Bones were moved to make room for another body. This process was usually repeated every year or two.

It was certainly not common, though, for a second person to be buried in the same place before the previous resident was removed from the loculus or arcosolium. Hence, the man in 2 Kings 13:21 came into contact with the remains of Elisha, though it does not specify how long the man had been dead. The circumstances suggest that the burial itself was hasty (11). The story says that the burial party "suddenly" saw the band of raiders and that they "threw" the body into Elisha's tomb. But these hasty actions occurred at the time of usual burial, and it is quite unlikely that the interval of time from death to resurrection was short enough that the death could have been confused with simply a comatose or unarousable state. In fact, once again the Hebrew does not equivocate about the man's death and revival. The Hebrew *chayah*, which was used to describe resurrection, means "to save" or "to revive." In this report, likewise, there is no mention of any heavenly experience told to the bystanders. At the very least, this story suggests that NDEs, if existing at all, are uncommon.

Jonah

The account of Jonah is one of the most famous from the Bible. Jonah resisted God's calling to preach against the sin of Nineveh, a wicked city, and was banished to the stomach of a great fish for three days. Whether he actually died during the experience, though, is unknown.

> *But the* LORD *provided a great fish to swallow Jonah, and Jonah was inside the fish three days and three nights.*

> *From inside the fish Jonah prayed to the LORD his God. He said: "In my distress I called to the LORD, and he answered me. From the depths of the grave I called for help, and you listened to my cry. . . . When my life was ebbing away, I remembered you, LORD, and my prayer rose to you, to your holy temple."*
>
> —*Jonah 1:17—2:2, 7*

So Jonah spoke of being in "the depths of the grave." It is not clear whether Jonah was describing actually going to Sheol or was simply using a figure of speech to highlight his precarious position in the belly of the great fish. Jonah prayed from within the fish, at least in the early stage of his sojourn there, and we are left with an uncertainty about his vital status at the end of those three days. It would seem logical that he might have died in the confines of the fish's stomach, with its acidic juices and lack of oxygen, but from the wording in Jonah we cannot be sure. Certainly Jonah's residence in the fish has been taken as a prototype for the experience of Jesus who died and spent three days in the grave, then was resurrected in his bodily form.

> *"For as Jonah was three days and three nights in the belly of a huge fish, so the Son of Man will be three days and three nights in the heart of the earth."*
>
> —*Matthew 12:40*

But we cannot with certainty say that Jonah was dead, nor that he experienced either a resuscitation or a resurrection.

The Young Man at Nain

This story is found in Luke 7:11-17:

> *Soon afterward, Jesus went to a town called Nain, and his disciples and a large crowd went along with him. As he approached the town gate, a dead person was being carried*

> *out—the only son of his mother, and she was a widow. And a large crowd from the town was with her. When the Lord saw her, his heart went out to her and he said, "Don't cry."*
>
> *Then he went up and touched the coffin, and those carrying it stood still. He said, "Young man, I say to you, get up!" The dead man sat up and began to talk, and Jesus gave him back to his mother.*
>
> *They were all filled with awe and praised God. "A great prophet has appeared among us," they said. "God has come to help his people." This news about Jesus spread throughout Judea and the surrounding country.*

The young man had been dead for some time (here "dead" comes from *thnesko*, assuring us that he was really dead). The preparation of the body and the funeral had been completed; the procession to the graveyard was underway. At Jesus' command, he arose on the spot, sitting up in his coffin or bier. The throng of people recognized Jesus' power, and His fame increased. Once again, there is no mention of an NDE. What a wonderful opportunity it would have been for Jesus to help describe the beauty of heaven and the everlasting peace that heaven holds for us if there had been such a journey for the young man of Nain. But there is no mention of the tunnel, the light, or any other aspect of the NDE! This was clearly a resurrection without an NDE.

Lazarus

There are two Lazarus stories: one of death, and another of resurrection, both of which yield important information about the NDE.

The Beggar Lazarus

Luke 16:19-31 sheds light on the NDE (though not mentioning resuscitation or resurrection). This Lazarus was a beggar at the city gate:

"There was a rich man who was dressed in purple and fine linen and lived in luxury every day. At his gate was laid a beggar named Lazarus, covered with sores and longing to eat what fell from the rich man's table. Even the dogs came and licked his sores.

"The time came when the beggar died and the angels carried him to Abraham's side. The rich man also died and was buried. In hell, where he was in torment, he looked up and saw Abraham far away, with Lazarus by his side. So he called to him, 'Father Abraham, have pity on me and send Lazarus to dip the tip of his finger in water and cool my tongue, because I am in agony in this fire.'

"But Abraham replied, 'Son, remember that in your lifetime you received your good things, while Lazarus received bad things, but now he is comforted here and you are in agony. And besides all this, between us and you a great chasm has been fixed, so that those who want to go from here to you cannot, nor can anyone cross over from there to us.'

"He answered, 'Then I beg you, father, send Lazarus to my father's house, for I have five brothers. Let him warn them, so that they will not also come to this place of torment.'

"Abraham replied, 'They have Moses and the Prophets; let them listen to them.'

"'No, father Abraham,' he said, 'but if someone from the dead goes to them, they will repent.'

"He said to them, 'If they do not listen to Moses and the Prophets, they will not be convinced even if someone rises from the dead.'"

We learn two major lessons from this story, which is thought to be a real account rather than a parable, told by Jesus, who is the only One who has the power today to see into both heaven and hell:

1. There is no way to communicate to or from heaven or hell or between them.

2. Even the return of a dead person with stories from "the other side" would be useless to convince men to repent. We do indeed still have Moses and the Prophets today. This Lazarus story speaks strongly against the NDE!

Lazarus, Jesus' Close Friend

The best-known resurrection story, other than Christ's, is that of Lazarus in John 11:1-45:

> *Now a man named Lazarus was sick. He was from Bethany, the village of Mary and her sister Martha. This Mary, whose brother Lazarus now lay sick, was the same one who poured perfume on the Lord and wiped his feet with her hair. So the sisters sent word to Jesus, "Lord, the one you love is sick."*
>
> *When he heard this, Jesus said, "This sickness will not end in death. No, it is for God's glory so that God's Son may be glorified through it." Jesus loved Martha and her sister and Lazarus. Yet when he heard that Lazarus was sick, he stayed where he was two more days.*
>
> *Then he said to his disciples, "Let us go back to Judea." "But Rabbi," they said, "a short while ago the Jews tried to stone you, and yet you are going back there?" Jesus answered, "Are there not twelve hours of daylight? A man who walks by day will not stumble, for he sees by this world's light. It is when he walks by night that he stumbles, for he has no light."*
>
> *After he had said this, he went on to tell them, "Our friend Lazarus has fallen asleep; but I am going there to wake him up."*
>
> *His disciples replied, "Lord, if he sleeps, he will get better." Jesus had been speaking of his death, but his disciples thought he meant natural sleep.*
>
> *So then he told them plainly, "Lazarus is dead, and for your sake I am glad I was not there, so that you may*

believe. But let us go to him." Then Thomas (called Didymus) said to the rest of the disciples, "Let us also go, that we may die with him."

On his arrival, Jesus found that Lazarus had already been in the tomb for four days. Bethany was less than two miles from Jerusalem, and many Jews had come to Martha and Mary to comfort them in the loss of their brother. When Martha heard that Jesus was coming, she went out to meet him, but Mary stayed at home.

"Lord," Martha said to Jesus, "if you had been here, my brother would not have died. But I know that even now God will give you whatever you ask."

Jesus said to her, "Your brother will rise again." Martha answered, "I know he will rise again in the resurrection at the last day."

Jesus said to her, "I am the resurrection and the life. He who believes in me will live, even though he dies; and whoever lives and believes in me will never die. Do you believe this?"

"Yes, Lord," she told him, "I believe that you are the Christ, the Son of God, who was to come into the world." And after she had said this, she went back and called her sister Mary aside. "The Teacher is here," she said, "and is asking for you." When Mary heard this, she got up quickly and went to him. Now Jesus had not yet entered the village, but was still at the place where Martha had met him. When the Jews who had been with Mary in the house, comforting her, noticed how quickly she got up and went out, they followed her, supposing she was going to the tomb to mourn there.

When Mary reached the place where Jesus was and saw him, she fell at his feet and said, "Lord, if you had been here, my brother would not have died."

When Jesus saw her weeping, and the Jews who had come along with her also weeping, he was deeply moved in spirit and troubled. "Where have you laid him?" he asked.

"Come and see, Lord," they replied.

Jesus wept.

Then the Jews said, "See how he loved him!"

But some of them said, "Could not he who opened the eyes of the blind man have kept this man from dying?"

Jesus, once more deeply moved, came to the tomb. It was a cave with a stone laid across the entrance. "Take away the stone," he said.

"But, Lord," said Martha, the sister of the dead man, "by this time there is a bad odor, for he has been there four days." Then Jesus said, "Did I not tell you that if you believed, you would see the glory of God?"

So they took away the stone. Then Jesus looked up and said, "Father, I thank you that you have heard me. I knew that you always hear me, but I said this for the benefit of the people standing here, that they may believe that you sent me."

When he had said this, Jesus called in a loud voice, "Lazarus, come out!" The dead man came out, his hands and feet wrapped with strips of linen, and a cloth around his face.

Jesus said to them, "Take off the grave clothes and let him go."

Therefore many of the Jews who had come to visit Mary, and had seen what Jesus did, put their faith in him.

Lazarus had died. There is no doubt from this passage that everyone present was convinced that he was dead. All the verses in this passage use a Greek word for death (*thanatos*), except for verse 11, where Jesus says, "Our friend Lazarus has fallen asleep," where he uses *koimao*, the term used interchangeably for sleep and death. However, Jesus later in verse 14 says unequivocally, "Lazarus is dead" (*apothnesko*, meaning dead, not asleep). Lazarus had been in the grave for four days, and his sister thought that severe decomposition would have begun, causing a stench if Jesus removed the stone from the grave. He was wrapped in grave clothes.

Nevertheless, Jesus raised Lazarus from the grave—truly a resurrection rather than a resuscitation. But there is no mention whatsoever of any NDE!

If the NDE is a valid message about the afterlife, why didn't Lazarus report one? Lazarus certainly had been dead long enough to have completed an NDE journey. But there is no mention of any physical sensations, no bright lights, no encounter with God, no blissfully peaceful feelings!

John 12 goes on to tell of further events that gave opportunity for Lazarus to give an account of what had transpired during those four days. Lazarus sat at a banquet table, and many people came to see the man raised from the grave. This was a perfect time to tell of his experience. Personal testimony time! But nothing! So if the NDE exists, and if it is supposed to be an opportunity to witness to the glory of God and bring people to God, both Lazarus and Jesus missed the chance! One has to wonder, is the NDE real, or is it an invention of a brain needing to make sense out of an unusual physiologic event? More importantly, is it a deception that turns people *away* from the real God of resurrection?

The account of Lazarus has, at times, been misinterpreted. Iverson in his book *In Search of the Dead: A Scientific Investigation of Evidence for Life After Death* (12) contends that Lazarus had a bad otherworldly experience during his death and time in the grave, though there is no evidence whatsoever in the Bible for this position. Iverson claims that *legend* holds that Lazarus never smiled after his resurrection, a notion difficult to accept, considering that Lazarus was not only restored to life but to life with the living Christ, one of Lazarus' best friends.

On the contrary, William McBirnie tells us of the tradition that has come down throughout the ages of the productive ministry of Lazarus after his resurrection (13). He supposedly left the Jerusalem area in about A.D. 60-63, went to Cyprus, and was the leader of the Christian church there. He later went to Marseilles, France, or his remains were moved there after he died.

Tabitha

Another account of resurrection involves Peter's praying to revive the disciple Tabitha, recorded in Acts 9:36-42:

> *In Joppa there was a disciple named Tabitha (which, when translated, is Dorcas), who was always doing good and helping the poor. About that time she became sick and died, and her body was washed and placed in an upstairs room. Lydda was near Joppa; so when the disciples heard that Peter was in Lydda, they sent two men to him and urged him, "Please come at once!"*
>
> *Peter went with them, and when he arrived he was taken upstairs to the room. All the widows stood around him, crying and showing him the robes and other clothing that Dorcas had made while she was still with them. Peter sent them all out of the room; then he got down on his knees and prayed. Turning toward the dead woman, he said, "Tabitha, get up." She opened her eyes, and seeing Peter she sat up. He took her by the hand and helped her to her feet. Then he called the believers and the widows and presented her to them alive. This became known all over Joppa, and many people believed in the Lord.*

It was unlikely that Tabitha was simply unconscious, considering the many witnesses to her death, the fact that her body had been washed in preparation for burial, and the placement of the body in an upper room. It was customary for a person to be buried soon after death. Inside Jerusalem the burial had to be performed within one day. Outside Jerusalem, up to three days were allowed before the body had to be buried. If the burial could not be performed immediately, it was also the Jewish custom to place the body in an upper room.

Tabitha's friends obviously wanted Peter to attempt an even greater miracle than the healing of Aeneas described earlier in the same chapter of Acts. The term *apothnesko* was used to describe her death, meaning real death and not just a deep sleep. Peter followed Jesus' example by asking all of the people to leave the upper room, and then he prayed for Tabitha. Miraculously she arose, just as Jesus' miracles had accomplished. Though the Bible describes the subsequent conversion of many because of this miracle, there is no mention of any NDE.

Resurrection of the Saints

At Jesus' death there occurred another series of resurrections that have been overshadowed by the account of Jesus' own resurrection. Matthew 27:51-53 relates concerning the moment of Jesus' death:

> *At that moment the curtain of the temple was torn in two from top to bottom. The earth shook and the rocks split. The tombs broke open and the bodies of many holy people who had died were raised to life. They came out of the tombs, and after Jesus' resurrection they went into the holy city and appeared to many people.*

This passage is explained nowhere else in the Bible. It simply says that "*many* holy people" were raised, but not how many. They came out of their tombs, but they waited until Jesus' resurrection before revealing themselves to the people of Jerusalem. Some scholars think this was the resurrection of all saints who had died up to that time, rising to paradise to await the final return of Jesus to earth. Other scholars surmise that those resurrected were simply some of the recently departed saints who had known Jesus during His earthly ministry. It is impossible to clarify this passage further. Nothing is said of them thereafter. Did they rise to paradise? Did they live more earthly life, later to die again? We don't know, but the absence of any further description suggests that they did not remain here on earth for any great length of time.

Jesus' Resurrection

Of course, the most important resurrection of all time occurred when Jesus conquered death and rose on the third day after His crucifixion. Here it was God the Father who did the miracle, though sadly there are still many who deny Christ's bodily resurrection.

The ordeal of crucifixion has been evaluated only from the distance that time has placed between us and the most recent executions by this method (14-27). Because it was an ancient form of torture and execution, it has not been the subject of direct observation by modern scientific or medical techniques. Edwards examined the medical aspects of crucifixion, and he reported them in the *Journal of the American Medical Association* (14).

Crucifixion was preceded by the ordeal of scourging. This torture involved the beating of the prisoner with a whip made of small leather strips to which were attached bones, rocks, and small pieces of metal. One or two Roman soldiers trained in the punishment of criminals wielded the scourge or whip. The purpose of the flogging was to inflict wounds that were just short of death, to weaken the prisoner before nailing him to the cross. The soldiers usually applied thirty-nine stripes to the prisoner, one short of the Jewish law allowing the application of forty stripes, to assure that no law was broken if the person counting the stripes made a small mistake in the tally. The whip usually caused multiple lacerations from the hard objects attached to it, and it was common for the whips to cut to the muscle or bone with each lash. This punishment usually left the prisoner in a weakened state from the pain of the whipping and the tearing of his flesh, but also from the blood loss that accompanied the lacerations. The duration of survival on the cross itself was related to the severity of the scourging. The more severe the scourging, the quicker the death on the cross.

The Bible tells us that Jesus was too weak from His scourging even to carry His own cross. The object that the prisoner was required to carry was actually the horizontal part of the cross, the patibulum, which weighed from seventy-five to 125 pounds. Jesus was supposed to carry this wooden beam for a distance of about one-third of a mile, although the exact locations of the crucifixion and burial sites are debated. The traditional site (now the location of the Church of the Holy Sepulchre) is located slightly further from the Praetorium than the alternate site represented by Gordon's Garden Tomb, though both were outside the city walls at that time. Simon of Cyrene, apparently just an innocent bystander, was pressed into service to carry the cross to Golgotha for Jesus.

The major physical stress from crucifixion was thought to be the difficulty of breathing in the upright position. The body was hung from the cross by nails driven through the feet and wrists, and it was difficult for the prisoner to exhale in this position. It required a muscular effort to lift the body enough to expel air from the lungs. Contrary to normal breathing, where exhalation is mostly a passive process, during crucifixion exhalation is the active process, requiring energy and strength. After the prisoner was weakened sufficiently from the ordeal, he would die from asphyxia, unable to summon the strength to breathe.

Death was sure due to the shock from the blood loss of the scourging, the rigors of carrying the cross, the crucifixion itself, and the exposure from hanging for a prolonged period of time. It could take days for the prisoner to die, though some died within a few hours. If the criminal was progressing too slowly toward death, the soldiers would often break the prisoner's legs to impair respiratory efforts, making it impossible for the prisoner to lift his body so he could exhale.

Of course, no one survived this punishment. Josephus in A.D. 66 recorded a single example of a man who survived crucifixion, but his death sentence was commuted before the punishment was complete. He was purposefully removed from the cross before dying, and he was then nursed back to health (28).

To insure that the person was dead at the end of the crucifixion, the Roman soldiers commonly thrust a spear into the body of the criminal. This was done both (1) to render a painful stimulus and so cause the person to move and show whether he was still alive, and (2) to hasten death with another new wound if life persisted. Unresponsiveness to the spear wound would indicate that the person was indeed dead. Roman soldiers were known for their cruelty, and the Roman forces had specialists in crucifixion to insure both suffering for the criminal and ultimate death, as well as providing a spectacle for the populace and to discourage others from breaking the law.

So Jesus had two groups of people present to assure His death—both the Roman soldiers and the Jewish officials who wanted him to die in the first place. It is unlikely that death was misdiagnosed with these combined witnesses and executioners. This man Jesus was the most important person ever to have been sentenced to execution by crucifixion. The Romans and Jewish leaders were not about to let Him down from the cross until He was indeed dead. While many explanations have been rendered for the physiology of Jesus' death by crucifixion (heart attack [myocardial infarction], cardiac rupture, stroke, hypovolemic shock, cardiac arrhythmia), it is clear that He was indisputably dead when taken down from the cross.

Even after Edwards and coworkers' paper, considerable discussion persisted in medical circles, exemplified by the publication by M. Lloyd Davies and T. A. Lloyd Davies who denied the biblical account of the resurrection (16). Their arguments were not new, but the reemergence of objections to the biblical accounts stimulated discussion. Originally published in the prestigious *Journal of the Royal College of Physicians of London*, they contended that Jesus simply fainted from the ordeal of the early stages of the crucifixion and that He did not die. They claimed that His resurrection was a matter of awakening from the hypotension produced by His punishment and was not a resurrection after all. They argued that His disappearance from the tomb simply never occurred because He was never placed in the tomb. Jesus' later appearances allegedly had no bearing on the resurrection story because they believed that He never died. They stated, "The Church will be stronger if it accommodates proven knowledge within its creeds. If it does not, all that is left is blind belief, far beyond the credulity of most people." Of course, they must have believed that their thesis represented the "proven knowledge" of which they spoke, though they presented only unsubstantiated theory.

As expected, their paper spawned an outcry from both the medical and religious community. All of Lloyd Davies' arguments were refuted by the respondents to their paper. The evidence for belief in the death and resurrection of Jesus is solid. The reader is referred to Josh McDowell's excellent scholarly works on the topic of Jesus' historical death and resurrection: *Evidence That Demands a Verdict* (21), *He Walked Among Us: Evidence for the Historical Jesus* (27), and *A Ready Defense* (24).

So Jesus died and was resurrected. Resurrection no longer occurs. Resuscitations are common, but Jesus had the last recorded resurrection, other than Tabitha's, in the book of Acts. And if descriptions of the afterlife from those who have "died" and come back are important for our understanding of theology, then Jesus missed His chance to teach us an important message.

Jesus' atoning sacrifice for us was also a trip from death to life, but we see nothing in His stories after His resurrection to suggest what happened to Him during these three days. Jesus Himself refused to describe the details of His three days in the grave. He could have told the most remarkable NDE story ever recorded, and He would have told it in a way to glorify God if He had thought it would have been useful. But He never said a word about what He experienced in those three days before the resurrection. Why didn't He tell us about brilliant lights, about angels, about the pains of hell, or about the glory of heaven awaiting Christians after our life here on earth? He didn't. That's about all that we can say. He taught. He ate with the disciples. He served them. But He did not use His experiences during the three days in the grave to lead men to Him. That example should tell us that we should beware of any messengers bearing stories of the hereafter.

There is even dispute about where Jesus spent this time. Some say He was in paradise or heaven, based upon His statement to the thief on the cross: "I tell you the truth, today you will be with me in paradise" (Luke 23:43). But 1 Peter 3:18-20 says:

> *For Christ died for sins once for all, the righteous for the unrighteous, to bring you to God. He was put to death in the body but made alive by the Spirit, through whom also he went and preached to the spirits in prison who disobeyed long ago when God waited patiently in the days of Noah while the ark was being built.*

This passage is interpreted by some theologians to suggest that Christ spent those three days in hell. Indeed, the Apostles' Creed speaks of Jesus descending into hell. However, some modern theologians vehemently deny that Jesus spent time in hell. Certainly Jesus took our sins and paid the price for us, but whether this time was spent in hell for our sakes or not is unclear. In Ephesians 4:9-10 we read:

> *What does "he ascended" mean except that he also descended to the lower, earthly regions? He who descended*

> *is the very one who ascended higher than all the heavens, in order to fill the whole universe.*

Whether in heaven or hell or both, Jesus had ample opportunity to tell of otherworldly sights during His forty days on the earth after His resurrection. And He saw or spoke to over 500 people during this time. But He spoke no words about an NDE! No story brought back from the grave, even by Jesus. Another strike against the NDE!

11

OTHER BIBLICAL EVIDENCE

Life Is Tough And Then You Die

Melissa Hunter was not supposed to see medicine from this angle. She was a cardiologist, and she knew about the problems that you can encounter during routine medical care. Her husband was also a physician, a pulmonologist and intensive care specialist. So the family's total knowledge of medicine was extensive. Nevertheless, here she was, about to undergo a cesarean section for their first child.

Melissa was young, hardly thirty, but she had a long history of high blood pressure. It had been discovered and evaluated extensively when she was in her early twenties, and her doctors had found no primary cause. So she simply had needed to take some medication for blood pressure control. Until now. The pregnancy had worsened her blood pressure, and her obstetrician decided that a C-section was needed to keep her from experiencing any further rise in her pressure.

Never one to worry much, Melissa was simply excited about the birth of their first child. She didn't exactly relish the idea of surgery, but she knew that it would be the best for both her and the baby. So here she was in the operating room. The anesthesiologist had performed an epidural block, a technique that would render her free of any pain or feeling in the abdomen. It was all going as planned. Her husband, Brent, was present, also unaccustomed to viewing medicine from the consumer's aspect; but he was trying to detach himself from the surgical procedure and concentrate on supporting his wife. Only a few years ago he would never have been allowed to stay in the operating room, even though he was a part of the medical fraternity; but hospital policy had changed.

Melissa was about to undergo the surgery. Numb beyond belief, she knew that soon her baby daughter (the ultrasound had told them it was a girl) would be in her arms. She had no apprehension as the C-section began. She knew that spinal anesthesia was the best anesthesia that could be used for her blood pressure, and she knew—more importantly—that it was the best for the baby, too. Within minutes Emily was born.

Her husband was ecstatic. Everything was going perfectly. After all, he was a lung specialist, and he couldn't help assessing the medical aspects of the situation. The anesthesiologist was also pleased. He even excused himself for a minute to go to the recovery room to see another patient who was in pain and needed some additional medication. However, immediately after he left the operating room, Melissa began to feel nauseated. She quickly vomited, although there was not much in her stomach. Melissa was now getting agitated, and before the obstetrician could express his concern or call the anesthesiologist back to the room, Melissa became disoriented. She developed a look of terror on her face and tried to sit up. The anesthesiologist came running back into the room and quickly gave her some intravenous sedation. Her skin color then turned blue as she began to breathe poorly.

The anesthesiologist rapidly controlled her ventilation with a face mask as he squeezed the bag that forced oxygen into Melissa's lungs. The artificial respiration worked rapidly and well. Within a few seconds Melissa's color went from dark blue to light blue to pink. Her husband observed this entire sequence, helpless to intervene as his reflexes demanded. Ventilation with the mask and Ambu bag kept her pink, but Melissa didn't seem to have any mental or emotional response to the crisis. She seemed oblivious—even comatose. Bag placed firmly against the face, no air leaks. Squeeze the bag. Release. Squeeze the bag. Release. The anesthesiologist was ready to insert a tube into her trachea, if necessary, but she finally began to breathe after some additional medicine was given to reverse the effects of the sedation. This was not what he had planned!

Brent felt helpless, wanting to do something, but knowing he must now stand aside and let the others do their work. What had happened? Did she have an embolus to her head? Would she recover? These were questions that raced through Brent's mind. He was afraid to think about the possible answers.

The next few hours were exhausting for Brent. Melissa began to breathe on her own, but she remained disoriented and initially combative. Then she settled into a rather deep sleep, and after four or five hours she began to respond sluggishly, then normally. No, there had been no embolus. No permanent damage.

The anesthesiologist was surprised and embarrassed to learn that both Melissa and Brent were physicians. You want all procedures to go smoothly, especially for fellow members of your profession. But Melissa was unharmed. "All's well that ends well" seemed to be the key thought for the day.

The rest of the day was less exciting. Fine, healthy baby. Mom and Dad a bit frazzled by the experience, but their apprehension would soon disappear into the recesses of their minds as the demands of the new child took their attention away from the anesthesia problems.

Melissa, though, later remembered the events quite well. The panic at the end of the C-section. The rapid intravenous medication. The sensation of being unable to breathe. The air hunger. The dimming of vision. The loss of consciousness. Then awakening confused with a four-hour gap in her memory. She had heard about heavenly experiences that some people had reported with such events. But neither Melissa nor Brent were particularly religious, so she thought that such visions must be reserved for the true believers.

Was she right? Do visions near death represent messages from God exclusively for the elect? Or was her lack of a near-death experience typical?

WHAT ELSE DOES THE BIBLE HAVE TO SAY ABOUT THE NDE?

God's Glory

No man can see God and live. Exodus 33:20 tells us that God is too powerful and glorious for mere man to behold. Today's cults, especially those espousing New Age doctrine, equate man with God, even declaring that man is, or can be, God. Proponents of this religious position have no difficulty envisioning man talking with God the Father literally, face-to-face, even having a rather casual relationship with God. Eadie talks of conversations with God held during her purported journey in *Embraced by the Light* (1). But biblical principles dictate otherwise. We can never stand before God and survive.

God's Omniscience

In Hebrews 9:27 we see that "It is appointed unto men *once* to die, but after this the judgment" (KJV, emphasis mine). If we can die only once, then a near-death experience is an oxymoron. God, in His omnipotence, certainly knows the time of our true death—when our spirit is to be released to go to our eternal home. He would not release anyone's spirit from the body until the real time of death had arrived. The very concept of the NDE mocks God. It contends that circumstances on earth can fool God into allowing a spirit to depart the body to go to heaven or hell before the person actually is destined to die.

I personally would be unwilling to worship God, who is supposed to be omnipotent, omniscient, and omnipresent, if He doesn't know when I am destined to die. If He could be fooled (as in some Indian NDE accounts) (2-3) by a "mistaken" identity, allowing the wrong person to die because one person's name was similar to another's, then I would have to question His wisdom.

More commonly, the NDE stories include a statement that the person had to return to earth to complete his tasks there. It seems implausible that an all-knowing God would allow death and then reverse His decision and tell a person, "It's not your time. You have work left to do on earth." Shouldn't an all-knowing God be aware that the person had work left to do on earth before the person "died" and went to heaven? If I worship a God like that, I'm in trouble.

God's Omnipotence

Another scenario has the "dying" person *choosing* to return to earth for some reason. God seems to be out of control in this situation. I can't imagine that my God relegates this decision to us. It says in Hebrews 9 that our death is "appointed," not "chosen." These accounts of the NDE that attribute to man a conscious choice of staying in heaven or returning to earth deny the power of Jesus described in Revelation 1:18, where it says that Jesus holds the keys to death. We are not given the choice for the timing of our own death.

God's Judgment

God's judgment is certain:

> *But he continued, "You are from below; I am from above. You are of this world; I am not of this world. I told you that*

> *you would die in your sins; if you do not believe that I am the one I claim to be, you will indeed die in your sins."*
>
> *—John 8:23-24*

> *God is just: He will pay back trouble to those who trouble you and give relief to you who are troubled, and to us as well. This will happen when the Lord Jesus is revealed from heaven in a blazing fire with his powerful angels. He will punish those who do not know God and do not obey the gospel of our Lord Jesus. They will be punished with everlasting destruction and shut out from the presence of the Lord and from the majesty of his power on the day he comes to be glorified in his holy people and to be marveled at among all those who have believed. This includes you, because you believed our testimony to you.*
>
> *—2 Thessalonians 1:6-10*

Our Duty to Discern

We read in 1 John 4:1-3:

> *Beloved, do not believe every spirit, but test the spirits to see whether they are from God, because many false prophets have gone out into the world. This is how you can recognize the Spirit of God: Every spirit that acknowledges that Jesus Christ has come in the flesh is from God. But every spirit that does not acknowledge Jesus Christ is not from God. This is the spirit of the antichrist, which you have heard is coming and even now is already in the world.*

Mark 13:22 tells us that Christ said:

> *"For false Christs and false prophets will appear and perform signs and miracles to deceive the elect—if that were possible."*

Many Christians have been seduced by the NDE concept, and early in its publication, even Christian bookstores stocked Eadie's book under the misconception that it represented a voice from God. *Embraced by the Light* and the NDE concept have been revealed to be deception (4-18).

> *For the time will come when men will not put up with sound doctrine. Instead, to suit their own desires, they will gather around them teachers to say what their itching ears want to hear. They will turn their ears away from the truth and turn aside to myths.*
>
> —*2 Timothy 4:3-4*

> *I am astonished that you are so quickly deserting the one who called you by the grace of Christ and are turning to a different gospel—which is really no gospel at all. Evidently some people are throwing you into confusion and are trying to pervert the gospel of Christ. But even if we or an angel from heaven should preach a gospel other than the one we preached to you, let him be eternally condemned!*
>
> —*Galatians 1:6-8*

People in the 1990s want their ears tickled. They desperately want tales of the supernatural. Such stories are more entertaining than sound biblical doctrine. Why else does the *National Enquirer* survive? The world wants the reassurance of the tenets of the NDE:

That all is well.
That sin doesn't matter.
That everyone will experience peace after death.
That death itself is not a reality.
That we have control over death and that we can even choose to return to the earth after death if we want, giving us a second chance.
That death is really synonymous with peace and love.

That God is only love and not a righteous judge of our sins.
That God does not demand our allegiance and worship.
That our earthly actions are of no consequence.
That we are not called to righteousness.
That all religions are acceptable.

Such theology is dangerous and must not be tolerated. From a Christian's point of view, the NDE is counterfeit because it lures us into all of these false doctrines. John Wesley rightly taught that the Christian must prove the truth of teachings by:

1. The Bible.
2. The tradition of the church.
3. Experience.
4. Reason.

We must not let visions be the sole authority base for testing a teaching. All visions must square with Scripture, tradition, and reason as well—and especially Scripture. If the universal experience of the NDE is peace and love, even for non-Christians—Buddhists, Muslims, atheists—where is the truth? Where is the imperative for telling the world about Christ?

After reading all of the works describing the NDE, one is impressed that glory is not given to Jesus, the Holy Spirit, or God the Father. In fact, the emphasis is usually placed upon the earthly person or the experience itself, not on the call to repentance required by God.

Our Duty to Spread the Gospel

The NDE often contains no redemption message. Furthermore, there is no Great Commission imperative. One might expect that if Jesus were to give us another message in an NDE, it would be the message that He gave His disciples as He left the earth:

> *"Therefore go and make disciples of all nations, baptizing them in the name of the Father and of the Son and of the Holy Spirit, and teaching them to obey everything I have commanded you. And surely I am with you always, to the very end of the age."*
>
> —*Matthew 28:19-20*

WHAT IS THIS LIGHT?

What, then, is this wonderful light that people see at the end of the tunnel or in the beautiful garden? Jesus is the Light of the world. Isn't Jesus this light?

> *When Jesus spoke again to the people, he said, "I am the light of the world. Whoever follows me will never walk in darkness, but will have the light of life."*
>
> —*John 8:12*

Here is where we must be discerning. It also says in 2 Corinthians 11:13-14:

> *For such are false apostles, deceitful workmen, masquerading as apostles of Christ. And no wonder, for Satan himself masquerades as an* angel of light. *(emphasis mine).*

Not all that appears good is good. The "being of light" virtually never identifies himself. If it is Jesus, why doesn't He simply identify Himself? The person who has an NDE often attaches a name to this being that is consistent with the beliefs of his religion. It may be Jesus, but it may also be Buddha, Allah, the turtle god, God the Father, an angel, a cow, or the "higher self." In the NDE the bright light that seems to encompass the person in warmth and love (even if appearing to be Jesus) could indeed be a trick of the deceiver, the great imitator, Satan.

We must be diligent to recognize the enemy. He tries to counterfeit everything that is good, and the message of the NDE seems to be that everyone will achieve warmth and love at death, so not to worry! By reassuring us that death is pleasant, this "being of light" may be removing the imperative to accept Christ. Satan seems to be saying, "Don't bother with this Jesus! Everything will be fine at your death. What you do in this life is unimportant. You don't need to make a decision about Christ as your Savior!"

> *The Spirit clearly says that in later times some will abandon the faith and follow deceiving spirits and things taught by demons.*
>
> *—1 Timothy 4:1*

A fine deception indeed!

12

MORE QUESTIONS

Death Is Just a Speed Bump On the Road to Eternity

Bill Johansen had been a Christian since he was eighteen. That was fifty years ago, and a lot had happened since then. A wife. Three children. A long career. His wife's death. And now a lot of time on his hands.

Bill had never been a scholar, but he liked to read. Usually his Bible, but occasionally other books. Even with a Bible school degree and fifty years of reading the Bible, though, he still was easily distracted into questionable theology.

A friend told him about a new book that she had just read. *Embraced by the Light*, it was called. It was about this wonderful Christian lady who had died and gone to heaven to visit with Jesus. But she came back to earth when she realized her work here was incomplete. Bill just had to read this book.

He was intrigued by the topic. This was just like the miracles described in the Bible. He liked the part about seeing Jesus. He really longed to see Jesus. His wife was with Jesus now, and Bill couldn't wait until the day he could join them.

But then Bill's friend Sam Andrews burst Bill's bubble. He

told Bill that the Jesus in *Embraced by the Light* was different from the Jesus they both knew. Eadie's Jesus didn't seem to be telling the redemption message of the Bible. And this Jesus seemed to be saying that it really doesn't make any difference what you believe. All religions are equally valid, according to Eadie. Each one holds its own truth, and a person can progress in completeness from one to another. How discouraging. Bill didn't want to hear it. It just wasn't possible that Betty Eadie could be wrong. Or was it?

WHAT, THEN, IS DEATH?

In simplest terms, death is the end of our mortal life here on earth. But that definition is not very helpful. There seem to be some gray zones where the distinction between life and death becomes blurred. We must remember that God through Jesus holds the keys to life and death.

> *"I am the Living One; I was dead, and behold I am alive for ever and ever! And I hold the keys of death and Hades."*
>
> —*Revelation 1:18*

In the mind of the Christian there is a constant tension between the desire to be with Christ in heaven and to remain on earth to do the work of His kingdom here.

> *For to me, to live is Christ and to die is gain. If I am to go on living in the body, this will mean fruitful labor for me. Yet what shall I choose? I do not know! I am torn between the two: I desire to depart and be with Christ, which is better by far; but it is more necessary for you that I remain in the body.*
>
> —*Philippians 1:21-24*

Man wants to conquer death, but death is final. And it only occurs once.

> *Just as man is destined* to die once, *and after that to face judgment.*
>
> —*Hebrews 9:27, emphasis mine*

Death is the result of original sin, beginning with Adam's transgression in the garden.

> *For as in Adam all die, so in Christ all will be made alive.*
>
> —*1 Corinthians 15:22*

Death is the separation of body and spirit.

> *And the dust returns to the ground it came from, and the spirit returns to God who gave it.*
>
> —*Ecclesiastes 12:7*

So death is final—the point at which God removes our spirit for eternity. Multiple death experiences don't exist.

Death is inherently negative. If not, there would be no need for God. God is just and will judge us for what we did with Jesus in our earthly lives.

> *Then I saw a great white throne and him who was seated on it. Earth and sky fled from his presence, and there was no place for them. And I saw the dead, great and small, standing before the throne, and books were opened. Another book was opened, which is the book of life. The dead were judged according to what they had done as recorded in the books.*
>
> —*Revelation 20:11-12*

But Jesus has power over death.

WHY NOT ACCEPT THE NDE?

So why not just believe the NDE "for what it's worth"? Why not accept the experience as valid? There are some good Christians who have reported the NDE and who believe it holds truths that can help all mankind. After all, it changes lives, some for the better. And many in the clergy do not see any conflict between the concept of the NDE and the Bible (1). So why the fuss about some details that seem irrelevant?

The answer is that the NDE is deceptive, leading many unwary listeners astray. The NDE is telling man what he wants to hear, and most NDEs have just enough ring of truth to make the lie appealing. It is subjective and cannot be validated. Man wants to believe in the afterlife. It is inherently unacceptable to think that our existence is terminated at our death. Man needs to have a god (or gods), whether real or imaginary. The NDE superficially satisfies that need because it has a religious veneer that seems to answer some of the questions most of us have about eternity. Death becomes sublime. Don't worry; be happy. A Savior is not only unimportant but irrelevant.

But we must not worship either the NDE or the person who claims to have had the experience. Here are just a few of the reasons why the "spiritual light" of the NDE should be denounced:

It assures us that the death process is peaceful and pleasant.

It makes the claim that we are not really responsible for our lives and actions on this earth; everyone (or almost everyone) will encounter peace and love in the end, no matter what we have done with our lives, whether or not we have accepted Jesus as Savior. It gives the believer in the NDE what Dietrich Bonhoeffer (2) called "cheap grace"—a gift from God without commitment to God—"no-fault eternity" (3). Terry Mattingly decries the rise of the cult of the NDE, suggesting that New Age philosophy has replaced the God of the light of the world with God Lite (4).

It denies original sin and man's guilt.

It holds the lure that we may likely be resuscitated from our "first death" to be given another chance to evaluate our lives and our relationship to God through Jesus.

It tells us that all religions are equally valid, from Buddhism to Islam to Hinduism to Christianity.

It assures us that we will have a heavenly reward without an earthly commitment.

And finally, it opens the door for euthanasia because it claims that death and its consequences are so pleasant that we should never allow pain when such a good place awaits us all during and after death.

We must not believe any details about paradise, heaven, hades, or hell that we do not find in the Bible. Even though the NDE may lead some to Jesus (a somewhat doubtful claim), we must beware that the NDE not lead us to an experiential religion in which the NDE dominates the believer's life and belief system.

Christianity should not be an experience-based religion. It is grounded in a theology that is historical and that is contained in the Holy Scriptures. It has clearly defined rules and guidelines regarding the acceptance of individual experience. The emotional high of a mystical vision must agree precisely with the Bible; otherwise we must reject the vision. Truth cannot be determined based solely upon subjective, unverifiable personal experience. If a vision contradicts Scripture, then Scripture wins. The short-term benefits of any personal vision must be measured by the long-term fruits that emanate from that vision.

> *Test everything. Hold on to the good.*
>
> *—1 Thessalonians 5:21*

> *Do not put out the Spirit's fire; do not treat prophecies with contempt.*
>
> *—1 Thessalonians 5:19-20*

> *What you heard from me, keep as the pattern of sound teaching.*
>
> —*2 Timothy 1:13*

> *We demolish arguments and every pretension that sets itself up against the knowledge of God.*
>
> —*2 Corinthians 10:5*

The NDE is an experience that falls short of this measure of truth required of Christians. It contains false doctrine, leading the unwary astray. While some Christians may hold to the NDE as a divine revelation from God, either as a personal experience or as a belief in another's experience, the NDE is virtually never consistent with Scripture, often glorifies man, and leads Christians into a self-centered life that can detract from true service to God.

IS THERE ANY DANGER TO BELIEF IN THE NDE?

Yes; the NDE promotes a number of dangerous religions and practices.

The New Age. We have seen that the proponents of the NDE talk in terms of "cosmic unity," "life force," "energy balance," "morphic resonance," "inner awareness," "oneness with the universe," "life energy," "psychic awakening," and other phrases that should be an immediate clue to be wary. These concepts are derivatives of many Far Eastern religions that have been appropriated in New Age philosophy. They emphasize universal love at the expense of ignoring man's depravity, sin, and the ultimate judgment that is coming. They deny the primacy of God and the existence of the Holy Trinity. They ignore Jesus as the salvation of the world. They reject the need for repentance and the provision of grace for all mankind.

Hinduism. Many of the New Age beliefs are actually drawn directly from the Hindu religion. Hinduism teaches that there are millions of gods and that man is reincarnated to future lives based on his conduct during the current life. Karma is the principle that guides your life, and there is no forgiveness in karma.

Both Kieffer (5) and Greyson (7) emphasized that the power of the NDE is like the kundalini force that is taught in the Hindu religion. Kundalini force is said to be the potential energy in each of us that is likened to the power of a coiled spring in the spine, often represented by a snake waiting to strike. This snake imagery should remind us of Satan. NDE proponents want us to believe that the kundalini force is present in each of us and can be unleashed by the NDE. The kundalini force is alleged to be responsible for all sorts of miraculous feats including changes in the "rhythm of the body," massive outpourings of energy, wisdom, and verbal enlightenment. Indeed, the adherents to the kundalini concept believe that it will transform mankind and bring about a glorious age of awakening and evolution into a grand society.

However, this concept suggests that we are all gods ourselves and that we only need to "realize" our potential. It denies the power of God and appropriates that power for man. Without acknowledging the imagery of Satan as the serpent, Kieffer (6) also claims value in any connection with the kundalini serpent power in the spine: "The benefits of knowing even a little bit about the Serpent Power are incalculable."

Furthermore, Greyson tries to legitimatize the kundalini hypothesis by comparing it to something that is real, a deceptive trick to make us feel comfortable with the lie. He says (6), "Though the vocabulary of the Kundalini hypothesis is foreign to Westerners, the concept bears some resemblance to the more familiar Holy Spirit." Satan counterfeits anything that is real to his advantage. We must remain diligent or we will be fooled.

Reincarnation. The writings of many of the NDE proponents contain direct references to reincarnation, and Moody is the most blatant about this belief. His book *Coming Back: A Psychiatrist*

Explores Past-Life Journeys (8) promotes reincarnation as a valid belief system.

Divination and other occult practices. Moody (8-13) and Stevenson (14-21) both have written books describing conversations with the dead; however, even the non-scientific community has had a hard time accepting any of these claims.

Mormonism. The Mormon religion has pre-existence of the soul as a prominent part of its doctrine. Return from the dead is also a major part of Mormon teachings.

Can we authenticate all NDEs? No. Clearly many (if not most, or even all) NDEs offer misleading theology. We are to test the spirits, to discern the true Gospel of Jesus Christ, to engage in spiritual warfare, and to judge the validity of testimony by the fruits resulting from the experience. Is it consistent with Scripture? Is God glorified? Does it point to God or to man? Does it prompt repentance and holy living?

> *Finally, be strong in the Lord and in his mighty power. Put on the full armor of God so that you can take your stand against the devil's schemes. For our struggle is not against flesh and blood, but against the rulers, against the authorities, against the powers of this dark world and against the spiritual forces of evil in the heavenly realms. Therefore put on the full armor of God, so that when the day of evil comes, you may be able to stand your ground.*
>
> —*Ephesians 6:10-13*

> *"Ye shall know them by their fruits."*
>
> —*Matthew 7:16,* KJV

> *Be self-controlled and alert. Your enemy the devil prowls around like a roaring lion looking for someone to devour. Resist him, standing firm in the faith, because you know that your brothers throughout the world are undergoing the same kind of sufferings. And the God of all grace, who called you*

> *to his eternal glory in Christ, after you have suffered a little while, will himself restore you and make you strong, firm and steadfast. To him be the power for ever and ever. Amen.*
>
> *—1 Peter 5:8-11*

WHAT ABOUT CHRISTIAN NDES?

People frequently ask about the wonderful NDEs reported by professed Christians. What about them? Must we deny the witness that they provide?

I do not discount the possibility that some sincere Christians may have visions sent from God. But the difference is in the interpretation of these visions. They do not represent a voyage to heaven and back. God says that such trips of the dead are forbidden. The visions may contain real messages to the ill or to those who hear the stories. But they simply don't equate with a trip to heaven. Often these visions are simply a manifestation of prior beliefs and in that sense are not really new messages sent from God. They reflect the person's prior concept of God and do not really contain new information. They are not a record of dying, going to heaven, and coming back.

Even Christian-based NDEs are intensely personal, unverifiable, and not subject to rational confirmation. Certainly it is true that some Christians have reported the NDE. However, their stories are often suspect as well, but not because we imply that these loving people are committing fraud or are creating these stories with financial motives. If the NDE is simply the mind's way of integrating the many sensory inputs that occur during a near-death event, then it is reasonable that the Christian would put a Christian interpretation on the event. In a context of true faith, these unusual sensory inputs are worded in the realm of orthodox Christian beliefs. But the events are no less a creation of the mind of the Christian than the events of a Hindu's vision of Shiva is a creation of the Indian's mind.

Even if you grant that some NDEs could be real messages from God, all would still have to be judged by the yardstick of Scripture. The overwhelming majority of NDEs simply do not measure up to the standards and principles of the Bible. In fact, their principles contradict Scripture. All but a miniscule few would have to be declared counterfeit. Thus, no NDE can be taken at face value but can be accepted only insofar as it corresponds entirely with the Bible.

So each NDE is simply a reflection of the sum of expectations for death, the memory of others' accounts of death experiences, the particular sensory input that accompanies the medical catastrophe, and the memory retained by the person near death after he recovers from the medical crisis. Thus we would expect that a Dwight Moody (22-25) or David Livingstone (26-28) would have an experience at near-death or death that was consistent with biblical teachings. Moody on his deathbed was said to have declared (29), "Earth recedes; heaven opens before me." His son, Will, tried to arouse him from his dream. "No, this is no dream, Will," the great evangelist replied. "It is beautiful. It is like a trance. If this is death, it is sweet. There is no valley here. God is calling me, and I must go."

Moody may have seen heaven, or he may simply have known from his lifetime experience and faith what heaven would be like. We will never know. But it was not an NDE by modern accounts.

We would not expect that the details of any purported journey would actually correspond to the story that would have been told if the person had truly experienced death. The color of Jesus' hair or the description of the gates to heaven would be a figment of the imagination of these men, even though they were sincere Christians—some truly giants of the faith. And even their descriptions are very different from popular NDE accounts.

In our lives we should assign importance to subjects in proportion to the attention given to them in the Bible. If the Bible talks about a subject frequently, then it is probably worthy of a lot of our attention. If it is covered infrequently, we need not dwell upon it much in our lives. If it is not covered at all, we should ignore it. Arguably, the NDE is never mentioned in the Bible.

ARE ALL NDES FABRICATIONS?

We must finally ask if the NDE is entirely a fabrication, exaggeration, grand suggestion, coercion, or deception. Is it the object of the fantasy-prone?

Are all visions and deathbed stories during physical travail creations of manipulating minds? Are all NDEers seeking to promote an agenda, to gain fortune or fame? Possibly, but I doubt it. We know the physical and anatomic reasons for the sensations reported by those who have had serious medical conditions. The descriptions often are simply the brain's attempt to integrate these complex inputs.

Why do men and women write about the NDE? Is it entirely to gain the fame and fortune that accompanies such endeavors? Probably not. Many authors writing about the NDE began as skeptics, writing as reluctant reporters, later claiming to become believers. The religiously-inclined would say they were simply deceived. The cynical would argue that the authors feigned initial disbelief to provide an element of authenticity to their works. The cynic would also continue by saying that they write in a simple literary style in order to achieve a "common man" appearance. The NDE believer would counter by saying that the paranormal elements of the NDE (the reporting of events that occurred in a distance or in the future) authenticate the experience. The skeptic would say that in no case has the paranormal component of the NDE ever been proven independently. The NDE brings the scientist into a new realm. The NDE is not subject to the usual rigorous inspection that typifies other scientific endeavors. The techniques are themselves subjective. The interview is hardly science but is more of an art form. It challenges rational experimentation and discovery.

If virtually all of the reported NDEs are generated by deceptions, misinterpretations, or misconceptions, then the NDE has no validity whatsoever, and it loses *any* chance of having value for our instruction. All aspects of the NDE must be precisely in accordance with Scripture, but NDEs seem to be overwhelmingly counterfeit. If *any* aspect of the story is at variance with Scripture, then the *entire* story must be rejected. Thus, an otherworldly account has no chance of instructing or edifying us. If it is not already in the Bible, reject it!

SO WHY BOTHER WITH THE NDE?

We cannot fathom our own death. We want to believe in our own immortality. The NDE is an escape mechanism that allows us to transform the death process into a spectator event. It gives us the assurance that we may have a few rehearsals before the real thing.

But the NDE is an illusion. While seeming to be real—even more vivid than real—it deceives us. Our minds cannot accept our own death, and when it seems that death is near, we construct an alternate existence that allows us to deal with the trauma. We take our sensory input and construct an acceptable scenario that allows us to cope. The fact that reported NDEs are similar means simply that man's sensory inputs and his defense mechanisms are similar around the world. The fact that there are crucial differences in the reported NDEs means they are really not journeys to the afterlife but instead elaborate constructions of our pressured minds. The detachment provided by this construction relieves us of the physical pain of the event and the mental, emotional, and spiritual pain of the realization of the certainty of ultimate death. But again, it is all an illusion—a dangerous counterfeit to truth.

13

CONCLUSIONS

How Shall We Then Die?

So what is to be the Christian's response to the evidence presented in this book? Many Christians, upon hearing the medical and biblical evidence against the NDE as reported in the popular press, are disappointed, even reluctant to believe the facts. We all want the fantastic voyage, the exciting. We want miracles. We want a life that has a peaceful and loving conclusion, regardless of the choices we make during our stay on earth. We want no consequences to our sinful actions. But the truth remains—there is not a single unequivocal example of the NDE in the entire Bible. And there is nothing in the NDE that cannot be explained by current medical knowledge. God simply has not given the same cookie-cutter vision to eight million people as claimed by the pollsters and the NDE proponents.

So what do we make of the descriptions that seemed so powerful and compelling at first glance? To be sure, some people experience real sensations at the time of impending death, interrupted "death," or real death. The sensations, the sensory experiences, are real; but the interpretations of the sensations are what have been incorrect. These are not excursions to the beyond; they are not a glimpse of heaven. They are complex sensory messages that must be interpreted by the brain and that are resolved by the melding of the sensory input with the memories and life patterns programmed by the person's entire life experience. Nothing more, nothing less. Not a message from God. More likely a deceptive message from Satan who is himself a false messenger of light, seeking whom he may devour.

So the Christian must rely less on experience and more on biblical principles for his guidance. The road that leads to accepting Jesus as Savior and living for Jesus is difficult to take when there appears to be a simple alternative, one that requires no confession of sins, no repentance, no commitment, no daily walk, no prayer life, no service. But that apparently easier road from the NDE leads only to destruction—to a life that at best is void of purpose for the Christian who buys into the concept of the NDE and at worst is surrender to cultism or New Age beliefs. For the non-Christian, the NDE can lead to ultimate rejection of Jesus and eternal separation from God.

Yes, you will die.But *will you wake before you die?* Will there be a temporary trip to heaven? No. Will you be resuscitated? Maybe. But more importantly, you must make a decision. Will you wake up to the fact that you must make a decision about Jesus? Is He truth or is He a lie? Only He can transform death into life. The choice is yours. Will you wake before you die?

BIBLIOGRAPHY

When All Is Said and Done, All of What's Done Will Be Said

CHAPTER 2

1. Kubler-Ross, E. *On Death and Dying.* New York: Macmillan, 1969.
2. "The Conversion of Kubler-Ross." *Time.* November 12, 1979, p. 81.
3. Alnor, W.M. *Heaven Can't Wait: A Survey of Alleged Trips to the Other Side.* Grand Rapids, Mich.: Baker Books, 1996.
4. Abanes, R. *Embraced by the Light and the Bible.* Camp Hill, Penn.: Horizon Books, 1994.
5. Moody, R.A. *Life After Life: The Investigation of a Phenomenon—Survival of Bodily Death.* New York: Bantam Books, 1976.
6. Ibid., pp. 4-5.
7. Ibid., p. 16.
8. Ibid., pp. 25-107.
9. Plato. *The Republic.* Trans. Cornford, F.M. New York: Oxford University Press, 1945.
10. *The Tibetan Book of the Dead, or The After Death Experiences on the Bardo Plane, According to Lama Kazi Dawa-Samdup's English Rendering.* Ed. Evans-Wentz, W.Y. London: Oxford University Press, third edition, 1960.
11. Swedenborg, E. *Heaven and Hell.* New York: Swedenborg Foundation, 1928.
12. Swedenborg, E. *Compendium of the Theological and Spiritual Writings of Emanuel Swedenborg.* Boston: Crosby and Nichols, 1853.

13. Moody, R.A. *Reflections on Life After Life.* New York: Bantam Books, 1977.
14. Ibid., p. 33.
15. Ibid., p. 36.
16. Ibid., pp. 125-126.
17. Moody, R.A. and Perry, P. *The Light Beyond.* New York: Bantam Books, 1988.
18. Gallup, G., Jr. and Proctor, W. *Adventures in Immortality.* New York: McGraw-Hill, 1982.
19. Moody, 1988, p. 5.
20. Ibid., pp. 31-44.
21. Ibid., p. 69.
22. Lundahl, C.R. "Near Death Experiences of Mormons." In Lundahl, C.R., ed. *A Collection of Near Death Readings.* Chicago: Nelson Hall Publishers, 1982, pp. 165-179.
23. Moody, 1988, p. 70.
24. Ibid., p. 70.
25. Ibid.
26. Moody, R.A. and Perry, P. *Coming Back: A Psychiatrist Explores Past-Life Journeys.* New York: Bantam Books, 1991.
27. Ibid., p. 1.
28. Ibid., p. 104.
29. Ibid., p. 58.
30. Moody, R.A. and Perry, P. *Reunions. Visionary Encounters with Departed Loved Ones.* New York: Villard Books, 1993.
31. Ibid., p. 46.
32. Moody, R.A. "Evoking Apparitions of the Deceased." *Journal of the Medical Association of Georgia*, 1993; 82: 533-535.
33. Colson, C. "The Year of the Neopagan." *Christianity Today*, March 6, 1995; 39(3): 88.
34. Stevenson, I. and Greyson, B. "Near-Death Experiences. Relevance to the Question of Survival After Death." *Journal of the American Medical Association (JAMA)*, 1979; 242: 265-267.
35. Stevenson, I. "Research into the Evidence of Man's Survival After Death. A Historical and Critical Survey with a Summary of Recent Developments." *Journal of Nervous and Mental Disease*, 1977; 165: 152-170.
36. Stevenson, I. "Comments on 'The Reality of Death Experiences: A Personal Perspective.'" *Journal of Nervous and Mental Disease*, 1980; 168: 271-272.
37. Stevenson, I. "Research into the Evidence of Man's Survival After Death. A Historical and Critical Survey with a Summary of Recent Developments," pp. 152-170.
38. Stevenson, I. "Reply to the Comments of Dr. Lief and Dr. Ullman." *Journal of Nervous and Mental Disease*, 1977; 165: 181-183.
39. Pasricha, S. and Stevenson, J. "Near-Death Experiences in India: A

Preliminary Report." *Journal of Nervous and Mental Disease*, 1986; 174: 165-170.

40. Greyson, B. and Stevenson, I. "The Phenomenology of Near-Death Experiences." *American Journal of Psychiatry*, 1980; 137: 1193-1196.
41. Owens, J.E., Cook, E.W. and Stevenson, I. "Features of 'Near-Death Experience' in Relation to Whether or Not Patients Were Near Death." *Lancet*, 1990; 336: 1175-1177.
42. Owens, J.E., Cook, E.W. and Stevenson, I. "Near-Death Experience." *Lancet*, 1991; 337: 1167-1168.
43. Lief, H.I. "Commentary on Dr. Ian Stevenson's 'The Evidence of Man's Survival After Death.'" *Journal of Nervous and Mental Disease*, 1977; 165: 171-173.
44. Ullman, M. "Discussion of Dr. Stevenson's Paper: 'The Evidence of Man's Survival After Death.'" *Journal of Nervous and Mental Disease*, 1977; 165: 174-175.
45. Roll, W. "Comments on Dr. Ian Stevenson's Paper. Some Assumptions Guiding Research on Survival." *Journal of Nervous and Mental Disease*, 1977; 165: 176-180.
46. Brody, E.B. "Research in Reincarnation and Editorial Responsibility. An Editorial." *Journal of Nervous and Mental Disease*, 1977; 165: 151.
47. Blacher, R.S. "The Near-Death Experience. In Reply." *JAMA*, 1980; 244: 30.
48. Sabom, M.B. "The Near-Death Experience." *JAMA*, 1980; 244: 29-30.
49. Blacher, R.S. "To Sleep, Perchance to Dream . . ." *JAMA*, 1979; 242: 2291.
50. Wilkerson, R. *Beyond and Back. Those Who Died and Lived to Tell It.* Anaheim, Calif.: Melodyland Publishers, 1977.
51. Ibid., p. 53.
52. Ibid., p. 93.
53. Ibid., p. 102.
54. Greyson, B. "The Psychodynamics of Near-Death Experiences." *Journal of Nervous and Mental Disease*, 1983; 171: 376-381.
55. Greyson, B. and Bush, N.E. "Distressing Near-Death Experiences." *Psychiatry*, 1992; 55: 95-110.
56. Greyson, B. "Varieties of Near-Death Experiences." *Psychiatry*, 1993; 56: 390-399.
57. Greyson, B. "Near-Death Experiences and Personal Values." *American Journal of Psychiatry*, 1983; 140: 618-620.
58. Greyson, B. "The Near-Death Experience Scale. Construction, Reliability, and Validity." *Journal of Nervous and Mental Disease*, 1983; 171: 369-375.
59. Rodin, E.A. "The Reality of Death Experiences. A Personal Perspective." *Journal of Nervous and Mental Disease*, 1980; 168: 259-263.
60. Moody, R.A., Jr. "Commentary on 'The Reality of Death Experiences: A Personal Perspective' by Ernst Rodin." *Journal of Nervous and Mental Disease*, 1980; 168: 264-265.

61. Sabom, M.B. "Commentary on 'The Reality of Death Experiences' by Ernst Rodin." *Journal of Nervous and Mental Disease*, 1980; 168: 266-267.
62. Schnaper. N. "Comments Germane to the Paper Entitled 'The Reality of Death Experiences' by Ernst Rodin." *Journal of Nervous and Mental Disease*, 1980; 168: 268-270.
63. Rodin, 1980, p. 262.
64. Roberts, G. and Owen, J. "The Near-Death Experience."*British Journal of Psychiatry*, 1988; 153: 607-617.
65. Osis, K. and Haraldsson, E. "Deathbed Observations by Physicians and Nurses: A Cross-cultural Survey." *Journal of the American Society of Psychical Research*, 1977; 71: 237-259.
66. Osis, K. and Haraldsson, E. *At the Hour of Death*. New York: Avon Books, 1977.
67. Roberts, 1988, p. 612.
68. Sabom, M.B. *Recollections of Death: A Medical Investigation*. New York: Harper and Row, 1982.
69. Sabom, M.B. and Kreutziger, S. "Near-Death Experiences." *Journal of the Florida Medical Association*, 1977; 64: 648-650.
70. Sabom, M.B. and Kreutziger, S. "The Experience of Near Death." *Death Education*, 1977; 1: 195-203.
71. Sabom, 1982, p. 3.
72. Ibid., p. 185.
73. Sabom, M.B. "Book review—*To Hell and Back: Life After Death—Startling New Evidence*, by Maurice S. Rawlings." *Journal of Near-Death Studies*, 1996; 14: 197-209.
74. Morse, M. "A Near-Death Experience in a 7-year-old Child." *American Journal of Diseases of Children*, 1983; 137: 959-961.
75. Morse, M., Conner, D. and Tyler, D. "Near-Death Experiences in a Pediatric Population. A Preliminary Report." *American Journal of Diseases of Children*, 1985; 139: 595-600.
76. Morse, M., Castillo, P., Venecia, D., Milstein, J. and Tyler, D.C. "Childhood Near-Death Experiences." *American Journal of Diseases of Children*, 1986; 140: 1110-1114.
77. Morse, M.L. and Neppe, V. "Near-Death Experiences." *Lancet*, 1991; 337: 858.
78. Morse, M.L. "Near Death Experiences and Death-Related Visions in Children: Implications for the Clinician." *Current Problems in Pediatrics*, 1994; 24: 55-83.
79. Morse, M.L., Venecia, D. and Milstein, J. "Near-Death Experiences: A Neurophysiologic Model." *Journal of Near-Death Studies*, 1989; 8: 45-53.
80. Morse, M. and Perry, P. *Closer to the Light: Learning from Children's Near-Death Experiences*. New York: Villard Books, 1990.
81. Ibid., p. xi.

82. Ibid., p. 8.
83. Morse, 1983, p. 960.
84. Morse, 1990, pp. 119-157.
85. Ibid., p. 124.
86. Ibid., p. 125.
87. Ibid., p. 89.
88. Morse, M. and Perry, P. *Transformed by the Light: The Powerful Effect of Near-Death Experiences on People's Lives.* New York: Villard Books, 1992.
89. Morse, 1994, p. 56.
90. Davis, L. "A Comparison of UFO and Near-Death Experiences as Vehicles for the Evolution of Human Consciousness." *Journal of Near-Death Studies*, 1988; 6: 240-257.
91. Dobson, M., Tattersfield, A.E., Adler, M.W. and McNicol, M.W. "Attitudes and Long-term Adjustment of Patients Surviving Cardiac Arrest." *British Medical Journal*, 1971; 3: 207-212.
92. Negovsky, V. "Death, Dying and Revival: Ethical Aspects." *Resuscitation*, 1993; 25: 99-107.
93. Negovsky, V.A. "Postresuscitation Disease." *Critical Care Medicine*, 1988; 16: 942-946.
94. Morse, 1994, pp. 59-60.
95. Ibid., p. 61.
96. Malz, B. *Angels Watching Over Me.* Grand Rapids, Mich.: Chosen Books, 1986.
97. Malz, B. *My Glimpse of Eternity.* Grand Rapids, Mich.: Chosen Books, 1977.
98. Sidey, K. "Doctors Dispute Best-selling Author's Back-to-Life Story." *Christianity Today*, July 22, 1991; 35(8): 40-43.
99. Eadie, B.J. *Embraced by the Light.* Thorndike, Maine: G.K. Hall and Co., 1992.
100. Abanes, R. "Readers Embrace the Light." *Christianity Today*, March 7, 1994; 38(3): 53.
101. Mattingly, T. "Culture Watch: Brilliant Orbs and God Lite." *Moody Monthly*, 1995; 95(1): 30.
102. Eadie, B. *Embraced by the Light* (Utah Edition). Placerville, Calif.: Gold Leaf Press, 1992.
103. Brinkley, D. and Perry, P. *Saved by the Light.* New York: Villard Books, 1994.
104. Ibid., p. 46.
105. Ibid., p. 48.
106. Ibid., p. 72.
107. Ibid., p. 141.
108. Ibid., p. 159.
109. Ibid., p. 160.

CHAPTER 3

1. Ring, K. *Life at Death—A Scientific Investigation of the Near-Death Experience.* New York: Coward, McCann and Geoghegan, 1980.
2. Ring, K. "Commentary on 'The Reality of Death Experiences: A Personal Perspective' by Ernst A. Rodin." *Journal of Nervous and Mental Disease,* 1980; 168: 273-274.
3. Ring, K. and Franklin, S. "Do Suicide Survivors Report Near-Death Experiences?" *Omega,* 1981; 12: 191-208.
4. Ring, *Life at Death—A Scientific Investigation of the Near-Death Experience,* pp. 24-25.
5. Ibid., p. 27.
6. Ibid., pp. 32-33.
7. Ibid., p. 40.
8. Ibid., p. 106.
9. Ibid., p. 110.
10. Ibid., p. 111.
11. White, J. "Beyond the Body: An Interview with Kenneth Ring." *Science of Mind,* November 1988, p. 89, as cited in Yamamoto, J.I. *Christian Research Journal,* 1992, Spring, p. 4.
12. Moody, R.A. and Perry, P. *The Light Beyond.* New York: Bantam Books, 1988.
13. Moody, R.A. *Life After Life: The Investigation of a Phenomenon—Survival of Bodily Death.* New York: Bantam Books, 1976.
14. Moody, R.A. *Reflections on Life After Life.* New York: Bantam Books, 1977.
15. Moody, R. and Perry, P. *Reunions: Visionary Encounters with Departed Loved Ones.* New York: Villard Books, 1993.
16. Moody, R.A. and Perry, P. *Coming Back: A Psychiatrist Explores Past-Life Journeys.* New York: Bantam Books, 1991.
17. Moody, R.A., Jr. "Commentary on 'The Reality of Death Experiences: A Personal Perspective' by Ernst Rodin." *Journal of Nervous and Mental Disease,* 1980; 168: 264-265.
18. Moody, R.A. "Evoking Apparitions of the Deceased." *Journal of the Medical Association of Georgia,* 1993; 82: 533-535.
19. Sabom, M.B. "The Near-Death Experience." *JAMA,* 1980; 244: 29-30.
20. Sabom, M.B. "Commentary on 'The Reality of Death Experiences' by Ernst Rodin." *Journal of Nervous and Mental Disease,* 1980; 168: 266-267.
21. Sabom, M.B. *Recollections of Death: A Medical Investigation.* New York: Harper and Row, 1982.
22. Sabom, M.B. and Kreutziger, S. "Near-Death Experiences." *Journal of the Florida Medical Association,* 1977; 64: 648-650.
23. Sabom, M.B. and Kreutziger, S. "The Experience of Near Death." *Death Education,* 1977; 1: 195-203.

24. Rawlings, M. *Life Wish. Reincarnation: Reality or Hoax?* Nashville: Thomas Nelson, 1981.
25. Rawlings, M. *Beyond Death's Door.* Nashville: Thomas Nelson, 1978.
26. Rawlings, M.S. *To Hell and Back: Life After Death—Startling New Evidence.* Nashville: Thomas Nelson, 1993.
27. Blackmore, S. *Dying to Live: Near-Death Experiences.* Buffalo, N.Y.: Prometheus Books, 1993.
28. Ibid., p. xii.
29. Blackmore, S.J. and Troscianko, T.S. "The Physiology of the Tunnel." *Journal of Near-Death Studies*, 1989; 8: 15-28.
30. Locke, T.P. and Shontz, F.C. "Personality Correlates of the Near-Death Experience: A Preliminary Study." *Journal of the American Society of Psychical Research*, 1983; 77: 311-318.
31. Greyson, B. and Stevenson, I. "The Phenomenology of Near-Death Experiences." *American Journal of Psychiatry*, 1980; 137: 1193-1196.
32. Greyson, B. and Bush, N.E. "Distressing Near-Death Experiences." *Psychiatry*, 1992; 55: 95-110.
33. Greyson, B. "Varieties of Near-Death Experiences." *Psychiatry*, 1993; 56: 390-399.
34. Greyson, B. "Near-Death Experiences and Personal Values." *American Journal of Psychiatry*, 1983; 140: 618-620.
35. Greyson, B. "The Near-Death Experience Scale. Construction, Reliability, and Validity." *Journal of Nervous and Mental Disease*, 1983; 171: 369-375.
36. Morse, M. and Perry, P. *Transformed by the Light: The Powerful Effect of Near-Death Experiences on People's Lives.* New York: Villard Books, 1992.
37. Morse, M. and Perry, P. *Closer to the Light: Learning from Children's Near-Death Experiences.* New York: Villard Books, 1990.
38. Morse, M. "A Near-Death Experience in a 7-year-old child." *American Journal of Diseases of Children*, 1983; 137: 959-961.
39. Morse, M., Castillo, P., Venecia, D., Milstein, J. and Tyler, D.C. "Childhood Near-Death Experiences." *American Journal of Diseases of Children*, 1986; 140: 1110-1114.
40. Morse, M., Conner, D. and Tyler, D. "Near-Death Experiences in a Pediatric Population. A Preliminary Report." *American Journal of Diseases of Children*, 1985; 139: 595-600.
41. Morse, M.L. and Neppe, V. "Near-Death Experiences." *Lancet*, 1991; 337: 858.
42. Morse, M.L. "Near Death Experiences and Death-Related Visions in Children: Implications for the Clinician." *Current Problems in Pediatrics*, 1994; 24: 55-83.
43. Morse, M.L., Venecia, D. and Milstein, J. "Near-Death Experiences: A Neurophysiologic Model." *Journal of Near-Death Studies*, 1989; 8: 45-53.
44. Blackmore, 1993, p. 111.

45. Ibid., pp. 128-135.
46. Iverson, J. *In Search of the Dead: A Scientific Investigation of Evidence for Life After Death*. San Francisco: HarperCollins, 1992.
47. Blackmore, 1993, p. xii.
48. Ibid., pp. 263-264.
49. Lindley, J.H., Bryan, S. and Conley, B. "Near-Death Experiences in a Pacific Northwest American Population: The Evergreen Study." *Anabiosis*, 1981; 1: 104-124.
50. Ibid., p. 114.
51. Zaleski, C. *Otherworld Journeys: Accounts of Near-Death Experience in Medieval and Modern Times*. New York: Oxford University Press, 1987.
52. Zaleski, C. "St. Patrick's Purgatory: Pilgrimage Motifs in a Medieval Otherworld Vision." *Journal of the History of Ideas*, 1985; 46: 467-485.
53. Zaleski, 1987, p. 14.
54. Ibid., p. 7.
55. *The Ancient Egyptian Book of the Dead*. Trans. Faulkner, R.O. Ed. Andrews, C. New York: Macmillan, revised edition, 1985.
56. *The Tibetan Book of the Dead, or The After Death Experiences on the Bardo Plane, According to Lama Kazi Dawa-Samdup's English Rendering*. Ed. Evans-Wentz, W.Y. London: Oxford University Press, third edition, 1960.
57. Gregory the Great. *Dialogues*. Trans. Zimmerman, O.J. New York: Fathers of the Church, 1959.
58. Zaleski, 1987, pp. 28-31.
59. bid., pp. 34-42.

CHAPTER 4

1. *The Ancient Egyptian Book of the Dead*. Trans. Faulkner, R.O. Ed. Andrews, C. New York: Macmillan, revised edition, 1985.
2. Ibid., p. 27.
3. Plato. *The Republic*. Trans. Cornford, F.M. New York: Oxford University Press, 1945, p. 351.
4. *The Tibetan Book of the Dead, or The After Death Experiences on the Bardo Plane, According to Lama Kazi Dawa-Samdup's English Rendering*. Ed. Evans-Wentz, W.Y. London: Oxford University Press, third edition, 1960.
5. Ibid., p. xiii.
6. Ibid., p. xvii.
7. Ibid., pp. 90-92.
8. Ibid., p. 103.
9. Heim, A. "Notizen Uber Den Tod Durch Absturz." *Jahrbuch des Schweizer Alpenclubs*, 1892; 27: 327-337. Trans. Noyes, R, and Kletti, R. "The Experience of Dying from Falls." *Omega*, 1972; 3: 45-52.

10. Ibid., p. 51.
11. Swedenborg, E. *Compendium of the Theological and Spiritual Writings of Emanuel Swedenborg*. Boston: Crosby and Nichols, 1853.
12. Swedenborg, E. *Heaven and Hell*. New York: Swedenborg Foundation, 1928.
13. Hallowell, I. "Spirits of the Dead in Saulteaux Life and Thought." *Journal of the Royal Anthropological Institute*, 1940; 70: 29-51.
14. McDermott, W.V. "Endorphins, I Presume." *Lancet*, 1980; 2: 1353.
15. Carr, D.B. "Endorphins at the Approach of Death." *Lancet*, 1981; 1: 390.
16. Livingstone, D. *Adventures and Discoveries in the Interior of Africa*. Philadelphia: Hubbard Brothers, 1872, p. 15.
17. Moody, W.R. *The Life of Dwight L. Moody*. London: Morgan and Scott, 1900.
18. Moody, P.D. *My Father: An Intimate Portrait of Dwight Moody*. Boston: Little, Brown and Company, 1938.
19. Day, R.E. *Bush Aglow: The Life Story of Dwight Lyman Moody. Commoner of Northfield*. Philadelphia: The Judson Press, 1936.
20. Pollock, J.C. *Moody*. New York: Macmillan, 1963, p. 316.
21. Greyson, B. "The Near-Death Experience Scale. Construction, Reliability, and Validity." *Journal of Nervous and Mental Disease*, 1983; 171: 369-375.
22. Blackmore, S.J. "Near-Death Experiences in India: They Have Tunnels Too." *Journal of Near-Death Studies*, 1993; 11: 205-217.
23. Osis, K. and Haraldsson, E. *At the Hour of Death*. New York: Avon Books, 1977, p. 7.
24. Lindley, J.H., Bryan, S. and Conley, B. "Near-Death Experiences in a Pacific Northwest American Population: The Evergreen Study." *Anabiosis*, 1981; 1: 104-124.
25. Gallup, G., Jr, and Proctor, W. *Adventures in Immortality*. New York: McGraw-Hill, 1982.
26. Ibid., p. 190.
27. Ibid., p. 17.
28. Blackmore, S. *Dying to Live: Near-Death Experiences*. Buffalo: Prometheus Books, 1993.
29. Blackmore, S.J. "Near-Death Experiences." *Lancet*, 1994; 344: 1298-1299.
30. Blackmore, S.J. and Troscianko, T.S. "The Psychophysics of Death." *Perception*, 1988; 17: 419.
31. Negovsky, V. "Death, Dying and Revival: Ethical Aspects." *Resuscitation*, 1993; 25: 99-107.
32. Dobson, M., Tattersfield, A.E., Adler, M.W. and McNicol, M.W. "Attitudes and Long-term Adjustment of Patients Surviving Cardiac Arrest." *British Medical Journal*, 1971; 3: 207-212.
33. Harris, B. and Bascom, L.C. *Full Circle: The Near-Death Experience and Beyond*. New York: Pocket Books, 1990.
34. Ibid., p. 247.

35. Schoonmaker, F. "Denver Cardiologist Discloses Findings After 18 Years of Near-Death Research." *Anabiosis*, 1979; 1: 1-2, as cited in Ring, K. *Life at Death—A Scientific Investigation of the Near-Death Experience.* New York: Coward, McCann and Geoghegan, 1980.
36. Lukoff, D., Lu, F. and Turner, R. "Toward a More Culturally Sensitive DSM-IV. Psychoreligious and Psychospiritual Problems." *Journal of Nervous and Mental Disease*, 1992; 180: 673-682.
37. Negovsky, V.A. "Postresuscitation Disease." *Critical Care Medicine*, 1988; 16: 942-946.
38. Druss, R.G. and Kornfeld, D.S. "The Survivors of Cardiac Arrest. A Psychiatric Study." *JAMA*, 1967; 201: 75-80.
39. Martens, P.R. "Near-Death-Experiences in Out-of-Hospital Cardiac Arrest Survivors. Meaningful Phenomena or Just Fantasy of Death?" *Resuscitation*, 1994; 27: 171-175.
40. Ehrenwald, J. "Out-of-the-body Experiences and the Denial of Death." *Journal of Nervous and Mental Disease*, 1974; 159: 227-233.
41. Hart, H. "ESP Projection: Spontaneous Cases and the Experimental Method." *Journal of the American Society of Psychical Research*, 1954; 48: 121-146.
42.. Palmer, J. "A Community Mail Survey of Psychic Experiences." *Journal of the American Society of Psychical Research*, 1979; 73: 221-251.
43. Palmer, J. and Lieberman, R. "The Influence of Psychological Set on ESP and Out-of-Body Experiences." *Journal of the American Society of Psychical Research*, 1975; 69: 193-213.
44. Palmer, J. and Lieberman, R. "ESP and Out-of-Body Experiences: A Further Study." *Research in Parapsychology*, 1976; pp. 102-106.
45. Palmer, J. and Lieberman, R. "The Influence of Psychological Set on ESP and Out-of-Body Experiences." *Journal of the American Society of Psychical Research*, 1975; 69: 257-280. Cited in Hillstrom, E.L. *Testing the Spirits.* Downers Grove, Ill.: InterVarsity Press, 1995, p. 88-89.
46. Tobacyk, J.J. and Mitchell, T.P. "The Out-of-Body Experience and Personality Adjustment." *Journal of Nervous and Mental Disease*, 1987; 175: 367-370.
47. Hillstrom, E.L. *Testing the Spirits.* Downers Grove, Illinois, InterVarsity Press, 1995.
48. Tart, C.T. "A Psychophysiologic Study of Out-of-the-Body Experiences in a Select Subject." *Journal of the American Society of Psychical Research*, 1968; 62: 3-27.
49. Sabom, M.B. *Recollections of Death: A Medical Investigation.* New York: Harper and Row, 1982.
50. Sabom, M.B. and Kreutziger, S. "Near-Death Experiences." *Journal of the Florida Medical Association*, 1977; 64: 648-650.
51. Sabom, M.B. and Kreutziger, S. "The Experience of Near Death." *Death Education*, 1977; 1: 195-203.

52. Ring, K. *Life at Death—A Scientific Investigation of the Near-Death Experience.* New York: Coward, McCann and Geoghegan, 1980.
53. Ring, K. "Commentary on 'The Reality of Death Experiences: A Personal Perspective' by Ernst A. Rodin." *Journal of Nervous and Mental Disease,* 1980; 168: 273-274.
54. Ring, K. and Franklin, S. "Do Suicide Survivors Report Near-Death Experiences?" *Omega,* 1981; 12: 191-208.
55. Vicchio, S. "Near-Death Experiences: Some Logical Problems and Questions for Further Study." *Anabiosis,* 1981; 1: 66-87.
56. Moody, R.A. and Perry, P. *The Light Beyond.* New York: Bantam Books, 1988.
57. Moody, R.A. *Life After Life: The Investigation of a Phenomenon—Survival of Bodily Death.* New York: Bantam Books, 1976.
58. Moody, R.A. *Reflections on Life After Life.* New York: Bantam Books, 1977.
59. Moody R. and Perry, P. *Reunions: Visionary Encounters with Departed Loved Ones.* New York: Villard Books, 1993.
60. Moody, R.A. and Perry, P. *Coming Back: A Psychiatrist Explores Past-Life Journeys.* New York: Bantam Books, 1991.
61. Moody, R.A., Jr. "Commentary on 'The Reality of Death Experiences: A Personal Perspective' by Ernst Rodin." *Journal of Nervous and Mental Disease,* 1980; 168: 264-265.
62. Twemlow, S.W., Gabbard, G.O. and Jones, F.C. "The Out-of-Body Experience: A Phenomenological Typology Based on Questionnaire Responses." *American Journal of Psychiatry,* 1982; 139: 450-455.
63. Gabbard, G.O., Twemlow, S.W. and Jones, F.C. "Do Near-Death Experiences Only Occur Near Death?" *Journal of Nervous and Mental Disease,* 1981; 169: 374-377.
64. Twemlow, S. and Gabbard, G. "The Influence of Demographic/Psychological Factors and Preexisting Conditions on the Near-Death Experience." *Omega,* 1984; 15: 223-235.
65. Stevenson, I. and Greyson, B. "Near-Death Experiences. Relevance to the Question of Survival After Death." *JAMA,* 1979; 242: 265-267.
66. Greyson, B. and Stevenson, I. "The Phenomenology of Near-Death Experiences." *American Journal of Psychiatry,* 1980; 137: 1193-1196.
67. Greyson, B. "The Psychodynamics of Near-Death Experiences." *Journal of Nervous and Mental Disease,* 1983; 171: 376-381.
68. Greyson, B. and, Bush, N.E. "Distressing Near-Death Experiences." *Psychiatry,* 1992; 55: 95-110.
69. Greyson, B. "Varieties of Near-Death Experiences." *Psychiatry,* 1993; 56: 390-399.
70. Greyson, B. "Near-Death Experiences and Personal Values." *American Journal of Psychiatry,* 1983; 140: 618-620.
71. Owens, J.E., Cook, E.W. and Stevenson, I. "Features of 'Near-Death

Experience' in Relation to Whether or Not Patients Were Near Death." *Lancet*, 1990; 336: 1175-1177.

72. Jansen, K.L.R. "Transcendental Explanations and Near-Death Experience." *Lancet*, 1991; 337: 244.
73. Jansen, K. "Near Death Experience and the NMDA Receptor." *British Medical Journal*, 1989; 298: 1708.
74. Jansen, K.L.R. "Neuroscience and the Near-Death Experience: Roles for the NMSA-PCP [sic] Receptor, the Sigma Receptor and the Endopsychosins." *Medical Hypotheses*, 1990; 31: 25-29.
75. Jansen, K.L.R. "The Near-Death Experience." *British Journal of Psychiatry*, 1989; 154: 883-884.
76. Siegel, R.K. "The Psychology of Life After Death." *American Psychology*, 1980; 35: 911-930.
77. Siegel, R.K. "Phencyclidine and Ketamine Intoxication: A Study of Four Populations of Recreational Users." In Peterson, R.C. and Stillman, R.C., eds. *Phencyclidine Abuse: An Appraisal.* Bethesda, Md.: National Institute of Drug Abuse, 1978, pp. 119-147.
78. Grinspoon, L. and Bakalar, S.B. *Psychedelic Drugs Reconsidered.* New York: Basic Books, 1981.
79. Walker, F.O. "A Nowhere Near-Death Experience: Heavenly Choirs Interrupt Myelography." *JAMA*, 1989; 261: 3245-3246.
80. Zaleski, C. *Otherworld Journeys: Accounts of Near-Death Experience in Medieval and Modern Times.* New York: Oxford University Press, 1987.
81. Harris, 1990, p. 247.
82. Davis, L. "A Comparison of UFO and Near-Death Experiences as Vehicles for the Evolution of Human Consciousness." *Journal of Near-Death Studies*, 1988; 6: 240-257.
83. Locke, T.P. and Shontz, F.C. "Personality Correlates of the Near-Death Experience: A Preliminary Study." *Journal of the American Society of Psychical Research*, 1983; 77: 311-318.
84. Kohr, R.L. "Near-Death Experiences, Altered States, and Psi-Sensitivity." *Anabiosis*, 1983; 3: 157-176.
85. Kellehear, A. "Culture, Biology, and the Near-Death Experience. A Reappraisal." *Journal of Nervous and Mental Disease*, 1993; 181: 148-156.
86. Kellehear, A. "The Near-Death Experience as Status Passage." *Social Science and Medicine*, 1990; 31: 933-939.
87. Kellehear, A., Heaven, P. and Gao, J. "Community Attitudes Toward Near-Death Experiences: A Chinese Study." *Journal of Near-Death Studies*, 1990; 8: 163-173.
88. Becker, C.B. "The Centrality of Near-Death Experiences in Chinese Pure Land Buddhism." *Anabiosis*, 1981; 1: 154-171.
89. Ibid., p. 163.
90. Muller, M. (ed. and trans.). *Sacred Books of the East*, Volume 49. Oxford: Clarendon Press, 1894. Quoted in Becker, C.B. "The Pure Land Revisited:

Sino-Japanese Meditations and Near-Death Experiences of the Next World." *Anabiosis*, 1984; 4: 51-68, p. 58.

91. Takakusu, J., trans. "The Amitayur-dhyana-sutra." In Muller, M., ed. *Sacred Books of the East*, Volume 49. Oxford: Clarendon Press, 1894. Quoted in Becker, C.B. "The Pure Land Revisited: Sino-Japanese Meditations and Near-Death Experiences of the Next World." p. 53.
92. Becker, C.B. "The Pure Land Revisited: Sino-Japanese Meditations and Near-Death Experiences of the Next World." *Anabiosis*, 1984; 4: 51-68.
93. Becker, C.B. "Views from Tibet: NDEs and the Book of the Dead." *Anabiosis*, 1985; 5: 3-20.
94. Becker, 1984, p. 53.
95. Ibid., p. 58.
96. Ibid., p. 61.
97. Pasricha, S. and Stevenson, J. "Near-Death Experiences in India: A Preliminary Report." *Journal of Nervous and Mental Disease*, 1986; 174: 165-170.
98. Pasricha, S. "Near-Death Experiences in South India: A Systematic Survey in Channapatna." *NIMHANS Journal*, 1992; 10: 111-118.
99. Blackmore, S.J. and Troscianko, T.S. "The Physiology of the Tunnel." *Journal of Near-Death Studies*, 1989; 8: 15-28.
100. Osis, 1977, p. 44.
101. Ibid., p. 177.
102. Ibid., p. 93.
103. Ibid., p. 98.
104. Pasricha, 1986, p. 167.
105. Ibid., p. 166.
106. Ibid.
107. Ibid., p. 167.
108. Osis, K. and Haraldsson, E. "Deathbed Observations by Physicians and Nurses: A Cross-cultural Survey." *Journal of the American Society of Psychical Research*, 1977; 71: 237-259.
109. Pasricha, 1986, pp. 168-169.
110. Gomez-Jeria, J.S. "A Near-Death Experience Among Mapuche People." *Journal of Near-Death Studies*, 1993; 11: 219-222.
111. Feng, Z. "A Research on Near-Death Experiences of Survivors in Big Earthquake of Tangshan, 1976." *Chinese Journal of Neurology and Psychiatry*, 1992; 25: 222-225.
112. Gallup, 1982, p. 91.
113. Alnor, A.M. "Heaven Can't Wait: A Survey of Alleged Trips to the Other Side." *Christian Research Journal*, 1993, Spring, p. 5.
114. Garfield, C.A. "More Grist for the Mill: Additional Near-Death Research Findings and Discussion." *Anabiosis*, 1979; 1: 5-7.
115. Grey, M. *Return from Death: An Exploration of the Near-Death Experience*. Boston: Arkana, 1985.

116. Tuttle, M.J. "Near-Death Experience Denied." *Canadian Medical Association Journal*, 1992; 146: 1700.
117. Brinkley, D. and Perry, P. *Saved by the Light.* New York: Villard Books, 1994.
118. Sutherland, C. "Psychic Phenomena Following Near-Death Experiences: An Australian Study." *Journal of Near-Death Studies*, 1989; 8: 93-102.
119. Atwater, P.M.H. *Beyond the Light: What Isn't Being Said About the Near-Death Experience.* New York: Birch Lane Press, 1994.

CHAPTER 5

1. Blacher, R.S. "To Sleep, Perchance to Dream . . ." *JAMA*, 1979; 242: 2291.
2. Sabom, M.B. "The Near-Death Experience." *JAMA*, 1980; 244: 29-30.
3. Blacher, R.S. "The Near-Death Experience. In Reply." *JAMA*, 1980; 244: 30.
4. James, P.F. "Near-Death Experiences." *Lancet*, 1989; 2: 1110-1111.
5. Wilson, J. "Near-Death Experiences." *Lancet*, 1989; 2: 1341.
6. Gordon, B.D. "Near-Death Experience." *Lancet*, 1989; 2: 1452.
7. Owens, J.E., Cook, E.W. and Stevenson, I. "Features of 'Near-Death Experience' in Relation to Whether or Not Patients Were Near Death." *Lancet*, 1990; 336: 1175-1177.
8. Thomas, D.J.B. "Near-Death Experiences." *Lancet*, 1991; 337: 116.
9. Rosen, S.D. "Near-Death Experiences." *Lancet*, 1991; 337: 116.
10. Jansen, K.L.R. "Transcendental Explanations and Near-Death Experience." *Lancet*, 1991; 337: 244.
11. Morse, M.L. and Neppe, V. "Near-Death Experiences." *Lancet*, 1991; 337: 858.
12. Owens. J.E., Cook, E.W. and Stevenson, I. "Near-Death Experience." *Lancet*, 1991; 337: 1167-1168.
13. Walker, F.O. "A Nowhere Near-Death Experience: Heavenly Choirs Interrupt Myelography." *JAMA*, 1989; 261: 3245-3246.
14. Tuttle, M.J. "Near-Death Experience Denied." *Canadian Medical Journal*, 1992; 146: 1700.
15. Harpur, T. "Near-Death Experience Denied." *Canadian Medical Journal*, 1992; 147: 1315.
16. Tuttle, M.J. "Near-Death Experience Denied." *Canadian Medical Journal*, 1992; 147: 1315-1316.
17. Williams, B. "Near-Death Experience Denied." *Canadian Medical Journal*, 1993; 148: 376.
18. Tuttle, M.J. "Near-Death Experience Denied." *Canadian Medical Journal*, 1993; 148: 376.
19. Jansen, K.L.R. "The Near-Death Experience." *British Journal of Psychiatry*, 1989; 154: 883-884.

20. James, P.F. "Near-Death Experiences." *Lancet*, 1989; 2: 1110-1111.
21. Wilson, J. "Near-Death Experiences." *Lancet*, 1989; 2: 1341.
22. Rea, M. "Near-Death Experiences." *Lancet*, 1989; 2: 1341.
23. McDermott, W.V. "Endorphins, I Presume." *Lancet*, 1980; 2: 1353.
24. Carr, D.B. "Endorphins at the Approach of Death." *Lancet*, 1981; 1: 390.
25. Blackmore, S.J. "Near-Death Experiences." *Lancet*, 1994; 344: 1298-1299.
26. Gordon, B.D. "Near-Death Experience." *Lancet*, 1989; 2: 1452.
27. Rodin, A. and Key, J. "Lazarus Complex (Lazarus Syndrome, Near-Death Syndrome)." *Ohio Medicine*, 1991; 87: 150-151.
28. Bray, J.G. "The Lazarus Phenomenon Re-visited." *Anesthesiology*, 1993; 78: 991.
29. Linko, K., Honakavaara, P. and Salmenpera, M. "Recovery After Discontinued Cardiopulmonary Resuscitation." *Lancet*, 1982; 1: 106-107.
30. Letellier, N., Coulomb, F., Lebec, C. and Brunet, C. "Recovery After Discontinued Cardiopulmonary Resuscitation." *Lancet*, 1982; 1: 1019.
31. Koblin, D.D. "The Lazarus Phenomenon Re-visited: I." *Anesthesiology*, 1993; 79: 1438.
32. Hill, D.J. "The Lazarus Phenomenon Re-visited: II." *Anesthesiology*, 1993; 79: 1438-1439.
33. Bray, J.G. "The Lazarus Phenomenon Re-visited: Reply." *Anesthesiology*, 1993; 79: 1439.
34. Heytens, L., Verlooy, J., Ghevens, J. and Bossaert, L. "Lazarus Sign and Extensor Posturing in a Brain Dead Patient." *Journal of Neurosurgery*, 1989; 71: 449-451.

CHAPTER 6

1. *Brain's Diseases of the Nervous System.* Ed. Walton, J. New York: Oxford University Press, tenth edition, 1994.
2. Adams, R.D. and Victor, M. *Principles of Neurology.* New York: McGraw-Hill, fifth edition, 1993.
3. Brown, M.M. and Hachinski, V.C. "Acute Confusional States, Amnesia, and Dementia." In *Principles of Internal Medicine.* Ed. Wilson, J.D., Braunwald, E., Isselbacher, K.J., Petersdorf, R.G., Martin, J.B., Fauci, A.S. and Root, R.S. New York: McGraw-Hill, twelfth edition, 1991, Chapter 30, pp. 183-193.
4. Kistler, J.P., Ropper, A.H. and Martin, J.B. "Cerebrovascular Diseases." In *Principles of Internal Medicine.* Chapter 351, pp. 1977-2002.
5. Truex, R.C. and Carpenter, M.B. *Strong and Elwyn's Human Neuroanatomy.* Baltimore: Williams and Wilkins, fifth edition, 1964.
6. Lassen, N.A. "Control of Cerebral Circulation in Health and Disease." *Circulation Research*, 1974; 34: 749-760.
7. Kovach, A.G. and Sandor, P. "Cerebral Blood Flow and Brain Function

During Hypotension and Shock." *Annual Review of Physiology*, 1976; 38: 571-596.

8. Bass, E. "Cardiopulmonary Arrest: Pathophysiology and Neurologic Complications." *Annals of Internal Medicine*, 1985; 103: 920-927.
9. Martin, G.B., Nowak, R.M., Paradis, N., Rosenberg, J., Walton, D., Smith, M., Eisiminger, R. and Welch, K.M.A. "Characterization of Cerebral Energetics and Brain pH by 31P Spectroscopy After Graded Canine Cardiac Arrest and Bypass Reperfusion." *Journal of Cerebral Blood Flow and Metabolism*, 1990; 10: 221-226.
10. Hevor, T.K. "Some Aspects of Carbohydrate Metabolism in the Brain." *Biochimie*, 1994; 76: 111-120.
11. Keele, A.C., Neil, E. and Joels, N. *Samson Wright's Applied Physiology*. Oxford: Oxford University Press, thirteenth edition, 1982, pp. 133-154.
12. Graham, D.I. "Hypoxia and Vascular Disorders." In *Greenfield's Neuropathology*. Eds. Adams, J.H. and Duchen, L.W. New York: Oxford University Press, fifth edition, 1992, Chapter 4, pp. 153-268.
13. Rossen, R., Kabat, H. and Anderson, J.P. "Acute Arrest of Cerebral Circulation in Man." *Archives of Neurology and Psychiatry*, 1943; 50: 510-528.
14. Aminoff, M.J., Scheinman, M.M., Griffin, J.C. and Herre, J.M. "Electrocerebral Accompaniments of Syncope Associated with Malignant Ventricular Arrhythmias." *Annals of Internal Medicine*, 1988; 108: 791-796.
15. Meduna, L.J. *Carbon Dioxide Therapy*. Springfield, Ill.: Charles C. Thomas, 1950.
16. Niedermeyer, E. "Consciousness: Function and Definition." *Clinical Electroencephalography*, 1994; 25: 86-93.
17. Culebras, A. "The Neurology of Sleep." *Neurology*, 1992; 42 (Suppl. 6): 6-8.
18. Culebras, A. "Neuroanatomic and Neurologic Correlates of Sleep Disturbances." *Neurology*, 1992; 42 (Suppl. 6): 19-27.
19. Mahowald, M.W. and Schenck, C.H. "Dissociated States of Wakefulness and Sleep." *Neurology*, 1992; 42 (Suppl. 6): 44-52.
20. Lugaresi, E. "The Thalamus and Insomnia." *Neurology*, 1992; 42 (Suppl. 6): 28-33.
21. Steriade, M. "Basic Mechanisms of Sleep Generation." *Neurology*, 1992; 42 (Suppl. 6): 9-18.
22. Wright, J.J. "Reticular Activation and the Dynamics of Neuronal Networks." *Biological Cybernetics*, 1990; 62: 289-298.
23. Stewart-Amidei, C. " Assessing the Comatose Patient in the Intensive Care Unit." *American Association of Critical-Care Nurses: Clinical Issues in Critical Care Nursing*, 1991; 2: 613-622.
24. Hess, C.W. and Bassetti, C. "Neurology of Consciousness and of

Consciousness Disorders." *Schweizerische Rundschau fur Medizin Praxis*, 1994; 83: 212-219.
25. Houdart, R. "Consciousness." *Encephale*, 1994; 20: 159-168.
26. Hulihan, J.F., Jr. and Syna, D.R. "Electroencephalographic Sleep Patterns in Post-Anoxic Stupor and Coma." *Neurology*, 1994; 44: 758-760.
27. Nogueira-de-Melo, A,. Krauss, G.L. and Niedermeyer, E. "Spindle Coma: Observations and Thoughts." *Clinical Electroencephalography*, 1990; 21: 151-161.
28. Plum, F. and Posner, J.B. *The Diagnosis of Stupor and Coma.* Philadelphia: F. A. Davis Company, third edition, 1980.
29. "Report of the Ad Hoc Committee of the Harvard Medical School to Examine the Definition of Brain Death. A Definition of Irreversible Coma." *JAMA*, 1968; 205: 85-88.
30. Safar, P. "Cerebral Resuscitation After Cardiac Arrest: A Review." *Circulation*, 1986; 74 (Suppl. IV): IV-138—IV-153.
31. Negovsky, V.A. "Postresuscitation Disease." *Critical Care Medicine*, 1988; 16: 942-946.
32. Safar, P. "Effects of the Postresuscitation Syndrome on Cerebral Recovery from Cardiac Arrest." *Critical Care Medicine*, 1985; 13: 932-935.
33. Caronna, J. "Diagnosis, Prognosis and Treatment of Hypoxic Coma." In Fahn, S., Davis, J.N. and Rowland, L.P, eds. *Advances in Neurology 26.* New York: Raven Press, 1979, pp. 1-19.
34. Heymans, C. "Survival and Revival of Nervous Tissues After Arrest of Circulation." *Physiology Review*, 1950; 30: 375-392.
35. Cummings, J.L., Tomiyasu, U., Read, S. and Benson, D.F. "Amnesia with Hippocampal Lesions After Cardiopulmonary Arrest." *Neurology*, 1984; 34: 679-681.
36. Volpe, B.T. and Hirst, W. "The Characterization of an Amnestic Syndrome Following Hypoxic Ischemic Injury." *Archives of Neurology*, 1983; 40: 436-440.
37. Bertini, G., Giglioli, C., Giovannini, F., Bartoletti, A., Cricelli, F., Margheri, M., Russo, L., Taddei, T. and Taiti, A. "Neuropsychological Outcome of Survivors of Out-of-Hospital Cardiac Arrest." *Journal of Emergency Medicine*, 1990; 8: 407-412.
38. Parkin, A.J., Miller, J. and Vincent, R. "Multiple Neuropsychological Deficits Due to Anoxic Encephalopathy: A Case Study." *Cortex*, 1987; 23: 655-665.
39. Finkelstein, S. and Caronna, J.J. "Amnestic Syndrome Following Cardiac Arrest." *Neurology*, 1978; 28: 389.
40. Caronna, J.J. and Finkelstein, S. "Neurological Syndromes After Cardiac Arrest." *Stroke*, 1978; 9: 517-520.
41. Jackson, J.H. *Selected Writings of John Hughlings Jackson on Epilepsy and Epileptiform Convulsions.* Ed. Taylor, J. London: Hodder and Stoughton, 1931.

42. Penfield, W. "The Twenty-ninth Maudsley Lecture: The Role of the Temporal Cortex in Certain Psychical Phenomena." *Journal of Mental Science*, 1955; 101: 451-465.
43. Penfield, W. "Temporal Lobe Epilepsy." *British Journal of Surgery*, 1954; 41: 337-343.
44. Penfield, W. and Perot, P. "The Brain's Record of Auditory and Visual Experience." *Brain*, 1963; 86: 595-696.
45. Gloor, P., Olivier, A., Quesney, L.F., Andermann, F. and Horowitz, S. "The Role of the Limbic System in Experiential Phenomena of Temporal Lobe Epilepsy." *Annals of Neurology*, 1982; 12: 129-144.
46. Penfield, 1955, p. 455.
47. Ibid.
48. Ibid., p. 614.
49. Ibid., p. 618.
50. Ibid., p. 458.
51. Gloor, P. "Experiential Phenomena of Temporal Lobe Epilepsy. Facts and Hypotheses." *Brain*, 1990; 113: 1673-1694.
52. Lenox, W.G. "Antonius Guainerius on Epilepsy." *Annals of Medical History* (third series) 1940; 2: 482-499.
53. Mulder, D.W. and Daly, D. "Psychiatric Symptoms Associated with Lesions of the Temporal Lobe." *JAMA*, 1952; 150: 173-176.
54. Halgren, E., Walter, R.D., Cherlow, D.G. and Crandall, P.H. "Mental Phenomena Evoked by Electrical Stimulation of the Human Hippocampal Formation and Amygdala." *Brain*, 1978; 101: 83-117.
55. Grosso, M. "Toward an Explanation of Near-Death Phenomena." *Anabiosis*, 1981; 1: 1-26.
56. Kieffer, G. "Kundalini and the Near-Death Experience." *Journal of Near-Death Studies*, 1994; 12: 159-176.
57. Becker, C.B. "Views from Tibet: NDEs and the Book of the Dead." *Anabiosis*, 1985; 5: 3-20.
58. Schnaper, N. "The Psychological Implications of Severe Trauma: Emotional Sequelae to Unconsciousness." *Journal of Trauma*, 1975; 15: 94-98.
59. Noyes, R. "Near Death Experiences: Their Interpretation and Significance." In Kastenbaum, R., ed. *Between Life and Death*. New York: Springer, 1979, pp. 73-88.
60. Olson, M. "The Out-of-Body Experience and Other States of Consciousness." *Archives of Psychological Nursing*, 1987; 1: 201-207.
61. Bengtsson, M., Holmberg, S. and Jansson, B. "A Psychiatric-Psychological Investigation of Patients Who Had Survived Circulatory Arrest." *Acta Psychiatrica Scandinavica*, 1969; 45: 327-346.
62. Blackmore, S. *Dying to Live: Near-Death Experiences*. Buffalo, N.Y.: Prometheus Books, 1993.
63. Ibid., pp. 79-80.
64. The Multi-Society Task Force on PVS. "Medical Aspects of the Persistent

Vegetative State." *New England Journal of Medicine*, 1994; 330: 1499-1508, 1572-1579.

65. Keren, O., Sazbon, L., Groswasser, Z. and Shmuel, M. "Follow-up Studies of Somatosensory Evoked Potentials and Auditory Brainstem Evoked Potentials in Patients with Post-Coma Unawareness (PCU) of Traumatic Brain Injury." *Brain Injury*, 1994; 8: 239-247.
66. Binnie, C.D. and Prior, P.F. "Electroencephalography." *Journal of Neurology, Neurosurgery, and Psychiatry*, 1994; 57: 1308-1319.
67. Bancaud, J., Brunet-Bourgin, F., Chauvel, P. and Halgren, E. "Anatomical Origin of Deja-vu and Vivid 'Memories' in Human Temporal Lobe Epilepsy." *Brain*, 1994; 117: 71-90.
68. French, J.A., Williamson, P.D., Thadani, V.M., Darcey, T.M., Mattson, R.H., Spencer, S.S. and Spencer, D.D. "Characteristics of Medial Temporal Lobe Epilepsy: I. Results of History and Physical Examination." *Annals of Neurology*, 1993; 34: 774-780.
69. Penfield, 1963, p. 658.
70. Ibid., p. 658.
71. Gloor, 1990, p. 1674.
72. Ibid., p. 1674.
73. Bancaud, 1994, pp. 71-72.
74. Penfield, 1955, p. 461.
75. Lempert, T., Bauer, M. and Schmidt, D. "Syncope and Near-Death Experience." *Lancet*, 1994; 344: 829-830.
76. Blackmore, S.J. "Near-Death Experiences." *Lancet*, 1994; 344: 1298-1299.
77. Comer, N.L., Madow, L. and Dixon, J.J. "Observations of Sensory Deprivation in a Life Threatening Situation." *American Journal of Psychiatry*, 1967; 124: 164-169.
78. Berg-Johnsen, J. "Action Mechanisms of Intravenous Anesthetics." *Tidsskrift for Den Norske Laegeforening*, 1993; 113: 565-568.
79. Javitt, D.C. and Zukin, S.R. "Recent Advances in the Phencyclidine Model of Schizophrenia." *American Journal of Psychiatry*, 1991; 148: 1301-1308.
80. MacDonald, J.F., Bartlett, M.C., Mody, I., Pahapill, P., Reynolds, J.N., Salter, M.W., Schneiderman, J.H. and Pennefather, P.S. "Actions of Ketamine, Phencyclidine and MK-801 on NMDA Receptor Currents in Cultured Mouse Hippocampal Neurones." *Journal of Physiology* (London), 1991; 432: 483-508.
81. Quirion, R., Dimaggio, D.A., French, E.D. et al. "Evidence for an Endogenous Peptide Ligand for the Phencyclidine Receptor." *Peptides*, 1984; 5: 967-978.
82. Siegel, R.K. "Phencyclidine and Ketamine Intoxication: A Study of Four Populations of Recreational Users." In Peterson, R.C. and Stillman, R.C., eds. *Phencyclidine Abuse: An Appraisal.* Bethesda, Md.: National Institute of Drug Abuse, 1978, pp. 119-147.

83. Grinspoon, L. and Bakalar, S.B. *Psychedelic Drugs Reconsidered.* New York: Basic Books, 1981.
84. Takakusu, J., trans. "The Amitayur-dhyana-sutra." In Muller, M., ed. *Sacred Books of the East*, Volume 49. Oxford: Clarendon Press, 1894. Quoted in Becker, C.B. "The Pure Land Revisited: Sino-Japanese Meditations and Near-Death Experiences of the Next World." *Anabiosis*, 1984; 4: 51-68, p. 53.
85. Barnes, D.M. "NMDA Receptors Trigger Excitement." *Science*, 1988; 239: 254-256.
86. Jansen, K.L.R. "Neuroscience and the Near-Death Experience: Roles for the NMSA-PCP [sic] Receptor, the Sigma Receptor and the Endopsychosins." *Medical Hypotheses*, 1990; 31: 25-29.
87. Hargreaves, R.J., Hill, R.G. and Iversen, L.L. "Neuroprotective NMDA Antagonists: The Controversy over Their Potential for Adverse Effects on Cortical Neuronal Morphology." *Acta Neurochirugica. Supplementum*, 1994; 60: 15-19.
88. Carter, A.J. "Many Agents That Antagonize the NMDA Receptor-Channel Complex in Vivo Also Cause Disturbances of Motor Coordination." *Journal of Pharmacology and Experimental Therapeutics*, 1994; 269: 573-580.
89. Millan, M.J. "Antagonists at the NMDA Recognition Site and Blockers of the Associated Ion Channel Induce Spontaneous Tail Flicks in the Rat." *European Journal of Pharmacology*, 1991; 203: 315-318.
90. Desmond, N.L., Colbert, C.M., Zhang, D.X. and Levy, W.B. "NMDA Receptor Antagonists Block the Induction of Long-term Depression in the Hippocampal Dentate Gyrus of the Anesthetized Rat." *Brain Research*, 1991; 552: 93-98.
91. Dalayeun, J.F., Nores, J.M. and Bergal, S. "Physiology of Beta-Endorphins. A Close-up View and a Review of the Literature." *Biomedicine and Pharmacotherapy*, 1993; 47: 311-320.
92. Morse, M., Castillo, P., Venecia, D., Milstein, J. and Tyler, D.C. "Childhood Near-Death Experiences." *American Journal of Diseases of Children*, 1986; 140: 1110-1114.
93. Jansen, K. "Near Death Experience and the NMDA Receptor." *British Medical Journal*, 1989; 298: 1708.
94. Jansen, K.L.R. "The Near-Death Experience." *British Journal of Psychiatry*, 1989; 154: 883-884.
95. ansen, K.L.R. "Transcendental Explanations and Near-Death Experience." *Lancet*, 1991; 337: 244.
96. McDermott, W.V. "Endorphins, I Presume." *Lancet*, 1980; 2: 1353.
97. Carr, D.B. "Endorphins at the Approach of Death." *Lancet*, 1981; 1: 390.
98. Olson, G.A., Olson, R.D. and Kastin, A.J. "Endogenous Opiates: 1991." *Peptides*, 1992; 13: 1247-1287.
99. James, P.F. "Near-Death Experiences." *Lancet*, 1989; 2: 1110-1111.

100. Wilson, J. "Near-Death Experiences." *Lancet*, 1989; 2: 1341.
101. Rea, M. "Near-Death Experiences." *Lancet*, 1989; 2: 1341.
102. Livingstone, D. *Adventures and Discoveries in the Interior of Africa.* Philadelphia: Hubbard Brothers, 1872, p. 15.
103. Greyson, B. "Varieties of Near-Death Experiences." *Psychiatry*, 1993; 56: 390-399.
104. Negovsky, V. "Death, Dying and Revival: Ethical Aspects." *Resuscitation*, 1993; 25: 99-107.
105. Eadie, B.J. *Embraced by the Light.* Thorndike, Maine: G.K. Hall and Co., 1992.

CHAPTER 7

1. Manolis, A.S. "The Clinical Spectrum and Diagnosis of Syncope." *Herz*, 1993; 18: 143-154.
2. Schaal, S.F., Nelson, S.D., Boudoulas, H. and Lewis, R.P. "Syncope." *Current Problems in Cardiology*, 1992; 17: 205-264.
3. Schraeder, P.L., Lathers, C.M. and Charles, J.B. "The Spectrum of Syncope." *Journal of Clinical Pharmacology*, 1994; 34: 454-459.
4. Manolis, A.S., Linzer, M., Salem, D. and Estes, N.A.M. "Syncope: Current Diagnostic Evaluation and Management." *Annals of Internal Medicine*, 1990; 112: 850-863.
5. Kapoor, W.N. "Syncope in Older Persons." *Journal of the American Geriatrics Society*, 1994; 42: 426-436.
6. Wayne, H.H. "Syncope. Physiological Considerations and an Analysis of the Clinical Characteristics in 510 Patients." *American Journal of Medicine*, 1961: 30: 418-438.
7. McHenry, L.C., Fazekas, J.F. and Sullivan, J.F. "Cerebral Hemodynamics of Syncope." *American Journal of Medicine, Science*, 1961; 241: 173-178.
8. Lempert, T., Bauer, M. and Schmidt, D. "Syncope and Near-Death Experience." *Lancet*, 1994; 344: 829-830.
9. Ibid., p. 830.
10. Moody, R.A. and Perry, P. *The Light Beyond.* New York: Bantam Books, 1988.
11. Whinnery, J.E. and Whinnery, A.M. "Acceleration-Induced Loss of Consciousness. A Review of 500 Episodes." *Archives of Neurology*, 1990; 47: 764-776.
12. Forster, E.M. and Whinnery, J.E. "Recovery from Gz-Induced Loss of Consciousness: Psychophysiologic Considerations." *Aviation, Space, and Environmental Medicine*, 1988; 59: 517-522.
13. Marks, M. and Greene, H.L. "Sudden Cardiac Death." In *Cardiac Arrhythmias.* Ed. Mandel, W.J. Philadelphia: J. B. Lippincott, third edition, 1995, pp. 1189-1203.
14. Taylor, G.J., Rubin, R., Tucker, M., Greene, H.L., Rudikoff, M.T. and

Weisfeldt, M.L. "External Cardiac Compression. A Randomized Comparison of Mechanical and Manual Techniques." *JAMA*, 1978; 240: 644-646.

15. Taylor, G.J., Tucker, W.M., Greene, H.L., Rudikoff, M.T.and Weisfeldt, M.L. "Importance of Prolonged Compression Duration During Cardiopulmonary Resuscitation in Man." *New England Journal of Medicine*, 1977; 296: 1515-1517.
16. Duggal, C., Weil, M.H., Gazmuri, R.J., Tang, W., Sun, S., O'Connell, F. and Ali, M. "Regional Blood Flow During Closed-chest Cardiac Resuscitation in Rats." *Journal of Applied Physiology*, 1993; 74: 147-152.
17. Halperin, H.R., Tsitlik, J.E., Guerci, A.D., Mellits, E.D., Levin, H.R., Shi, A-Y., Chandra, N. and Weisfeldt, M.L. "Determinants of Blood Flow to Vital Organs During Cardiopulmonary Resuscitation in Dogs." *Circulation*, 1986; 73: 539-550.
18. Bill, A. and Sperber, G.O. "Control of Retinal and Choroidal Blood Flow." *Eye*, 1990; 4: 319-325.
19. Rodin, A. and Key, J. "Lazarus Complex (Lazarus Syndrome, Near-Death Syndrome)." *Ohio Medicine*, 1991; 87: 150-151.
20. Bray, J.G. "The Lazarus Phenomenon Revisited." *Anesthesiology*, 1993; 78: 991.
21. Linko, K., Honakavaara, P. and Salmenpera, M. "Recovery After Discontinued Cardiopulmonary Resuscitation." *Lancet*, 1982; 1: 106-107.
22. Letellier, N., Coulomb, F., Lebec, C. and Brunet, C. "Recovery After Discontinued Cardiopulmonary Resuscitation." *Lancet*, 1982; 1: 1019.
23. Koblin, D.D. "The Lazarus Phenomenon Re-visited: I." *Anesthesiology*, 1993; 79: 1438.
24. Hill, D.J. "The Lazarus Phenomenon Re-visited: II." *Anesthesiology*, 1993; 79: 1438-1439.
25. Bray, J.G. "The Lazarus Phenomenon Re-visited: Reply." *Anesthesiology*, 1993; 79: 1439.
26. Heytens, L., Verlooy, J., Ghevens, J. and Bossaert, L. "Lazarus Sign and Extensor Posturing in a Brain Dead Patient." *Journal of Neurosurgery*, 1989; 71: 449-451.
27. Penfield, W. and Perot, P. "The Brain's Record of Auditory and Visual Experience." *Brain*, 1963; 86: 595-696.
28. Penfield, W. "The Twenty-ninth Maudsley Lecture: The Role of the Temporal Cortex in Certain Psychical Phenomena." *Journal of Mental Science*, 1955; 101: 451-465.
29. Penfield, W. "Temporal Lobe Epilepsy." *British Journal of Surgery*, 1954; 41: 337-343.
30. Keele, A.C., Neil, E. and Joels, N. *Samson Wright's Applied Physiology*. Oxford: Oxford University Press, thirteenth edition, 1982, pp. 133-154.
31. Bill, A. "Circulation in the Eye." In *Handbook of Physiology*. Section 2:

"The Cardiovascular System," Vol. IV, Chapter 22: "Microcirculation," Part 2, pp. 1001-1034. Bethesda, Md.: American Physiological Society, 1984.

32. Lewis, D.W. and Watson, M.E. "Explaining the Phenomena of Near-Death Experiences." *American Journal of Diseases of Children*, 1987; 141: 828.
33. Lovasik, J.V. and Kergoat, H. "Influence of Transiently Altered Retinal Vascular Perfusion Pressure on Rod/Cone Contributions to Scotopic Oscillatory Potentials." *Ophthalmic and Physiological Optics*, 1991; 11: 370-380.
34. Gellhorn, E. "The Effect of O^2-Lack, Variations in the CO^2 Content of the Inspired Air, and Hyperpnea on Visual Intensity Discrimination." *American Journal of Physiology*, 1936; 115: 679-684.
35. Gordon, B.D. "Near-Death Experience." *Lancet*, 1989; 2: 1452.
36. Wong, C.W., Chen, T.Y., Liao, J.J. and You, D.L. "Serial Regional Blood Flow and Visual Evoked Responses in Transient Cortical Blindness." *Acta Neurochirugica*, 1993; 120: 187-189.
37. Daniel, P.M.and Whitteridge, D. "The Representation of the Visual Field on the Cerebral Cortex in Monkeys." *Journal of Physiology*, 1961; 159: 203-221.
38. Blackmore, S. *Dying to Live: Near-Death Experiences*. Buffalo, N.Y.: Prometheus Books, 1993.
39. Blackmore, S.J. and Troscianko, T.S. "The Physiology of the Tunnel." *Journal of Near-Death Studies*, 1989; 8: 15-28.
40. Cowan, J.D. "Spontaneous Symmetry Breaking in Large-Scale Nervous Activity." *International Journal of Quantum Chemistry*, 1982; 22: 1059-1082, as cited in Blackmore, S. *Dying to Live: Near-Death Experiences*, pp. 82-83.

CHAPTER 8

1. Morris, H.M. *Theophany*. El Cajon, Calif.: Institute for Creation Research, December 1994.
2. Moody, R.A. and Perry, P. *The Light Beyond*. New York: Bantam Books, 1988.
3. Moody, R.A. *Life After Life: The Investigation of a Phenomenon—Survival of Bodily Death*. New York: Bantam Books, 1976.
4. Moody, R.A. *Reflections on Life After Life*. New York: Bantam Books, 1977.
5. *International Standard Bible Encyclopedia*. Eds. Bromiley, G.W., Harrison, E.F., Harrison, R.K., LaSor, W.S. and Smith, E.W. Grand Rapids, Mich.: William B. Eerdmans, 1979.
6. Martin, R.P. *Word Biblical Commentary*. Eds. Hubbard, D.A., Barker, G.W., Watts, J.D.W. and Martin, R.P. Volume 40: 2 *Corinthians*. Waco, Tex.: Word, 1986, pp. 390-424.
7. Hughes, P.E. *Paul's Second Epistle to the Corinthians*. London: Marshall, Morgan and Scott, 1961, pp. 424-455.

8. Bruce, F.F. *Paul: Apostle of the Heart Set Free.* Grand Rapids, Mich.: William B. Eerdmans, 1977.
9. "The Vision of Paul." In Menzies, A. *The Ante-Nicene Fathers: Translations of the Writings of the Fathers Down to* A.D. 325. Grand Rapids, Mich.: William B. Eerdmans, 1969, fifth edition, Vol. X, pp. 149-166.
10. Wilkerson, R. *Beyond and Back: Those Who Died and Lived to Tell It.* Anaheim, Calif: Melodyland Publishers, 1977.
11. Prophet, E.C. *Forbidden Mysteries of Enoch.* Livingston, Mont.: Summit University Press, 1983.
12. Bruce, F.F. *The Canon of Scripture.* Downers Grove, Ill.: InterVarsity Press, 1988.

CHAPTER 9

1. *International Standard Bible Encyclopedia.* Eds. Bromiley, G.W., Harrison, E.F., Harrison, R.K., LaSor, W.S. and Smith, E.W. Grand Rapids, Mich.: William B. Eerdmans, 1979.
2. Prophet, E.C. *Forbidden Mysteries of Enoch.* Livingston, Mont.: Summit University Press, 1983.

CHAPTER 10

1. Wilkerson, R. *Beyond and Back: Those Who Died and Lived to Tell It.* Anaheim, Calif: Melodyland Publishers, 1977.
2. Rodin, A. and Key, J. "Lazarus Complex (Lazarus Syndrome, Near-Death Syndrome)." *Ohio Medicine,* 1991; 87: 150-151.
3. Bray, J.G. "The Lazarus Phenomenon Revisited." *Anesthesiology,* 1993; 78: 991.
4. Linko, K., Honakavaara, P. and Salmenpera, M. "Recovery After Discontinued Cardiopulmonary Resuscitation." *Lancet,* 1982; 1: 106-107.
5. Letellier, N., Coulomb, F., Lebec, C. and Brunet, C. "Recovery After Discontinued Cardiopulmonary Resuscitation." *Lancet,* 1982; 1: 1019.
6. Koblin, D.D. "The Lazarus Phenomenon Re-visited: I." *Anesthesiology,* 1993; 79: 1438.
7. Hill, D.J. "The Lazarus Phenomenon Re-visited: II." *Anesthesiology,* 1993; 79: 1438-1439.
8. Bray, J.G. "The Lazarus Phenomenon Re-visited: Reply." *Anesthesiology,* 1993; 79: 1439.
9. Heytens, L., Verlooy, J., Ghevens, J. and Bossaert, L. "Lazarus Sign and Extensor Posturing in a Brain Dead Patient." *Journal of Neurosurgery,* 1989; 71: 449-451.
10. Ritmeyer, L. and Ritmeyer, K. "Akeldama. Potter's Field or High Priest's Tomb?" *Biblical Archaeology Review.* November/December 1994; 20(6): 22-35, 76.

11. Kee, H.C. *Medicine, Miracle and Magic in New Testament Times.* Cambridge, England: Cambridge University Press, 1986.
12. Iverson, J. *In Search of the Dead: A Scientific Investigation of Evidence for Life After Death.* San Francisco: Harper Collins, 1992.
13. McBirnie, W.S. *The Search for the Twelve Apostles.* Wheaton, Ill.: Tyndale House, 1973.
14. Edwards, W.D., Gabel, W.J. and Hosmer, F.E. "On the Physical Death of Jesus Christ." *JAMA*, 1986; 255: 1455-1463.
15. Paraskos, J.A. "Biblical Accounts of Resuscitation." *Journal of the History of Medicine and Allied Sciences*, 1992; 47: 310-321.
16. Lloyd Davies, M. and Lloyd Davies, T.A. "Resurrection or Resuscitation?" *Journal of the Royal College of Physicians* (London), 1991; 25: 167-170.
17. Mahler, R. "Editor's Note: Resurrection or Resuscitation?" *Journal of the Royal College of Physicians* (London), 1991; 25: 268.
18. Leinster, S.J. "Resurrection or Resuscitation?" *Journal of the Royal College of Physicians* (London), 1991; 25: 268-269.
19. Wright, V. "Resurrection or Resuscitation?" *Journal of the Royal College of Physicians* (London), 1991; 25: 269-270.
20. Fowler, A.W. "Resurrection or Resuscitation?" *Journal of the Royal College of Physicians* (London), 1991; 25: 270.
21. Barnardo, D. "Deceased or Deceit?" *Journal of the Royal College of Physicians* (London), 1991; 25: 270-271.
22. Porter, A.M.W. "The Crucifixion." *Journal of the Royal College of Physicians* (London), 1991; 25: 271.
23. Dunstan, G.R. "Comment: Resurrection or Resuscitation?" *Journal of the Royal College of Physicians* (London), 1991; 25: 271-272.
24. McDowell, J. *A Ready Defense.* Comp. Wilson, B. San Bernadino, Calif.: Here's Life Publishers, 1990.
25. McDowell, J. *Evidence That Demands a Verdict.* San Bernadino, Calif.: Campus Crusade for Christ, 1972.
26. Morrison, F. *Who Moved the Stone?* London: Faber and Faber, 1930.
27. McDowell, J. *He Walked Among Us: Evidence for the Historical Jesus.* San Bernardino, Calif.: Here's Life Publishers, 1988.
28. Josephus, F. "Life of Flavius Josephus, 75." In *The Complete Works of Josephus*, trans. Whiston, W. Grand Rapids, Mich.: Kregel Publications, 1981, pp. 20-21.

CHAPTER 11

1. Eadie, B.J. *Embraced by the Light.* Thorndike, Maine: G.K. Hall and Co., 1992.
2. Pasricha, S. and, Stevenson, J. "Near-Death Experiences in India: A Preliminary Report." *Journal of Nervous and Mental Disease*, 1986; 174: 165-170.

3. Pasricha, S. "Near-Death Experiences in South India: A Systematic Survey in Channapatna." *NIMHANS Journal*, 1992; 10: 111-118.
4. Brooke, T., *The Other Side of Death.* Wheaton, Ill.: Tyndale House, 1979.
5. Habermas, G.R. and Moreland, J.P. *Immortality: The Other Side of Death.* Nashville: Thomas Nelson, 1992.
6. Gram, R.L. *An Enemy Disguised.* Nashville: Thomas Nelson, 1985.
7. Clapp, R. "Rumors of Heaven." *Christianity Today*, October 7, 1988; 32(14): 16-21.
8. Saunders, D. "Books Reviewed." *Christianity Today*, June 17, 1977; 21: 33.
9. Groothuis, D. "To Heaven and Back?" *Christianity Today*, April 3, 1995; 39(4): 39-42.
10. Groothuis, D. *Deceived by the Light.* Eugene, Ore.: Harvest House, 1995.
11. Hillstrom, E.L. *Testing the Spirits.* Downers Grove, Ill.: InterVarsity Press, 1995.
12. Page, A.F. *Life After Death: What the Bible Says.* Nashville: Abingdon Press, 1987.
13. Hick, J. *Death and Eternal Life.* Louisville: Westminster/John Knox Press, 1994.
14. Phillips, P. *Angels, Angels, Angels: Embraced by the Light . . . Or . . . Embraced by the Darkness?* Lancaster, Penn.: Starburst Publishers, 1995.
15. Abanes, R. *Embraced by the Light and the Bible: Betty Eadie and Near-Death Experiences in the Light of Scripture.* Camp Hill, Penn.: Horizon Books, 1994.
16. Alnor, W.M. *Heaven Can't Wait: A Survey of Alleged Trips to the Other Side.* Grand Rapids, Mich.: Baker Books, 1996.
17. Connelly, D. *After Life.* Downers Grove, Ill.: InterVarsity Press, 1995.
18. Rhodes, R. *The Undiscovered Country.* Eugene, Ore.: Harvest House, 1996.

CHAPTER 12

1. Royse, D. "The Near-Death Experience: A Survey of Clergy's Attitudes and Knowledge." *Journal of Pastoral Care*, 1985; 39: 31-42.
2. Bonhoeffer, D. *The Cost of Discipleship.* New York: Collier Books, Macmillan, 1959, pp. 43-60.
3. Phillips, P. *Angels, Angels, Angels: Embraced by the Light . . . Or . . . Embraced by the Darkness?* Lancaster, Penn.: Starburst Publishers, 1995, p. 215.
4. Mattingly, T. "Culture Watch: Brilliant Orbs and God Lite." *Moody Monthly*, 1995; 95(1): 30.
5. Kieffer, G. "Kundalini and the Near-Death Experience." *Journal of Near-Death Studies*, 1994; 12: 159-176.
6. Ibid., p. 175.
7. Greyson, B. In Harris, B. and Bascom, L.C. *Full Circle: The Near-Death Experience and Beyond.* New York: Pocket Books, 1990, p. 268.

8. Moody, R.A. and Perry, P. *Coming Back: A Psychiatrist Explores Past-Life Journeys*. New York: Bantam Books, 1991.
9. Moody, R. and Perry, P. *Reunions: Visionary Encounters with Departed Loved Ones*. New York: Villard Books, 1993.
10. Moody, R.A. *Life After Life: The Investigation of a Phenomenon—Survival of Bodily Death*. New York: Bantam Books, 1976.
11. Moody, R.A. *Reflections on Life After Life*. New York: Bantam Books, 1977.
12. Moody, R.A. and Perry, P. *The Light Beyond*. New York: Bantam Books, 1988.
13. Moody, R.A. "Evoking Apparitions of the Deceased." *Journal of the Medical Association of Georgia*, 1993; 82: 533-535.
14. Stevenson, I. and, Greyson, B. "Near-Death Experiences. Relevance to the Question of Survival After Death." *JAMA*, 1979; 242: 265-267.
15. Stevenson, I. "Research into the Evidence of Man's Survival After Death: A Historical and Critical Survey with a Summary of Recent Developments." *Journal of Nervous and Mental Disease*, 1977; 165: 152-170.
16. Greyson, B. and Stevenson, I. "The Phenomenology of Near-Death Experiences." *American Journal of Psychiatry*, 1980; 137: 1193-1196.
17. Stevenson, I. "Comments on 'The Reality of Death Experiences: A Personal Perspective.'" *Journal of Nervous and Mental Disease*, 1980; 168: 271-272.
18. Stevenson, I. "Research into the Evidence of Man's Survival After Death. A Historical and Critical Survey with a Summary of Recent Developments." *Journal of Nervous and Mental Disease*, 1977; 165: 152-170.
19. Stevenson, I. "Reply to the Comments of Dr. Lief and Dr. Ullman." *Journal of Nervous and Mental Disease*, 1977; 165: 181-183.
20. Owens, J.E., Cook, E.W. and Stevenson, I. "Features of 'Near-Death Experience' in Relation to Whether or Not Patients Were Near Death." *Lancet*, 1990; 336: 1175-1177.
21. Owens, J.E., Cook, E.W. and Stevenson, I. "Near-Death Experience." *Lancet*, 1991; 337: 1167-1168.
22. Pollock, J.C. *Moody*. New York: Macmillan, 1963, p. 316.
23. Moody, W.R. *The Life of Dwight L. Moody*. London: Morgan and Scott, 1900.
24. Moody, P.D. *My Father. An Intimate Portrait of Dwight Moody*. Boston: Little, Brown and Company, 1938.
25. Day, R.E. *Bush Aglow: The Life Story of Dwight Lyman Moody. Commoner of Northfield*. Philadelphia: The Judson Press, 1936.
26. Livingstone, D. *Adventures and Discoveries in the Interior of Africa*. Philadelphia: Hubbard Brothers, 1872, p. 15.
27. McDermott, W.V. "Endorphins, I Presume." *Lancet*, 1980; 2: 1353.
28. Carr, D.B. "Endorphins at the Approach of Death." *Lancet*, 1981; 1: 390.
29. Moody, W.R., 1900, p. 473.

SCRIPTURE INDEX

GENERAL INDEX